My Almost Certainly Real Imaginary Jesus

en, children. Having heard about him from my earliest memory, I found that he spilled God all over me.

This, then, is the story of a journey that pauses at the threshold of one of a growing number of churches who, in opening the door to me and other gay people, welcomed Jesus back inside as well. It is my attempt to leave a record of the early signs of the turning and softening of a collective heart. What follows is the only proof I can offer of the love and protection I have felt, and the life I have been given by my oldest and dearest and, yes, imaginary friend.

Preface

There are an enormous number of people—and I am one of them—whose native religion, for better or worse, is Christianity. We were born to it; we began to learn about it before we became conscious; it is, whatever we think of it, an intimate belonging of our being; it informs our consciousness, our language, and our dreams.

—Wendell Berry

Dear reader, it might bother you, I know, when I speak of Imaginary Jesus. You can't make your own Jesus out of thin air, you'll say, just to suit yourself. You might even say I have stolen the savior and fashioned a mealy-mouthed figment, that I have taken the parts of him I like and left out the rest. Moreover, a certain majority will agree I cannot be a Christian; they won't let me: If I don't believe certain literal things about Jesus—that he managed to be conceived without a human father, that he walked on water, that his dead body revived, stood up, spoke, and flew up to heaven—then I can't really believe.

To each one of these statements, my only defense is to say that I could accuse them of the very same things. Belief in who we imagine Jesus to have been—to be—puts us all in the same indefensible position. So we put the ineffable down on paper. Look, it's something you can hold in your hands.

Here is how I understand it. From what we know about him, Jesus learned how to be completely human. He had kindness, confidence, and insight the likes of which no one had seen before. He was more aware than most of the Creativity around him, and this had emerged uniquely through him. He was so full of the Sacred, maybe even of God—if that term still fits for you—that some spilled out of him, and he made a mess that some people are still playing in and others are still trying to clean up. He got God all over people he shouldn't have: lepers, Samaritans, wom-

Pat Kehde and Mary Lou Wright and Heidi Raak and Lisa Stockton, former and current owners, respectively, of Lawrence, Kansas' Raven Bookstore, the finest and leanest little bookstore in the world. (And a special thanks to Heidi for her impeccable proofreading skills.) I have spent some of my finest days among The Raven's shelves. Not only have these women provided me precious income over the years, but they have shared my central passion for books.

I'm also thankful for my spiritual communities: Trinity Presbyterian Church in Independence, Missouri; Broadway Baptist and Crossroads Church in Kansas City, Missouri; and Plymouth Congregational Church, and Kawsmos in Lawrence, Kansas. Your collective love and support over the years has midwived many a painful but necessary transition.

I also owe a debt of gratitude to the brave people from my faith tradition who have been willing to view the church with a critical eye and take me and others by the hand to lead us to higher ground: Frederick Buechner, Peter Gomes, Marcus Borg, Mel White, and especially, John Shelby Spong. Thanks also to Soulforce and Beyond Ex-Gay for their clarifying and nourishing presence in the midst of so much hate, heterosexism, and bigotry masquerading as "Christian concern."

Thanks also to two fine counselors, Ann Hakan and Emily Kofron. Without their attentiveness and insight, I never would have finished the manuscript or, for that matter, that last fifteen years of my life.

With help from my mother, my father and three sisters have consistently loved and tried to understand their little odd one, which is all I could have asked for. I love each of you beyond words, and I hope that shows on these pages.

Finally, I owe this book and, quite literally, my life to Lisa Grossman, my daily sounding, my horizon, my heart, and my home. I am pink and breathing proof that we are created by the love of another.

Acknowledgments

It isn't wise to write a memoir about your spirituality. I could have more easily painted a portrait of a hummingbird. I needed every last little bit of help and encouragement the following individuals offered to help me bring it finally to fruition. Thanks to early manuscript readers: rabble-rouser Jennifer Newlin, fellow recovering fundamentalist Robert Tims, and Caryn Mirriam-Goldberg especially for her astute editorial comments and dogged persistence in asking where the manuscript was. Thanks also to Lawrence, Kansas, friends and chapter readers Amy Stuber, Mary Wharff, and Laura Moriarty and to fellow University of Montana writing program survivors Mike Lancaster and Penny Orwick for plowing through the first epic-length draft. Deep bows also to Elizabeth Schultz, who offered sage writing advice and encouragement, not to mention invaluable generosity in keeping me employed one way or another so that I could pay the bills while I wrote. To fellow University of Montana writing program graduate and editorial saint, Leigh Tillman-Partington, I offer my most heartfelt gratitude for wading through not just one, but two overwrought drafts. Without her unflagging interest and almost clairvoyant ability to see what this book could be, it would never have been.

Many, many thanks to Red Hen Press and to Eloise Klein Healy of Arktoi Books for their collective willingness to take a chance on this manuscript. I'll be forever grateful that Eloise understood my story and for the rare opportunity she has presented to make it available to a wider audience. I am also indebted to her for her invaluable skills as a poet and wordsmith. Thanks also to Arktoi Books publicist Nickole Brown, who saved this book from being incomprehensible for those outside the fold. Her kind yet incisive comments transformed the manuscript.

Thanks to the following two publications that allowed reprints of previously published chapters here: The chapter "Lovingkindness" appeared in *Love Shook My Heart 2*, edited by Jess Wells (Alyson Books, New York, 2001), and "Raise Up a Child in the Way She Should Go" appeared in *Muse & Stone* (2011).

I have had many supporters on the sidelines as well. I'm ever grateful for the mentoring of my first writing teacher, Maryfrances Wagner, and writing group leader, Donna Trussell. They are the best of poets and friends. Many thanks to

Wendell Berry's quote is from *Sex, Economy, Freedom, & Community*, copyright © 1992, 1993 by Wendell Berry. Reprinted courtesy of Pantheon Books,
a division of Random House, Inc. Frederick Buechner's quote is from *Beyond
Words*, copyright © 2004 by Frederick Buechner. Reprinted courtesy of HarperCollins Publishers. Thomas Moore's quote is from *The Soul of Sex*, copyright
© 1998 by Thomas Moore. Reprinted courtesy of HarperCollins Publishers.
John Shelby Spong's quote is from *The Sins of Scripture*, copyright © 2005 by
John Shelby Spong. Reprinted courtesy of HarperCollins Publishers.

Book design and layout by David Rose

Library of Congress Cataloging-in-Publication Data
Barth, Kelly, 1964–
 My almost certainly real imaginary Jesus : a memoir / Kelly Barth.—1st ed.
  p. cm.
 Includes bibliographical references and index.
 ISBN 978-0-9800407-5-3 (alk. paper)
 1. Barth, Kelly, 1964– 2. Christian biography—United States. 3. Lesbi-
ans—United States—Biography. I. Title.
 BR1725.B3475A3 2012
 277.3'083092—dc23
 [B]
                    2012006480
The Los Angeles County Arts Commission, the National Endowment for
the Arts, the Los Angeles Department of Cultural Affairs, the James Irvine
Foundation and the Ahmanson Foundation partially support Red Hen Press.

First Edition
Published by Arktoi Books
An imprint of Red Hen Press, Pasadena, CA
www.arktoi.com
www.redhen.org

My Almost Certainly Real Imaginary Jesus

a memoir

Kelly Barth

Arktoi Books | *Pasadena, CA*

Jesus said, "I am the light that is over all things. I am all.
From me all came forth, and to me all extends.
Split a piece of wood, and I am there.
Lift up the stone, and you will find me there."
                                        —Gospel of Thomas 77

1

Searching for Imaginary Jesus

Unlike another imaginary friend of mine, whose face I had drawn in red Magic Marker on an English walnut to prove his existence, Jesus had actually been seen by people. From my earliest memory, my family told me he was everywhere. All I had to do was look. I couldn't grasp *everywhere* in the sense of St. Augustine's "circle whose center is everywhere and whose circumference is nowhere." Everywhere was where I lived, in our split-level house on a quarter-acre of what had recently been part of a dairy farm. We could still hear the farmer's reduced herd lowing from the backyard. We lived in a burgeoning suburb of Kansas City, Missouri, called Raytown after its founder, William Ray, who operated a blacksmith shop along the Santa Fe Trail.

Trying to find Jesus is one of the first things I remember doing. Fascinated by microcosm, I imagined I'd find him shining up from the dirt like a lost dime, cloaked and sandaled, tiny as a foil-covered chocolate Easter egg forgotten in a lampshade ruffle. I looked for him in my sock drawer, under footstools, beneath rocks in the garden, and in the holes of electrical outlets, which lured me although I had been told to stay away from them because something unbelievably powerful other than Jesus would come out of them and yank me away from Momma forever. (This was a compelling warning. I'd fallen even more hopelessly in love with Momma than had any of my sisters before me. During bouts of childhood insomnia, I memorized her sleepy brown eyes, her thick dark bangs that tickled me when she kissed my cheek. She must have memorized the dimple on my left cheek and the big ears that my hair couldn't cover.) I thought that if I were very still and actually did see my tiny Imaginary Jesus, he might crawl onto my hand and let me pet him.

Though my shy, insular parents didn't have company over very often, they made an exception where my Imaginary Jesus was concerned. They gave him the run of the house. Every night, we thanked him for putting food on our table and giving us safety on the roads and rest in our beds. My Jesus wasn't family, but I knew from a very early age that I could trust him completely. We owed him a debt of gratitude for a host of kindnesses. Momma especially appreciated him showing up at the last possible moment to collect my dying grandmother, who had only just started going to church, and to escort her safely to heaven. She had roused from a three-day coma to say he had done so. There seemed to me to be nothing my Jesus would not or could not do if we asked him, even if he had to set the whole world in his imaginary hands down for a bit to do it. The picture in my children's Bible showed how he stopped right in the middle of healing the sick or raising the dead to let children like me climb onto his lap. When there was no one else to play with, there was always Jesus to hunt for.

My oldest sister, Karen, invited Jesus into her heart as a teenager during a very un-Presbyterian altar call after a Baptist friend visited our church to do religious magic tricks. With my parents' permission, she started having Jesus Time with me, just before naps. I remember always standing up in my crib, sliding first one leg then the other through the slats, flirting—the last of four children to use this squeaky crib, I slept in it until I was so big I had to sleep curled up. Momma also dressed me in the toddler one-piece footy pajamas for too long. Finally, my sister Kathy, who was taking junior high biology, pointed out to her that in my pajamas

I walked not quite erect, like Australopithecus. Tall, skinny, and bullied unmercifully at school, Kathy had to keep all of us as "normal" as possible so we wouldn't bring any more abuse upon her. I loved Kathy's long brown hair and thought of her as my *beautiful* sister.

"Zaccheas was a wee little man, and a wee little man was he. He climbed up in the sycamore tree for the Lord he wanted to see. And as the Savior passed that way, He looked up in the tree, and He said, 'Zaccheas, you come down, for I'm going to your house today, for I'm going to your house to pray.'" Karen pointed to a place between her emerging breasts, where I'd recently been told to no longer pound, and said, "Jesus is right in here." Of course he'd fit. I imagined that at night he slept in a tidy little room in Karen's heart and that she let him run free during the day.

Though I spent early childhood holding out hope that I'd see him in the flesh, Imaginary Jesus continued to keep himself safely tucked behind the baseboard or the petals of a peony. Nevertheless, I knew he was always with me. We exchanged jokes. I saved and put out choice bits of food for him. People finally stopped asking, "Who's she talking to?" One night he ducked quickly into a ventricle of my own heart where Karen helped me invite him. Wonder of wonders, he could live in her heart and mine all at once. That night, he sang me to sleep.

✦ ✦ ✦

There were limits to Imaginary Jesus's powers to help a family of Presbyterians. Even though they had been raised with old-time evangelical cousins and Billy Graham crusades and had been trained by a pastor with a lazy eye and a literal mind who saw Jesus everywhere, my parents shared a distrust of the happiness Jesus supposedly promised. They were classic examples of what religion scholar William James called "the sick soul." They were bracing for all sorts of bad things to happen. They were bracing for me, the child I know they had to reassure themselves wasn't gay. All evidence indicated I was.

My parents worked hard to reconcile their trust in God with a profound disbelief in accident. When they saw how perfectly the torn edges of their abandonment issues fit together, they felt predestined to have met. Both of them had fathers who had left the family when they were children, and sickly mothers who had depended too much on them as a consequence. As children, my sisters and I absorbed their collective hunch that all we loved would at any moment be snatched away. Daddy's chest pains weren't nothing but required a three-month stay in Cleveland and one of the first open-heart surgeries ever performed. A month later, Momma wheeled him off the airplane, a skeletal man in black horn-rimmed glasses and a black suit. God, Jesus's daddy, had decided not to take him away from us. When we were all gathered around the tree that Christmas, Daddy unbuttoned his shirt to show us the scar that ran from just below his Adam's apple to his groin, a raised purple reminder of how right we were to suspect the worst. When Karen and her fiancé Roger were late for dinner one drizzly night, the telephone ringing into the silence of the living room came as no surprise. Their car had been hit head-on, and Karen had had to be cut from it. Of course, she had nearly died from a fatty embolism, a phrase repeated over and over even though none of us would ever really understand what it meant. Like most Presbyterians, we tried not to blow our cover as a contented, normal family, resting in God.

Daddy sometimes forgot impending doom and let his guard down. When happiness sideswiped him, he flapped his hands in front of him as if he'd touched something burning hot. You could never tell when or where he'd flap. I'm told that when I copied him as a toddler, Momma decided something must be done. When she saw him start in, she grabbed his hands and looked him straight in the eye, which charmed the flap right out of him.

My own Presbyterian tendencies manifested around age four, when Momma felt I was old enough to move into a big-girl bed on the other side of the room from my sister Kim and join her in a bedtime prayer. I wanted to go wherever Kim was, which she didn't permit. I loved her straight, shiny gold hair and how she could spray water between her two front teeth and use the telephone by herself. When she wasn't looking, I crept to her bed and smelled her pillow and played with her stuffed rabbit. Prayers came after vitamins, tooth brushing, and a chapter from a Thornton W. Burgess nature book. If it were winter, prayers came after Momma plugged in the vaporizer and slathered my chest with Numotizine, a pink poultice prescribed to treat my frequent bouts of croup. (A whiff of creosote, one of Numotizine's active ingredients, still makes me feel reverent.) These preparations finished, Momma would position herself at the foot of my bed—her back against the same wall so many nights that she left a dark shape of herself on it—to hear us recite our "God blesses," a litany I said so many times that even thirty years later it still pours from me whole like a released breath. I assumed that, as Jesus's daddy, God must be as upset, overworked, and as on the verge of a stress-induced heart attack as my daddy. I must have also absorbed an understanding of Imaginary Jesus as rodeo clown to this Old Testament longhorn daddy God, who would just as soon gore us as look at us. Despite being sheltered from the most violent of Bible stories, I knew God could get plenty angry. If he encouraged his chosen people to kill every living thing in Jericho, even women, children, cattle, and sheep, just because they had the misfortune of being in the way, I knew we all needed Jesus to calm him down. At 5:00 p.m. when Daddy's carpool dropped him off from a long day at the office where people didn't always do what he said, my sisters and I needed Jesus and my mother for the same reason. Kim and I finished our prayers with "Now I Lay Me," the boilerplate rhyme that slowly but surely turned me into an insomniac. Every night, like a little old man with lung cancer, I would kiss Momma for what I knew was the last time. I was convinced I would die before I woke and that God would take my soul or not, depending on his mood. I didn't understand that this prayer had been written before the invention of antibiotics, which I certainly would have died without, as many children did. Nor did I understand that the writer of the prayer, probably a good Presbyterian, believed the doctrine of original sin. If you didn't baptize infants, their little pink unused souls would travel straight to hell. From Adam and Eve, even babies had inherited a putrid inner core. I can't blame Momma. Everyone said "Now I Lay Me." Exhausted mothers could help children rattle it off with no preparation like a boil-in-a-bag meal of chipped beef in gravy. It had just enough of the obsessive-compulsive in it to make Momma believe nothing could happen to us if she'd heard us recite it.

Because I had caught croup so often, I was repeatedly exposed to a similarly unsettling book in Dr. Swisher's waiting room. *Little Visits with God* always fell open to the same stained page, its binding cracked there by the hands of countless sick and uneasy children whom it was mistakenly placed there to comfort. In this story, a boy's puppy runs into the street. The boy runs after it and is hit by a car. On the story's last page, the boy dies. A shaft of light beams into the brown fog of death around his bed. The dead boy didn't look exactly at peace. Once, I showed it to Momma, who said, "See why I tell you to stay away from the street!" Intentionally avoiding a discussion about heaven and hell, she knew if she didn't get my mind (and her own for that matter) off death, she would get nothing else done the rest of the day. She had three other daughters coming home from school in a few hours and a hungry husband to feed.

◆ ◆ ◆

As I did on the other days I was required to leave home for the official world, I associated Sundays and church with binding leotards and restricted movement rather than with Imaginary Jesus. My parents didn't condone Wee Kirk, the Presbyterian Church nursery. Neither did they take us to the cry room at the back of the sanctuary where you could still see but not hear screaming children. They believed learning to sit through a worship service came only with practice, practice, practice.

Thankfully, there were a few things to do other than pay attention during church. I could imagine swinging from one big, wooden, Celtic light fixture to the next. On paper kept in Momma's purse, I drew birds and the tops of trees I could see out the sanctuary's second-story window, things that I would be permitted to enjoy once church was over. Sometimes I was also allowed to crawl over laps to sit next to my sister Kim. I loved her silent but dramatic imitations of Dovie the organist flipping buttons, depressing pedals, and rapidly turning pages. Up in the choir Anka, the Latvian war bride who sang soprano solos, provided Kim with fodder, too. She imitated Anka's bright pink lips wobbling as if to keep an egg in her mouth. Momma put an end to each of Kim's performances by reaching across me to pinch a tiny piece of skin on the underside of her arm. When all else failed to stop my fidgeting, Momma gave me her hands to play with. It worried me that other children's mothers didn't have raised blue veins. Nevertheless, for that one hour I could have her hands all to myself.

After most every benediction, in my hurry outside I launched from my chair and cracked my head on one of the several floor-to-ceiling wooden sanctuary arches. After that I had only one more Sunday hurdle to surmount: carsickness. I learned to control myself until the car stopped. I then got immediately out and emptied my stomach onto the parking lot of whatever restaurant my parents decided to go to for Sunday dinner—usually Nichols Lunch at 39th and Southwest Boulevard where transvestite waitresses fooled Daddy into flirting. Momma didn't cook on Sundays. That was her day. A chain-reaction of vomiting traveled from one sister to the next. We were never able to pinpoint the exact cause. It could have been an overzealous car heater, the oxygen-poor air full of English Leather and Ambush in the front seat where I sat squeezed between my parents, lack of food (not a breakfast eater herself, Momma couldn't get any of us to eat it either), or some combination of them all topped with the rush of relief that I could push my trucks through the sand pile my father had put inside an old tractor tire or, if it were cold or raining, move the plastic animals up and down the gangplank of the metal Noah's ark that I set up behind Momma's recliner.

✦ ✦ ✦

When I was old enough to attend the kindergarten Sunday school class, Momma could no longer hide that I was clinically shy. I had spent every day of my life rarely more than twenty feet from her. I followed her around while she vacuumed up Lite Brite pegs, ironed Daddy's handkerchiefs, waxed the furniture with Lemon Pledge, and chipped things out of the freezer to thaw for dinner. During coffee breaks, we listened to "Thoroughly Modern Millie" on our stereo. I could pull off a convincing Carol Channing. To me, other children were unpredictable and disturbing.

On the Sunday after Rally Day, a fall event designed to commit people to enrolling both themselves and their children in the Sunday school program, Momma took me down the basement steps into the cold, dark, windowless kindergarten classroom to learn about God. We sat in two tiny chairs beside a tiny Formica table covered with dried glue and glitter to wait for the teacher.

"This is Mrs. Alders," Momma said when a lady appeared with an armload of supplies. Standing erect, she was nearly six feet tall. I stared up at her orange hair. "Say hello," Momma said. I've seen children stare like I must have then, as if they've never seen another human being. "She's usually so friendly," Momma lied, as she disentangled her hand from mine.

Other children eventually straggled in who would become as familiar as my Mary Janes, because I would have to spend so much time with them over the years. That morning, Mrs. Alders balanced a flannel graph on an easel and pulled Jonah, a couple of Ninevites, and the whale from an envelope. Curled with age, the whale repeatedly fell on the floor. Each time I handed it back to Mrs. Alders, she called me helpful, which was almost enough to make me want to go back to her class.

Subsequent Sunday school classes merged into a vague swirl of Old Testament stories that floated in and out of the curriculum over the years like scary reruns: almost-sacrificed children, unsinged men in fiery furnaces, a good brother thrown down a well, Jericho's walls crumbled from stomping. One class stands out, in particular, because I was selected to play the part of the only slave with a speaking part. I was to be beaten for not producing enough bricks by a boy playing one of Pharaoh's henchmen. "I could pretend this is my straw," I told the teacher, kneeling over the polyester fringe of my shawl. When it came time for me to be beaten, I felt unpleasantly helpless, the way I had felt when I watched June Lockhart twist her ankle trying to flee from a bad man Lassie and Timmy had eluded. Her frailty made me sick.

I suddenly stood up from my brick-making before the skinny boy playing Moses had a chance to rescue me. I didn't need his help. I planned my own escape from another boy beating me ever so slightly with the black belt he had pulled from his Toughskins. From my hiding place behind a wing-backed chair someone had donated to our classroom, I plotted how to save, not just myself, but all the other slave girls. Why couldn't Moses the Deliverer have been a girl? (Where other little girls dreamed of marrying their daddy, I imagined one day being a daddy, which then seemed no more impossible than the parting of the Red Sea. I happily and secretly loved one little girl after another, dreaming each would be my wife.) Her lesson in tatters, the teacher called us together to look at a display of the ingredients used in making Egyptian bricks—a pile of straw, a pile of dirt, and a pitcher of water. I remained in my hiding place, disappointed with the Bible lesson: women were weak, men strong, the same lesson I learned in so many other areas of my life. We were shielded from the exceptions: the story of Israel's judge, Deborah, and her female compatriot Jael, who killed an enemy warlord with a tent peg through the temple, and the apocryphal tale about Judith, who saved her people from King Nebuchadnezzar's henchman Holofernes by getting him drunk and whacking off his head with his own scimitar.

I recall only one lesson about Jesus. The Sunday school teachers at Trinity Presbyterian seemed much more comfortable teaching Bible stories about what had happened to people they were sure were dead. Not being able to tell where Jesus really was made mainline Presbyterians nervous. This Sunday school lesson brought on one of a series of spiritual crises I would begin having far earlier than my parents liked. At the time, Presbyterian seminaries were trying to figure out what to do with the Jesus Movement, the 1970s countercultural version of Christianity, how to enfold it without seeming too literal. The pastor's wife, Phyllis, herself a seminary student, gathered all of the grades together for a joint class to see a film.

"When it's over," she said, "we'll have a little talk because I know the man who made the film, and he wants to know what boys and girls like you think of it."

Here's what I thought of it. Afterward, I wanted to find Momma and sit on her lap, even though I was getting too big for that. The star of the film, a white-faced, bald clown, helped other clowns, even sad, dirty ones who no one else liked, even one with a clubfoot, which the camera dwelled on for an eternity. Toward the end of the film, a group of clean, well-dressed clowns began to push the nice clown around between themselves. Before long, they had turned him into a puppet with strings tied to his hands and feet. Several girls around me started to cry. When the clean clowns finally hung him from a set of playground bars. It was too much, even for me.

"Why'd they do that?" I whispered loudly to Kim over the projector. "Is he dead?"

"Shh," she said. "Dying. I think it's Jesus."

"The clown isn't Jesus," I said. "Jesus isn't dead!" I had not yet connected the Messianic dots—Christmas, Good Friday, Easter, "Sitteth on the right hand of God the Father"—and was suddenly very worried about my friend, even if that wasn't at all what I imagined he looked like. And they left him hanging there. The End. The background music turned finally sinister. The screen went white. The lights flicked on.

"What did you learn?" Phyllis said into stunned silence. I finally raised my hand. "You shouldn't be mean to clowns?" I said.

That same year of third grade, I reached the age when human minds inevitably begin to lose their elasticity, when imaginary things are imperiled. No one thinks to offer children the wonder

of the world, real and equally as lovely as it is, to take these things'
place. Talk had started that Santa Claus wasn't real. Not ready
to give him up, the rumors still made me wonder how he brought
toys to every single child in the world all in one night. If Santa
had elves, why did some of the things he brought me have half-
removed price stickers? What about the poor girl up the street
from me who tried to be happy when Santa got her a new set of
drinking glasses because her family needed them? Finally, during
a Saturday night bath, I mustered up the courage to ask Momma.
She looked at my shampooed head with unveiled sadness and said,
"What do you think?"

Santa's demise started a chain reaction of loss. "No Easter
Bunny, no Tooth Fairy, no Jesus?"

"Now wait—there's no Easter Bunny or Tooth Fairy—those
are me—but there is a Jesus," Momma said, but I could see she
was scrambling. I wanted it all to come out. "I've never seen Jesus either," I said. "But you can sense that he's there," she said. I
could, but I needed help to understand, help she herself needed.
Just as I had, without a word from her mouth, absorbed her fear of
lightning, I could sense Momma's uncertainty, a very reasonable
intelligent human uncertainty. Oh, how it would have helped to
acknowledge it, to have gotten down to brass tacks about who Jesus was and who he wasn't, what amazing things that, as a human
being like us, he could and could not have done.

Instead, we floundered together. She hurried to explain resurrection. She tired me out with her reassurances that she'd col-
luded in a big lie only about only three imaginary benevolent be-
ings, not four. But I pretended to believe her. I wanted to believe
in Imaginary Jesus even if he and Santa were only for babies. After
all, he was my oldest friend. The damage had been done. I knew
that the time had come for tiny Imaginary Jesus to be taken away.
My Presbyterian self had been caught loving too much. Despite
his daily mention at home, a torrent of doubt pushed him from
my heart. I stopped hearing his whispers. Searching for his tiny
self became something else that, the older I grew, I wouldn't think
was fun anymore. And without a more solid sense of the very real

wonder that had given rise to him and to me and to everything else, for that matter, I wouldn't search for him again until my church told me to.

2

Lovingkindness

At twelve, the age of spiritual accountability, the age my imaginary friend had debated Talmud with the teachers in the temple, I couldn't have given an account for a great number of things. I lied about having periods so I could be excused from taking showers in gym class. I masturbated and then lost sleep worrying about it. I did not defend my frail best friend, Margaret, from the daily attacks of a large-breasted bully, Frannie, because I feared Frannie would turn her abuse on me. I had huge ridged white teeth, my father's bulbous nose, curly hair that wouldn't feather, and I was beset with worry. I hadn't imagined Imaginary Jesus skittering around in my life for years. I lived in the cold enamel of junior high where he would have been eaten alive as I already had been. Jesus and I had our unpopularity in common. Also, as he had as a twelve-year-old, I wanted to go to church as often as possible, especially Wednesdays. Wednesdays meant youth group meetings and Mary Ellen Adams, the pastor's daughter. She made me a zealot.

I loved her the first time I met her, at age nine, when my parents had suggested the two of us play Barbies while they and her father discussed the possibility of his becoming our pastor. Usually, I played Barbies with no one but Margaret, who, like me, involved her Barbie and the Sunshine Family ('70s hippie Barbie knockoffs) in tense hostage situations. Even though her Barbie played Mommy, her dialogue was flat, and her plot was dismal, I loved Mary Ellen. From my hiding place behind the Barbie 747, I peered at her. She was bouncing Barbie up and down and asking Ken what he wanted for dinner, telling him how nice he looked. I waited to be filled with the disgust that never manifested.

So desperately did I want to go to Mary Ellen—what church had become to me—that one Wednesday night, when our sky-blue Ford XL was in the shop and Momma had no way to take me to youth group, I had a textbook pubescent event. I yelled. I rolled across my bed into my bedroom wall, which was wallpapered with tiny clowns.

Wearing nothing but her panties and bra, Momma took breaks from fixing potato-hamburger patties to stand in my bedroom door and monitor my condition. She was going through what I heard her tell people on the phone was "the change." Every so often she would redden and lift her shirt to show us the sweat running down her stomach. "I think we can turn the heat down just a little," she'd say to the rest of us bundled in sweaters. Familiarity with her own mood swings must have given her enough empathy to keep from harming me.

She stood at my bedroom door, drying her hands on a dish-towel. "Do you see how silly this is? Do you see a car we can drive?"

"I'm going," I said. "I'll walk if I have to." I swung my legs over the side of the bed and put my shoes on. That day I had scored a touchdown for the wrong team in flag football, and in retaliation, Frannie tried to wring my hand off my arm. I was the timid chicken, hesitant at the feed pan, that either starves on the fringes or that the other birds eventually peck to death. At youth group, everything was different. People, especially Mary Ellen, liked me because I could make them laugh.

"You're not walking, Kelly," Momma said. "There are no side-walks on Chrysler. Someone will hit you. It's ten miles."

I'd had no intention of walking to church, but I had a way with Momma. For instance, she had believed me even when I told her my first grade teacher's father loaned her his farm animals—horses, cows, pigs, and eventually, when the stories no longer impressed, giraffes—to bring to our class. At a parent-teacher conference, Momma told my teacher to thank her father for his generosity. She found out he sold insurance.

"I'm certainly not walking with you," Momma said and left the doorway. The elastic had given out on one leg of her underwear and this made me feel sorry for her for a minute.

I resumed my tirade.

"I like the Bible studies," I said, pulling out the big guns. My parents so wanted God to be important to us.

"The patties are sticking," Momma said.

I threw myself against the wall again, imagining the youth group in the church kitchen without me. First, we cooked dinner together under the supervision of Barbara Mann, a short, heavy woman with a small mustache who worked part time as youth minister to defray the costs of divinity school. I imagined them making spaghetti and meatballs, and Mary Ellen dipping her fingers in the jar of sauce, smearing it across someone else's cheek instead of mine.

My sister telephoned.

"Your sister Kathy's getting her hair cut over by the church," Momma said. "She heard you screaming all the way in here and asked why—if you wanted a ride. After all that, I don't know if I should let you go." But I did go.

Mary Ellen missed youth group that night. She had cheerleading tryouts, which for her were only a formality.

✦ ✦ ✦

During Lent, those of us who would be twelve by Easter met in the Colonial Room—a long, carpeted room filled with early American furniture and heavy green drapes—for Confirmation Commissioning Class. By the end of the eight-week course, we would officially become Christians. We would take our first communion at the Maundy Thursday service to commemorate Jesus's last supper with his disciples.

After our communal supper on the first Wednesday of Lent, our teachers, Barbara Mann and Pastor Adams, Mary Ellen's father, a great bull of a man, handed out workbooks called *Serendipity*. The liberal-leaning, thinking brand of Presbyterian church we belonged to didn't like to scare people with too much unadulterated talk of Jesus. Instead, the workbooks had lots of innocuous cartoons and blank lines sprinkled throughout designed for penciling in answers to questions, such as "Martin Luther wrote the _____ and nailed them to the door of the _____."

A question on the first page read, "In your own words describe what it means to be a Presbyterian." I had only a rudimentary understanding of the faith. From a cup Barbara passed around, I took a pencil badly in need of sharpening and wrote, "It means trying to be a good person. You are sprinkled instead of dunked. Presbyterian is hard to spell. Maybe Presbyterians are smart. Our cross looks funny. It doesn't look like a cross. We are not Catholics. We are not Baptists." Then I ran out of lines.

To foster group cohesion, *Serendipity* also included sections called "rap sessions." Rap sessions went out of the vernacular in the 1960s, but being a frugal church, Trinity Presbyterian had purchased the workbooks in large quantities at a discount. They sat in a box in a sunless room in the basement, and so, aside from a slight smell of mold, each fresh workbook gave the illusion of being current. One rap session question said, "If the group were a car, I would be its a) gas tank, b) engine, c) battery, d) wheels, e) windshield wipers, f) exhaust pipe, or g) spark plug. I knew very little about cars, so I just picked the battery because I knew that it was square and had to be recharged occasionally.

Mary Ellen pointed at me and said, "I think this one's a spark plug. She makes us all crack up all of the sudden, like we'd stuck our finger in a light socket." Mary Ellen had chipping red fingernail polish, dark eyes, and smelled like a combination of Bonnie

Bell lip gloss and a cigarette falling apart in the bottom of her suede purse.

I knew how Mary Ellen smelled and how her skin felt because once, after class, she and I were the last two people left roaming the halls of the dark church playing Sardines, the youth group version of hide-and-seek. The rules said that as each person found those hiding, they crawled into the hiding place with them. Eventually, only a few stragglers remained, wandering the tile hallways alone with only the occasional light through the church's stern sixteen-paned windows to guide them. You didn't want to be the last one left. You could not end Sardines by calling out, "I quit." You had to keep looking until you found everyone waiting somewhere in the dark for you.

Mary Ellen and I found each other by the half-door to the crawl space in the wall of the fellowship hall where they stored folding tables between church suppers—a favorite hiding place because it could hold so many people. She touched my sleeve, and I swatted at her hand in the dark, like you would at a June bug trying to hang on.

"Shit! Sorry. Oh, my God," she said. "Who is this?"

I did not need to ask her.

"Thank God, it's you," she said.

"Have you seen anybody else?"

"Not for a long time," she said, whimpering a little.

"Shh," I said, taking charge. We stood still, Mary Ellen squeezing my arm. "That's it. They've all found each other," she said.

Another rule said you couldn't pair off to search. It unfairly minimized the fear and shock when you heard the collective rustle of clothing in the dark rising to greet you.

"I'm not letting go of your arm," Mary Ellen said. "Rule or no rule."

She pulled me into the crawl space. "Are we sure they aren't in here?"

We both felt into the darkness, touching spider webs, exposed cement blocks, the bowels of the church. On what felt like a table-top, I touched what I hoped was jelly. Aside from each other's, we felt no clothing or skin. "They aren't here," she said. She sat and pulled me down next to her. She put her fingers between mine.

"Whatever happens, don't let go of me," she said.

"I won't."

For different reasons, neither of us wanted to start seeking again.

"I refuse to keep looking," Mary Ellen said. "I've had a hard day. When we find them, I'll have a heart attack. You won't leave me, will you?"

"I wouldn't leave you," I said, and then I added, "I'm not going out there alone" so she wouldn't know how much I longed to stay there in the crawl space with her. We hid like that for what seemed like half an hour. For a while, she nervously rubbed her thumb back and forth over my hand. I tried to count the number of times just to keep myself from touching her back. If I had, she would have known I hadn't done so out of fear.

When Mary Ellen felt good and ready, we found the others in the chancel area, under the massive church organ. One of the boys lay camouflaged across its pedals in a black-and-white rugby shirt. Before someone turned on the lights, Mary Ellen squeezed my hand one last time and then turned it loose.

✦ ✦ ✦

In Confirmation Commissioning Class, we learned creeds: the Apostles' Creed and the Nicene Creed. We practiced reciting them as proof that we understood what it meant to eat the flesh and drink the blood of the Lord at Maundy Thursday service. After hearing them every Sunday for twelve years, they were as familiar and without meaning as the Pledge of Allegiance. For adults, they were part of the church's old game of theological pretend, caught as they now were between all that the authors of the creeds had not needed to know and all humans now did. No one dared breathe too hard on a creed, lest the whole thing crumble. It would be years before I would understand why a few in the congregation recited the creeds with crossed fingers. *I believe in*

God the Father Almighty, maker of heaven and earth and in Jesus Christ His only Son our Lord, who was conceived by the Holy Ghost, born of the Virgin Mary, suffered under Pontius Pilate, was crucified, dead, and buried; He descended into Hell; the third day He rose again from the dead; He ascended into heaven, and sitteth on the right hand of God the Father Almighty. From thence He shall come to judge the quick and the dead. I believe in the Holy Ghost, the Holy Catholic church, the communion of saints, the forgiveness of sins, the resurrection of the body, and the life everlasting. Jesus was the same as God, *Very God from Very God*, he was completely human though—not conceived from a sperm and an egg like other babies—but still carried in a womb, *begotten not made.* He was the plastic baby wrapped in felt in our manger scene and my long-lost imaginary friend dressed up for grown-ups. Still, I needed to believe he lived everywhere—in pockets, canyons, in lemonade, in the tip of a conch shell, between Mary Ellen's teeth. I learned and promptly forgot many things about John Knox, the founder of the Presbyterian church. I looked at maps of the Holy Land pulled like window shades from a metal scroll on the wall of the Colonial Room and followed dotted lines representing Jesus's movements on earth.

Barbara Mann gave all the girls a mustard seed trapped in a little ball of blown glass fastened to a necklace. The boys got tie clips. If I had faith even as small as a mustard seed, I could move mountains, Jesus said. I imagined breaking my necklace in a big fat hurry when I needed my old imaginary friend. I didn't wear the necklace but kept it snapped in my coin purse where I also kept a few hairs I plucked from the rug after my dog died of cancer. I took the mustard seed and the hairs out sometimes and held them in algebra class and hoped they would offer help with problems I couldn't solve.

Emboldened by my official status as Christian, I took it upon myself to remind my family to form a circle around the Advent wreath. My enthusiasm didn't bring anyone running. If Karen had still been around instead of living in a trailer with her new husband, she would have gladly joined in, but Advent time dragged the rest of my family away from things that required little of them—Daddy's favorite show, *Mannix*; clipping coupons; picking off chipping nail polish. So that I would stop pestering them, everyone turned everything off and set aside their various activities. We would then read together that night's meditation from the pamphlet we had, with good intentions, purchased from Trinity Presbyterian for $1.50 to help us focus on what Christmas really meant. Since no one else wanted to do it, I didn't need to beg to light the Christ candle. It dripped holy wax on the Bassett dining room table that we never used except on holidays. Momma had to gently scrape at the Advent remains with a butter knife and risk ruining the table until she figured out a linen Christmas table runner would do the trick. It wasn't all for naught though; Advent time caused my family and me holy discomfort. It made us feel that at the very least we should start being a little nicer to each other if we were going to keep repeating something so religious on school nights. The ritual made us acknowledge the vast chasm between how much the Advent pamphlet writers assumed we loved each other and the growing, awkward ambivalence my sisters and I felt toward Daddy and he toward us. By going through the motions, my family brushed hard enough against the Sacred that we had a difficult time finding our way back to whatever we'd been doing.

Sometimes, if I concentrated, I could conjure up a vision of my old friend Imaginary Jesus, the closest I had ever come to God. Sensing my confusion about things, Momma took me to Zondervan Music and Gift where I bought a pocket mirror with a picture of a white Jesus in striped clothes, knocking on a heavy wooden door of a stone house with a porch light. "Behold I stand at the door and knock. If anyone hear my voice and answer, I will enter in and sup with him, and he with me." I kept it in the bottom of my purse. When things got bad, I felt around in my purse until I found his blond face. I pulled him out and held him tight in my palm where no one else could see. I told him I had faith that he could take me away from the school bus with its smell of stale vomit, hot vinyl, and teenage boys. I had faith that he might help my parents find the money to buy me pants at the middle of the school year to replace the ones I had grown out of at the beginning. Over time, though, I grew tired of looking at the mirror, an ineffectual substitute for my old faithful friend.

✦ ✦ ✦

"I asked a boy who goes to your school, Pat Pernice, if he knew you. He said your name sounded familiar, but he couldn't remember you," Mary Ellen said the Wednesday before Easter. She went to a different school than I did. "I met him at a party."

"I know who he is," I said. "We're not friends or anything."

Pat Pernice rode my school bus. Every day, he blocked the aisle, and called Margaret and me "faggots." "He thinks we're girlfriends or something," Margaret said. Every day, a good girl with Jesus in my purse, I waited until Pat Pernice chose to let me pass. "It is not right to hate," Momma always said. For an hour or so every day after school, I hated myself instead.

"You know why you and Pat aren't friends?" Mary Ellen asked. "You don't smoke, and that's why you don't know people who smoke. He's a nice boy."

"It wouldn't help if I smoked," I said. I was too afraid to smoke and too afraid of people who did. If he'd lived in the late 1970s, Jesus would have hung out with people who smoked. This gave me one more thing to feel ashamed of.

"No," she said. "That's right. You couldn't smoke. You're one of those people who's going to live a long time. I don't know anyone else like you."

She was probably right, I thought. I would live a long time, but what for?

✦ ✦ ✦

At the end of the eight weeks, I received a certificate from the Presbyterian Church USA with my name on it saying I was a Christian.

"Lissa has decided she doesn't feel comfortable graduating from Confirmation Commissioning Class," Barbara Mann said at the last meeting before Maundy Thursday communion. Lissa Baker didn't want to be rushed into becoming a Christian. None of us said anything. All over again, I doubted everything anyone had ever told me about Jesus. What if it was all an elaborate hoax? What if he was just a picture on a pocket mirror?

"Does anyone want to ask any questions about Lissa's decision?" Barbara said. I felt sorry for Barbara and Pastor Adams. Mrs. Baker, Lissa's mother, had jet-black hair cut like Marlo Thomas's and had divorced her husband and gone back to college. Momma didn't like Mrs. Baker waving her modern ideas in everyone's face.

"Did she decide on her own?" I finally said.

"Yes, Lissa came to us on her own. It was a difficult thing for her to do."

"Well, how do any of us know we're ready?" Mary Ellen said.

Pastor Adams and Barbara had no ready-made answer, so they left the remaining six of us in the Colonial Room to talk about it without adults present.

It would never have occurred to me that I had the option of refusing the Lord's Supper, let alone the creeds, maps, group cohesion exercises, John Knox, or church governance.

After a while, Barbara and Pastor Adams came back into the room.

"Any questions?" Barbara said.

✦ ✦ ✦

All six of us came to church early on the night of Jesus's betrayal to walk through our part of the evening.

"All right," Pastor Adams said. "After 'Let Us Break Bread Together On Our Knees,' I will come down like this and offer you bread, and you'll take one of the cubes. You hold it until you hear me say, 'Take, eat, this is my body broken for you. Do this in remembrance of me.' Then you can eat your cube, and everyone else will, too." He stopped and smiled.

"How do you break bread on your knees?" I asked. Despite the solemnity of the moment, I couldn't live without the laugh I knew I would get from Mary Ellen.

I had never been allowed to partake before, and that, if for no other reason, made me look the slightest bit forward to communion. We all knew the drill. During moments of intense boredom, all of us had inevitably stumbled across the extra Communion Service leaflet glued to the inside back cover of our hymnals. Leader's words in red; people's words in black. I had begged for even a crumb of Momma's piece of the Lord, but she never once relented. Most of what I knew about the Lord's Supper was that for the past twelve years I hadn't been invited but had been made to sit among those who had, watching them chew and swallow.

"Now you'll stay seated, and I'll hand the person on the end the tray of cups," Pastor Adams said.

I winced. I feared the tray of cups more than the idea that Imaginary Jesus wasn't real. Made of solid brass and filled with four tiers of tiny glass cups filled with grape juice, the tray weighed about fifty pounds. Once, Mrs. Andrews, the palsied church librarian, dropped the tray. It made a sound I'll never forget. I remember the puddle of juice and broken glass under Mrs. Andrews's chair and the long purple stains down her legs. I remember the collective gasp and how, aside from the lady with blue wavy hair in the chair next to Mrs. Andrews attempting to put shards of the little cups back in the brass holes, everyone pretended as if nothing had happened, as if the Lord hadn't spilled all over the floor.

"Is it really blood?" Mary Ellen said and then grabbed my thigh, snickering. As always, I had to try hard to pretend I didn't like it more than I should.

Pastor Adams offered his daughter a serious explanation of transubstantiation, a Catholic belief we did not share, that at a certain point during the mass, the wine (in our case grape juice) did indeed become the blood.

Throughout the evening, Lissa Baker's refusal of Christianity hung in the air above us. Did anyone know Jesus well enough for all of this? Nevertheless, I and the six remaining confirmands each took our first sip of the Lord. I expected to feel something. But, I came to learn, Presbyterians don't *feel* spiritual things; they *think* them. Like the disciple Thomas, we had trouble seeing the Lord.

Easter Sunday morning, I hunted for chocolate eggs, a tradition none of us could give up even though I no longer believed. When I brought up Lissa that sunny afternoon, Momma said that the Bakers thought too much anyway. "Don't you worry about her."

After Easter services—He is risen; He is risen indeed—we ate ham with cherries. That Sunday night, with the first smell of wind and dirt and spring blowing through the window screens, I watched Charlton Heston part the Red Sea, and that was enough in one day for a twelve-year-old to believe.

✦ ✦ ✦

Later that year, I stepped out of the shower one morning onto an orange shag bath rug and confessed to the ceramic cherubs hanging on the wall with plastic flowers coming out of their heads that I was a lesbian. I knew Pat Pernice wouldn't be the last person to notice. A prayer grew in my head that my old friend Jesus would come to me and help me stop being a lesbian. In fact, I told him I had the faith that he could make me act or feel like everyone else.

✦ ✦ ✦

So well did I hide my real self, that by the time I turned fourteen, Kurt Dreiling, an older boy in the youth group, mistook me for a girl who liked boys. I saw, in him, an opportunity to appear normal for a short time. Nearly everyone in the youth group had, at sometime or another, paired off in the few weeks before the annual mission work trip. Potential couples intently watched each other during sermons.

Because I loved Mary Ellen, I'd never concerned myself with pre-work trip courtship displays. All I cared about was that she didn't like church boys and always left her current boyfriend at home and only carried a postage-stamp-size picture of him in a plastic sleeve of her wallet. Without attachments, she remained at my complete disposal. We rode together, ate together, slept in adjoining bunks.

The week before the work trip, while we all stood on the church steps in the darkness after the youth group meeting, Kurt's fingers, with their bitten-off nails, pushed their way into my balled-up hand. Reluctantly, I opened my fist. He never said a word to me. We had become a couple.

That year we went to the Presbyterian camp at Flathead Lake, Montana, to clean up ash from an eruption of Mount St. Helens. At a truck stop in Scott's Bluff, Nebraska, Kurt decided to leave me and sit at the back of the bus next to Jodie Hamilton. He'd found out she had broken up with her boyfriend before she left and, unlike me, let him put his hand up her shirt. He never returned to the seat I saved for him. At about two o'clock in the morning, somewhere in the West, Mary Ellen wobbled to the empty seat beside me, the light from a passing truck revealing the look of concern on her face.

"Are you all right?" she said.

She sat with me all the rest of that night past dark hills and radio towers until we saw the first light in the sky in Wyoming. She did not sleep but asked permission to lay her pillow on my shoulder. She leaned against me, telling me why Kurt might have left me for Jodie. It took concerted effort to pretend to mourn. I looked out the window, hoping she could not see my look of contentment reflected in the glass.

"He never liked me anyway," I said, taking advantage of the situation. Mary Ellen worried about my self-esteem, a concept discussed in our *Serendipity* workbooks.

"I like you," she said, milking my upper arm like an udder. "I mean, if you were a boy—you know what I mean."

+ + +

The bus broke down somewhere in Wyoming. The Presbyterian church that had planned to host us only one night graciously let us sleep on the floors of their Sunday school classrooms for an indeterminate amount of time. While driving the only backup vehicle into Laramie to pick up a mechanic, our bus driver pulled to the side of the road and had an aneurysm that doctors would say he was far too young to have suffered. Mary Ellen's mother, Joan, who had ridden with him, called from the hospital to tell us of their helicopter ride.

Every afternoon about three o'clock, an older boy, Kevin, took a baggie of pot from inside one of his tube socks. Everyone, including Mary Ellen, left to smoke it—everyone, that is, except a quiet boy named Paul, a fat girl named Debbie, and me. The only thing the three of us had in common was that we hadn't been invited.

An Eagle Scout, Paul sketched plants in a spiral notebook. I followed him through the dirt and sagebrush, squatting when he squatted. Debbie sat on the ground next to us. She loved Jesus with a fervor unknown to any other youth. She carried a white leather King James Bible with a zipper, given to her by her father. He had left Trinity because he said you couldn't find the Lord there. To find the Lord, Debbie's father had to become a Baptist. Debbie also wore a pin with a picture of a goose beneath the words "Honk If You Love Jesus." No one had the heart to point out to her that her mother was having a poorly concealed affair with another of the adult sponsors.

Over our heads, the blue sky stretched taut as the lid of a jar.

"Where is everybody?" Debbie said on the third day, standing up. Neither of us answered her. She had a lima bean-shaped patch of dirt pressed into her shorts. I hated her for not being Mary Ellen. Eventually, a line of the smokers reappeared on the crest of a foothill. For a few hours after smoking, Mary Ellen either took a nap or said things that didn't make any sense. "I'm sorry," she said every day. "You wouldn't want to come anyway. It isn't fun." She did not permit my following her.

Our fourth night of sleeping on the floor of the K-3 classroom, I walked in my sleep. Mary Ellen found me digging in a bucket of crayons searching for a doorknob. When I took a sip of the water she brought me, I awoke to an entire room of girls, blinking, irritated.

"How far do you think you'd have gone if I hadn't found you?" Mary Ellen whispered before we fell asleep.

"Not far enough," I said.

✦ ✦ ✦

A mechanic fixed the bus, and we made it to Flathead Lake Presbyterian Camp. The first day after cleaning volcanic ash, I stepped on a field mouse on my way out of the mess hall where I spent my break times reading *The Hobbit* while Mary Ellen smoked pot in the pine trees. I saw the mouse fly off the sole of one of my huge new hiking boots and lie on its side gasping. I cupped it in my hands until one of the adults took it away from me and killed it behind a cabin.

After dinner I went to my bunk and wrote on a piece of paper. "I want to go someplace else." I folded up this prayer and carried it my coat pocket.

A few nights before we went home, I tried to remember what Momma always said: "You have to make yourself part of the group. Get back on that horse." During devotions, we sang "Pass It On."

By the end of the song, I had determined to pass it on, whatever it was, so I secretly volunteered to play the ugly person in a group initiation game called the "Ugliest Person in the World." I shouldn't have done this. By participating, I hoped to rise in the social strata and gain further access to Mary Ellen. Those in the know about initiation games belonged to an exclusive group of only the most fearless teenagers.

"Okay," Joan said. "You remember what you're supposed to do?"

"Yes," I said. I'd seen "The Ugliest Person in the World" game before. I laughed and took several mincing steps into the kitchen, where Joan wrapped me in a green Army blanket and led me back into the center of the mess hall.

"Okay," she whispered, "have fun."

"Under this blanket," Joan said in a sideshow voice, "is the ugliest person in the world. Is anyone here brave enough to look?"

I lay on the floor chuckling quietly to myself. The two volunteers who knew the score each lifted the corner of the blanket, looked at me, screamed, and fell down on the floor near me, as if dead.

"Anyone else?" Joan said.

An inkling of worry crept into my brain. I was supposed to do something when the third person, one who did not know the joke, lifted the blanket. But what was it? Maybe I'd never known at all. It was really very simple. I was supposed to have screamed when the uninitiated person lifted the blanket, making them even uglier than me, the ugliest person in the world.

"I am ugly—and stupid," I thought, lying there. I imagined I looked like a turd someone had laid a blanket over. I considered creeping away, blanket and all, into the adjoining kitchen.

Joan handpicked Mr. Bradish as someone who enjoyed being laughed at. He lifted the blanket and peeked under.

I smiled and waved at him. He lifted it again, waiting for the punch line he knew must be coming.

I heard everyone laugh, then I felt Joan's foot slide under the blanket and hunt for me. "Oh, my, someone survived," she said and whispered something down to me that I couldn't quite hear.

"Ugly person," Joan said, "I'm sending Mrs. Bradish over to look at you." She said this loud and slow just in case I had missed the reminder that neither of the Bradishes knew the score. Mrs. Bradish also looked at me and lived to tell about it.

"Who is it?" I heard people whispering to each other and giggling.

Finally, I heard the floorboards squeaking near me and Mary Ellen's whisper, "You're supposed to scream," she said. "I'll take care of it. Scream when I look at you."

"Not my only daughter, Mary Ellen. Are you going to look? Brave girl, brave, brave girl."

I spent the closing hymn, "For Those Tears I Died," in the bathroom looking at myself in the cracked mirror over the toilet and saying "Idiot." When I did not follow everyone to the cabins, Mary Ellen came in after me. Instead of moving away from the spreading pool of embarrassment around me, she stepped right into it with me. She sat on my bunk and asked me to tell her stories about my Uncle Sam. They made her laugh. She sat on my bunk until she thought I had fallen asleep.

✦ ✦ ✦

While the youth group was away cleaning volcanic ash, the church voted to remove Pastor Adams from his position. At General Assembly, he had voted in favor of allowing gays to become full members of the church.

As soon as Joan and Mary Ellen returned from the work trip, the family packed all their things into boxes and moved out of the manse. I never saw Mary Ellen again. Momma said she didn't know where to take me to find her. When I asked why they had left, my parents told me the half-truth that Pastor Adams had had to leave because no one wanted to give money to the church anymore. Had I known the whole story, I would have known that I, not Lissa Baker, should have dropped out of Confirmation Commissioning Class. I would have believed that I had no right to eat the flesh of the Lord or to become a Presbyterian. And I would have thought I had no right to love Mary Ellen, through whom, though I was not yet aware of it, Imaginary Jesus himself showed *lovingkindness* to me.

3

Lost and Found

My sophomore year in high school, I knew I was lost. I couldn't give a clear description of Imaginary Jesus; we'd been separated for too long. I'd started looking for him again in a white-hot panic because I knew I was the only gay person in the world, or in Raytown, Missouri, at least. Being gay meant you were evil, a pervert. Anita Bryant, who Momma admired, thought so. Everyone in school thought so. Although I'd always gone to my parents with problems, this would have stretched "unconditional" love to the snapping point. Any time the subject came up, they thanked God none of their children was gay, which, looking back, must have been more a hope, a subtle warning even, than a statement of certainty. No, for this problem, I needed someone who, as I remembered, had always known what to do, who would know what to do with me. Trinity Presbyterian had tried to assure me its version was the right one, but from the description I'd gotten in Confirmation Commissioning Class, he seemed so ethereal I knew they'd lost the scent. Finally, I did what the lost must do; I stood still and waited. Fundamentalists have an eagle eye for the lost, who, like me, need tangibility. They would introduce me to their version of Jesus, and even though he wasn't the same as I remembered, I would spend far too many years thinking I was just remembering him wrong. The fundamentalists believed that gay people were evil perverts, too, but that they just needed to start over from scratch and be born again. It was that simple.

Because I'd completely absorbed the pervasive fear of homosexuality, I couldn't just quietly begin appreciating my "growing sexual feelings" as we had all been told to do in Sex Ed. class. Instead, I repressed myself in a perfectly normal series of passing crushes until my repression manifested itself in a lurid cartoon I drew on a piece of notebook paper during Physical Science. The first five squares showed me putting a mask over Jill's face—Jill was a cheerleader at lab table three—tying her up, and putting her in my parents' cement garden shed with the lawn mowers, rakes, potting soil, and Hippity Hops. In the next square, I pushed a plate of scribbled food under the shed door. In another, I rescued her. In the final block, she gave me her undying love and gratitude, which I couldn't figure out how to draw. I also had trouble with the plot. How would I keep her from figuring out I was both villain and hero? The little mask I had drawn on myself wouldn't have covered nearly enough of the long narrow face I'd inherited from Daddy. Besides, after doing all those handstands and round-offs, Jill was stronger than I was. I'd never have been able to pull my fantasy off. Despite my dangerous decision to write "Jill" on the shirt of one of the badly drawn figures, I couldn't destroy the cartoon; it gave me too much pleasure. I lived in constant fear of losing it or, worse, having it confiscated from my notebook and being called to the principal's office for being a psychopath. I did have good taste though; Jill was beautiful. I was realistic, too; she was only Junior Varsity.

I knew I must work on becoming an appealing person, someone people wouldn't have to be forced to pay attention to. Jill and several other nice students were members of Fellowship of Christian Athletes (FCA). I knew who belonged because they wore the same T-shirts with a Bible verse on the back and little crosses around their necks. They tried, even within the social meat grinder of high school, to be nice to people like me who just couldn't fade into the background, the most prudent course if one weren't talented, good-looking, or straight. I lacked early morning mental vigilance and would find myself at school wearing a pair of high-water Liberty overalls like the tomboy on *Hee-Haw*, a flannel shirt, and a stickpin with a basset hound on it—because I had a basset hound. In the early morning fog of self-confidence that had built slowly up in the fifteen hours since it had burned down in the school hallways the day before, my clothes had made sense. Once at school, though, my get-ups shouted that I didn't understand how to be a girl. Also, I was terrible at pretending to like boys. Most of them smelled like a mixture of silkscreen ink from long-unwashed concert T-shirts, B.O., and marijuana. My little bit of blue eye shadow just didn't cut it. Everything about me added up to gay.

The Christian athletes fascinated me. For one thing, they treated me like I deserved to live. For another thing, they weren't huddled on the social fringes like my tiny ghetto of odd friends. They were thriving. Some of the girls even looked a little bit like me, like they were growing into something other than young women and no one seemed to mind.

Unfortunately, most of us lured to Christianity by these happy athletes were destined not for FCA but for a sad, catchall group of fundamentalists called Youth for Christ (YFC). Where FCA members were hurdlers, quarterbacks, thinkers, and gymnasts, YFC admitted people with too many teeth, homemade haircuts, cheap jeans, and poorly concealed emotional problems they wanted quickly rid of. FCA members "fought the good fight and won the race." They witnessed to their fellow students by their mastery of life, not merely their ability to withstand it. YFC members, on the other hand, adopted the verse "Christ alone and Him crucified." Crucifixion they could understand. Instead of gym bags, YFC members carried Bibles zipped inside vinyl covers with crosses on them that made them look like religious shaving kits. I understood my place; I was made for Youth for Christ.

◆ ◆ ◆

I bought a journal. My creative writing teacher told us we should write everything that occurred to us for fifteen minutes without stopping to think. She called this freewriting. Because there were things I was afraid to see coming out the end of my pencil, I didn't freewrite very well. Though I did not lift the pencil, as I'd been told not to, the point of it often sat motionless as a stalled car at the end of a word. Nevertheless, I tried to freewrite every day at the back of the yard behind the cement shed where I had decided it would be wrong to hold anyone captive. I sat with my back against the electric pole with metal foot hooks I occasionally climbed, trying to work up the nerve to climb right out of Raytown. I would link into the electrical infrastructure, into the wild blue yonder with the squirrels, running from yard to yard until I made it to the Chalk Pyramids, odd geological formations my cooped-up father said rose out of the ground near his hometown of Healy, Kansas, wherever that was. I didn't ever have to come down if I didn't want to. Sitting there amid last summer's dead tomato vines and burst milkweed pods one evening, I wrote the cliché, "There has to be more to life than this." My teacher didn't like us to write in clichés. "They tell me nothing," I could hear her saying. I didn't know what I meant by it other than that I wanted to be happy. I heard my cliché verbatim on a Christian radio drama, "Unshackled." Each episode, a derelict left a life of sin that was scored by minor chords on the Wurlitzer, and, to an up-tempo hymn, asked Jesus to save him. That I'd been able to tune in anything, much less a program about a reunion with Jesus, between the crackles on my transistor radio sitting on the dirt beside me was, I thought, its own kind of miracle. Maybe, like the man on the radio, I'd caused all my own problems. Maybe I was gay because I had sinned. Maybe when I found Imaginary Jesus again, that's what he would tell me, and maybe he could help me stop.

During another freewrite, I wrote that Beth, a new friend in American Government, had finally picked up on my hints and invited me to an after-school YFC meeting. I took up several pages about her horse in the barn behind her house that occasionally ground his hoof into my foot while I brushed him. Beth said he did this only to people he liked. She carried the tiniest, most discreet Bible I had ever seen. She seemed a little more normal than the other people in YFC and made me feel like joining wouldn't mean complete social suicide.

I was already terminally awkward. In my spare time, I loosened my cuticles from their moorings and peeled them down on every finger at least to the first knuckle. My fingers bled on everything—the school's loaner textbooks, pencils, homework, and clothing. People quickly figured out my injuries were self-inflicted, no matter what story I invented to explain them. I chewed my cuticles whenever I felt afraid that someone might say or do something to make me feel worse about myself than I already did, something that took the better part of every day. It would be years before I learned the problem had a name—displacement behavior—or that animals in stress-filled situations do similar things to themselves such as preening out their feathers, the very things that would allow them to fly away. Beth also chewed her cuticles, which made me feel relieved; I had much less explaining to do. Her cuticles also worried me though, since she had already found Jesus. Her cuticles made me doubt that when I found him again, he would become the firewall I needed between me and everything that broke my heart.

By the afternoon of the YFC meeting, they could have showed a dental hygiene film and I would have been ready to give my life over. I didn't know what to do with it anymore. At first, the film held the promise of an "After School Special," which I liked for their instructive looks at modern teenage problems my parents would never allow me to have. "A Thief in the Night" focused not on a modern problem, however, but on a prophetic one: The Rapture. Within the first ten minutes, the attractive young star made a grave error: she neglected to accept Jesus Christ as her Personal Lord and Savior when an opportunity arose and the Rapture came. Represented cinematically by a bright flash of light rather than a low-budget interpretation of Christ descending from the clouds in glory, the Rapture took all of this girl's family and most of her friends. And it left quite a mess in its wake—car accidents, interrupted meetings. A cake the girl's mother had intended to bake for her after-school snack had splattered all around the kitchen from an instantly and permanently unattended mixer. The Antichrist, a man in a business suit who looked a little like Daddy's boss, appeared on the new global television broadcasts, urging people to drop by the closest government building to have 666 tattooed either on their forearm or forehead, whichever they preferred. The protagonist found an equally confused and orphaned neighbor boy, and the two formed an alliance that endured every trial and tribulation but the last, when they were finally apprehended for trying to purchase milk and a pop-top can of spaghetti without the mark of the beast. They were discreetly beheaded off-camera in a school parking lot with a host of other tardy converts. You could tell when the boy died because you could see the yellow balloon he'd been clutching floating into the ominous blue sky overhead. The girl was led quietly away after him with a prayer on her lips, secure in the knowledge that though she was one of those prophesied to suffer a horrible death because of her initial refusal of Jesus, she would be numbered among those who would spend eternity with him.

I'd never heard of the Rapture. I'd never heard of the fundamentalist's version of Jesus. If you didn't do what he said, if you didn't get born again, evict your real self and become a host for his Holy Spirit before the final trumpet sounded, he'd ignore you. Oh, he might feel bad about having to, but he'd ignore you anyway, which you didn't want because he was the only one who could make excuses for you to his father, God, who was meaner than he was. In this Jesus's big mean shadow, my imaginary friend didn't seem as real. Maybe my old pal was just for babies, and this one was the real one, just the one I needed to whip me into shape.

I sat shaking in a hard school chair with a squeaky back. The shop teacher, the YFC sponsor who had operated the projector and whom everyone said had once been a drunk, asked us to bow our heads. He asked if anyone of us wanted to ask Jesus into our heart. I recited the following prayer. "Dear Lord Jesus. I know that I am a sinner. Please forgive me of my sin and take me to heaven when I die." That was it, the end of the meeting. I didn't feel loved and comforted as I'd hoped, but terrified.

In the nick of time, out from behind some table saw or another popped my old imaginary friend. Before anyone had a chance to check if my conversion was genuine, which fundamentalists like to call follow-up, he and I scuttled out of the building into the parking lot where Momma sat idling in our long, whipped-cream-colored Le Sabre. It was too late to tell Imaginary Jesus I'd changed my mind. I'd already raised my hand and prayed the Sinner's Prayer.

"How was your meeting?" she said. I'd told her I'd joined French Club. I didn't want to get into a religious discussion with her because she might find out more than she wanted.

"Fine," I said, turning to look at the back seat, half-expecting to see the YFC version of Jesus sitting there, trumpet raised. Even then, I was having a fantasy about how I might have rescued the little girl in the film, even after I'd asked him to save me from my mutant gay self. Once home, Imaginary Jesus—who seemed just as kind as I'd remembered him—and I fled immediately to my room, where I had lived alone for a year since Kim went away to college. I felt sure I didn't want to share it with someone again, especially someone in charge of the Rapture. I sat atop my purple nylon bedspread, my teeth chattering.

"Well," I said into the silence. And this is the miracle. In those first moments back in my disturbed self again, Imaginary Jesus peeked out his tiny head and asked me how I'd been and told me he'd missed me. He said little of rejecting all I had been up until that point, as the man at YFC club had suggested. In fact, our conversation in my head had as little to do with YFC as possible. The film had embarrassed him. He sensed its ridiculously literal take on Revelation had terrified me back into a friendship with him and wanted to reassure me that he meant me no harm. It would take me years to learn that, in spite of what YFC suggested, I could try to repent of my genetic code and my personality, but they would still be there waiting for me when I turned back around. That's the way genetic codes and personalities are. Imaginary Jesus stretched out his tiny imaginary palm, like you would to a stray dog. It had a little love in it. Of course, I still didn't trust him, didn't trust that I even had the right one of him, but enough of me still remembered the feeling that I had had when I was a little girl, the feeling that I belonged in the world with everything else, just as I was, the feeling that had allowed me to imagine him in the first place.

When I was ready, we left my bedroom for supper, where we kept our secret to ourselves. I went back to my bedroom and did my freewriting while he settled back into his old home in my heart. I then did my algebra homework thoroughly and incorrectly as usual. Before bed, I brushed my teeth, something I forgot to take care of more often than not. I fell asleep feeling ever so slightly more hopeful.

4

Raise Up a Child in the Way She Should Go

I didn't join Youth for Christ club to become a social pariah or a rebellious, sickeningly religious child my parents didn't recognize: that came free with the new membership. I joined because YFC members talked about Jesus as if he were real. No matter that the Jesus they claimed bore no resemblance to my imaginary friend. At Trinity Presbyterian, which I still attended with my parents, he had slowly become a distant memory, the best of good, dead people. That wasn't good enough for me.

I soon found that becoming a pariah for Christ did have benefits. Most importantly, it distracted me from being gay, which was becoming ever more difficult to hide. Instead of a deviant, I could be a religious whacko. No longer simply strange, I had my faith to blame. I like to think that if I had found a club who declared I could be both Christian and gay, I would have joined and saved myself some backtracking. But that's unlikely. I wasn't ready for affirmation.

YFC had a whole host of ideas about ways we could get people to ridicule us, like carrying our Bibles everywhere, even to gym class. I may as well have gone to school dressed as Anne Bradstreet. Trying to pass out poorly licked-clean Popsicle stick crosses with other YFC members before the first bell on Good Friday did me no favors either. I was still too awkward to give my fellow students Imaginary Jesus's love, the love he quickly offered me when someone threw a Popsicle stick cross at my face. As an apprentice fundamentalist, it wasn't my place to question club activities, even if they weren't winning converts. No one asked me or any other YFC member the reason for "the hope that was within us" as the Bible verse we memorized. Obviously, we didn't have any hope.

I whiled away many hours at YFC learning how to become not only a pariah but a bigot as well. Satan loved an open mind, they said. Between brow-beatings about whom I shouldn't associate with and what I shouldn't wear, think, or say, they fed me cider and doughnut holes, sang with me, and sympathized. The way they explained it, people liked making fun of Jesus, *ergo* me. Always had, always would. Blessed was I when I was persecuted for his name's sake.

If I listened hard, I could hear my Jesus's quiet voice, even through YFC's thick fundamentalist filter. He said he hadn't commissioned me to be a victim. It worried me that he didn't seem to care that I was gay, when, as my new friends said, the Bible was so clear on that and so many other things. In fact, YFC led me to believe that Jesus had had to die because I was gay, and every time a gay person like me had another gay thought, it killed him all over again. Jesus's calls to life, mercy, and justice for myself as well as others and his quiet contradictions of the views of those in my new fundamentalist inner circle seemed so discordant, so off track, that I doubted they were his.

When Momma mentioned that I'd started going to YFC club, Karen rejoiced. With the best of intentions, as she had my whole life, Karen decided what was best for me. She would arrange for me to have a diet of spiritual meat rather than the thin baby formula Trinity Presbyterian offered to grown-up Christians like my parents who no longer needed it. With Daddy's temper, though, both of us knew better than to tell them so. I must set aside the plans I never had for Saturday night to go with her and her husband, Roger, and members of More Grace Baptist Church, which met in their living room, to the YFC Rally, a weekly gathering of its bedraggled local high school clubs. I must join the larger ranks of the weird.

The Rally happened every Saturday night at YFC headquarters, a hulking white cement block structure in midtown Kansas City. After the evening's fare of Bible verse quiz competitions, musical numbers, skits, sermon, and an altar call, droves of teenagers gathered downstairs to buy things from a Christian snack bar and say godly things to each other.

On the Saturdays that I went to the Rally instead of to Trinity with my parents, I could spend the night with Karen and go to Sunday school and church the next morning without ever leaving her house. All I had to do was crawl out of bed in her guestroom, wash my face, put on my dress, and wander into her yellow kitchen for Sunday school. Jean, a born-again divorcee, taught the high school class; I was the only student. Roger taught a circle of adults in folding chairs around the guestroom bed that I had vacated so recently the sheets were still warm. Karen taught the children in the sanctuary/living room, which she separated from the kitchen by a collapsible wall that blocked all but the loudest of happy outbursts. One Sunday, Jean and I sat on Karen's sticky yellow kitchen chairs reading the story of the feeding of the multitude. We were surrounded by metaphor: thirty some-odd, half-drunk glasses of juice and cereal bowls with circles of milk in their bottoms were left on every surface by the people Roger had collected on the More Grace Church bus that morning. No one ever left Karen's house/church hungry.

✦ ✦ ✦

Every teenager wanted to sing in a YFC music group. It got you on TV50, YFC's station. After they cleared away the tables and buzzers from team Bible quizzing at the Rally, each music group took the stage one at a time to perform—from the least to the most talented—dressed in gender-appropriate pastels. A cameraman filmed every last one of the singers.

The best musical performances aired repeatedly when TV50 had nothing else to broadcast, usually late on Friday nights when people with no better place to be could tune in and wind up getting saved a first, second, or even a third time because of their witness. I would sit in my dark living room alone in my pajamas watching the most tuneful group, Joyful Noise. I longed for the camera to pan across one particular soprano.

My sublimated desire for this girl resurfaced as a perfectly acceptable fundamentalist pursuit; I would audition for Joyful Noise. This did have some basis in reality because I could carry a tune. In fact, with Karen's encouragement, I sang a solo at a More Grace church service. I stood in front of her red and black living room curtains with the black pompoms sewed to the swag and sang "For Those Tears I Died." Karen said I sounded like Christian radio with the volume turned almost all the way down. I wobbled, terrified, and sang until there were no more verses, looking not up toward heaven as Karen had suggested, but out at an addict Roger had picked up from a HUD apartment complex who was trying to stay upright in his folding chair. My saliva gone and the rough edges of my plastic church shoes snagging in Karen's red shag, I crept back to my chair while still singing the last line, "I felt every teardrop, when in darkness you cried/ And I strove to remind you, that for those tears I died."

At the Rally, I reconnected with an old Trinity Presbyterian youth group friend Cheryl Tupper, a string bean of a girl who sang in one of the top YFC choirs. I hadn't seen her since she left Trinity to attend a Baptist church with her father and younger brother. Her mother and older sister stubbornly remained at Trinity, and Cheryl compared them to flood victims. "They're too stubborn to leave the house for the rescue boat." Unlike Presbyterians, she said, Baptists took Jesus seriously.

"Confirmation class didn't cut it," she said. "We both proved that. You don't become a Christian by turning twelve and going to a class." I nodded agreeably in the back seat of the car as she and her father drove me to choir auditions. Though I knew I shouldn't,

I found Trinity Presbyterian a respite from the rigors of YFC, like a tall, cool glass of milk after too much spicy chili.

I didn't tell Cheryl and her father that I was auditioning for Joyful Noise against my parents' wishes. Even though they had attended Rallies as teenagers, too, my parents didn't have much use for YFC anymore. When I asked if I could try out, Daddy said YFC took people away from their home church. "But it's a Christian group," I said. "I don't care if the angel Gabriel heard you sing and asked you to join a choir, you're not going to," he said. It was a blow to my parents, Daddy in particular, that the Presbyterianism that had nourished them hadn't been enough either for Karen or for me. We'd had to go outside of it hunting for Jesus. "You have a perfectly good church," he said. "You can sing in our choir." Their choir was full of liberal Presbyterians who Karen doubted were even saved. "Trinity's a dead church," she whispered to me, referring loosely to the message to the church at Ephesus, which had "forgotten its first love. . . ." "Momma and Daddy used to be on fire for the Lord, but not anymore." I lay awake one night worrying about Momma's salvation. I didn't worry about Daddy's, because for the past year we had failed to appreciate each other in any way. He did, however, drop me off on his way to his job as a drafting teacher at the Vo-Tech building, so I didn't have to ride the school bus. Now that I was his only daughter left at home, he obsessed about everything I did: the way I held my fork, the length of my showers, the tight navy blue sweatpants I wanted to wear to school. We couldn't seem to love each other, which distilled our commutes to pure silence. Imaginary Jesus tried to reassure me he wasn't worried about either of my parents' salvation; he didn't easily forget a face.

Before I could reconsider my disobedience, I found myself waiting my turn at one of five upright pianos, each with a person banging out "Amazing Grace" with one hand and directing with the other. The woman at my piano stopped playing and said, "Louder honey, sing it out, if you believe it. Do you believe it?"

"Yes," I squeaked. I had a hard time staying with her "Amazing Grace," since renditions were being churned out at various stages all over the room. At an adjoining piano, a reed-thin boy passionately mangled his version, perfectly holding notes not found on any piano. I felt myself pulled into his vortex. "Don't look at him," said my pianist. "You have a pretty voice. Sing it out."

"When we've been here 10,000 years, bright shining as the sun," I breathed. "We've no less days to sing God's praise than when we first begun."

"Fine," she said. "We'll be in touch." I would know in the fall whether or not I had made it into Joyful Noise with the beautiful soprano. On the remote chance that I would be chosen, I counted on my parents' pride at seeing me on TV to dilute their anger. I wandered into the cacophony of the audition hall, dizzy with rebellion.

+ + +

In the spring, I would rebel against my parents again by becoming excessively obedient. I would stop tying up the phone line having unnecessary conversations. I would clean up the sticky sheen my hairspray left on the bathroom wall without being asked and put my dirty clothes in the hamper instead of on the floor where my mother had had to make her own determination. I would change the channel for my father without rolling my eyes. I would come when called, await further instruction, and speak in a soft voice and only when spoken to, just like a Puritan. I would learn how to do this at the Bill Gothard Seminar sponsored by the Institute in Basic Youth Conflicts. Karen thought this would fertilize the tender shoot of my Christian life. From what she said about him, I had secret hopes that Bill Gothard could make me stop being gay.

Where other people my age begged for Alice Cooper tickets, I begged my parents to let me attend the Bill Gothard Seminar. Not only were they skeptical because the Institute in Basic Youth Conflict had no denominational affiliation, they also had no use for Bill Gothard's main cheerleader, Carl, the self-ordained preacher of More Grace Baptist. Karen didn't think it was crazy that Carl took a McDonald's jelly-covered copy of the *Kansas*

City Star home with him every morning to add to the bundles tied with string that lined each inside wall of his house. "No one should have that much newspaper," Momma said. She couldn't put her finger on exactly what else it was about Carl that bothered her so much. They were supposed to be on the same side, after all. Criticizing him left her looking somehow less devout.

Karen tried to assure my parents that Bill Gothard wasn't a Jim Jones. "How many cults do you know of that encourage people to obey their parents? He even obeys his now, and he's in his fifties." She finally wore Momma down.

"It won't affect my homework," I said in a sweet little voice neither Momma nor I had ever heard. "Plus, I'll learn to be submissive."

"She will, Momma," Karen said. "I promise."

I would become so good and so submissive I wouldn't even recognize myself.

I might have even become a heterosexual if Carl hadn't brought his pretty teenage daughter from a failed marriage. He had bribed her to come to the Seminar by promising to pay her car insurance. Carl worried about Laurel's unsaved soul aloud and in front of her. Her name had become Laurel against his wishes; his obstinately non-Christian ex-wife had found it in a book of Greek mythology.

Carl introduced me to Laurel as the young Christian woman he hoped would become her role model. With her curly brown hair and worn copy of *On the Road*, which Carl confiscated, Laurel distracted me from resolving my one Basic Youth Conflict. I fantasized that, in the small pond of More Grace misfits, I might even seem attractive. Laurel could choose to spend her entire week in silence, or she could talk to me. I could spend the week being afraid that she'd been sent by Satan to tempt me, or I could claim a new verse I'd just memorized at YFC club: "All things work together for good for those who love God, who are called according to his purpose."

✦ ✦ ✦

Bill Gothard had his work cut out for him where I was concerned. Sitting in my hard blue plastic chair that first night waiting for the Seminar to start, I daydreamed that I would become the son-in-law Carl had always imagined. I startled from my reverie when an usher handed me the blood-red, twenty-five-pound Seminar book which came with my enrollment. Scattered throughout were watercolors of eagles soaring near their mountain aeries. Not all looked flight-worthy. Eagles were important at the Institute for Basic Youth Conflicts, I guessed, because they weren't afraid of adversity and were too busy flying to fall victim to temptation.

The lights dimmed. A hush fell. At the other end of the aisle from me, Laurel's fingernail file rasped into the silent auditorium. She had a wad of toilet paper sprouting from each ear. I wanted to both run from her and hold her hand. In a profane moment of bravado, I stuck the cap of my pen in my nose and leaned forward to get her attention. Then I crossed my eyes and folded my hands as if in prayer. When she laughed, Carl slapped her on the back of her pretty head. I'd gone and done it—killed Imaginary Jesus all over again.

Suddenly, Bill Gothard's face loomed on a projection screen that unfurled from the ceiling of Municipal Auditorium. He rarely made it to Kansas City for his Seminar in person. Since at this time in the early '80s, VCRs had not yet come into common use, people had to gather in large groups even to see footage of him. In his blue suit with a red tie and math teacher hair, Bill Gothard looked very uncomplicated. Maybe even a little bit gay—a mental flicker I quickly tried to douse. Like other people who don't worry, he had a face without wrinkles. "I hope those of you watching me on a screen don't mind that my physical body is not present with you today," he said. "But rest assured, I am entirely with you in the Lord. Wherever you are, you are in competent hands."

At that, an enormous hand appeared atop an overhead projector trained on an enormous screen beside the one with Bill Gothard's face on it. The hand wrote, "Hello. My name is Cliff," then it arranged the first of many overhead duplicates of pages from the Seminar book atop the projector.

Bill Gothard said, "As the answers appear, you just fill in the blanks yourself." The blessed simplicity of it all. I would never have to wonder where we were in the workbook or what answer to write in the big empty spaces provided.

The first night, Bill Gothard explained why he still lived with his parents at fifty. Cliff drew a sketch of a diamond. Above it, he drew a chisel, and above that, a hammer. On the hammer, Cliff wrote "GOD." On the chisel, he wrote "PARENTS," and on the diamond, he wrote "ME." Bill Gothard said that only through the sculpting of our parents, who were tools in the hands of God, could we become jewels. Next, Cliff drew an umbrella, which he labeled "MOTHER" and "DAD." Having remained in his parents' home in obedience to what he thought God had asked of him, Bill Gothard believed it imperative that all other unmarried persons do the same. "I know it's not the world's way to live at home, but Mother and Dad are God's umbrella of protection over you," he said. Raining down from the top of the overhead, Cliff wrote words like "drugs," "alcohol," "pride," "premarital sex," "loneliness," "television," "idolatry," "credit card debt." I tried to write all these above my umbrella, which I had drawn too big for the space provided.

Someone in Bill Gothard's once-live audience asked if his hammer and chisel and umbrella illustrations still held true if a person's parents were alcoholics, child molesters, physically abusive, or worse, if they didn't follow Jesus. What if they just didn't seem worthy tools?

"That's a good question," he said, turning his unflappable face back toward the audience. We silently waited for him to defuse this bomb. "And this is the hardest for most people to believe, that God especially selects each person's parents as the perfect tool to shape and break her. No matter how abusive, licentious, and ungodly parents can be, a person should submit to their authority as humbly and respectfully as possible. God will honor that obedience to His plan by leading those parents in their task."

With this, Bill Gothard had coaxed me into a hidey-hole so attractive I couldn't imagine ever wanting to leave it again. If I didn't want to move out of my parents' house and marry a man, I didn't have to. Even if it meant living with my irritable daddy, I could and should stay with them until death did us part; whichever of us went first didn't really matter. I would never have to face my sexuality head on. Bill Gothard had handed me a ready-made explanation for the rest of my life.

On the way home on the More Grace bus that night with Roger careening too close to the guardrail on the ASB bridge, I rode unafraid, looking down into the black and frothing Missouri River. I relished the uncomplicated, sexless path unrolling before me as far as the eye could see. All I needed to do was sit still and obey, no matter what happened. I felt so relieved.

◆ ◆ ◆

Friday morning, Momma drove me to school with a note saying I could be excused to attend a special all-day session of the Bill Gothard Seminar. Her heart wasn't in it. My fervor wasn't sitting with her.

"Those are perfectly good record albums," she said. Bill Gothard had told us to purge our lives of rock and roll because it interfered with our heartbeat and made us licentious. "We paid good money for them. It seems silly to get rid of them because one man tells you to, a man you've never met."

After the raid, all I had left were some Disney Read-and-Play records, an early Captain and Tennille, and Barry Manilow. Like a Taliban official, I also took a little onyx Buddha my creative writing teacher had brought back for me from India downstairs to the basement and tried to crush it with a hammer. Bill Gothard urged us to find each and every questionable object we owned and destroy it lest Satan establish a hidden stronghold.

"Bill Gothard says some of the beats in rock music are Satanic."

"Well, that sounds like cockamamie."

We weren't having the right disagreement.

"Well, I think I'll just keep them myself until you grow out of this."

That cut me to the quick, the thought that I might grow out of Bill Gothard, but then I remembered I should obey.

"Okay, you do what you think," I said.

My soft response irritated her. She wondered aloud where I had gone and who had replaced me with this weirdo. Momma had worked hard all her life not to be a weirdo. She read magazines to learn how not to be one. During high school, she had participated in dances and debates and other social events that had terrified her because she wanted to conquer her shyness. She had encouraged all of her daughters to stay current and involved with life.

"Well, we can sell the records at a garage sale if you're so dead set against them," she said, trying to pick a fight.

"No, that's all right," I said. "I'll do what you think is best."

"Don't you make fun of me now," she said.

◆ ◆ ◆

On this last day of his Seminar, Bill Gothard finally covered my Basic Youth Conflict. He equated gay people with the frothing man whose demons Jesus had cast into a herd of pigs that ran pell-mell off a cliff. I had thought that if I tried hard enough not to be gay, I could overcome it, but Bill Gothard said no. He said that after the Seminar, he would be happy to exorcize demons in the privacy of one of the conference rooms. I felt grateful that no one at Municipal Auditorium made the same offer. Terrified of making a spectacle, I also could stop worrying about whatever poor beast would have received my gay demon through no fault of her own, probably a pigeon or a house sparrow since they were the only living things besides humans I'd seen in downtown Kansas City all week. It puzzled me how Imaginary Jesus and a demon could both live inside me; there just couldn't be enough room for both of them. I prayed that my demon would simply starve from lack of sexual activity.

Laurel was triumphant after having endured the week without making one mark in her Seminar book or giving any indication she wanted anything to do with Bill Gothard. With the end in sight, a year of car insurance paid, she coaxed me into losing dozens of games of tick-tack-toe during Bill Gothard's farewell Chalk Talk. Into the drawing of a beach, he drew a cross with fluorescent chalk that you couldn't see until he turned on a black light at the very end. The crowd gasped and applauded. I wrote down Laurel's phone number, and she wrote down mine. At 5:00, we closed our workbooks, and Bill Gothard said goodbye. Cliff turned him off and his head shrunk to a bright pinpoint. On our way out, I thought once more about my demon and threw Laurel's number in the trash.

Bill Gothard's teachings worked their way deep into my psyche like splinters. Had I not still been living in their house, my parents might have hired someone to kidnap and deprogram me. I measured every word. I never raised my voice, always came when called. I quickly tamped down any stray gay thoughts. This went on for weeks, the soft answers and the cheerful countenance. Daddy was itching for a fight.

✦ ✦ ✦

During a family dinner to celebrate my sixteenth birthday, the telephone rang. I crawled over several people in our dining room to answer it. A voice on the other end told me I'd been selected for Joyful Noise. Shocked, I stood in the door between the kitchen and dining room suddenly without enough saliva to finish chewing the dinner in my mouth. My forgotten act of defiance came flooding back. "You'll need to come for a dress fitting next week," she said.

"Just a minute," I said in a voice roughened by phlegm. I was battling my third case of strep throat in three months that, in honor of my birthday, everyone agreed to pretend I didn't have. I had a fever. My tonsils blossomed with white pustules.

I put a hand over the receiver and said, nonchalantly, "This is a lady from Youth for Christ." Everyone continued happily to eat. I'd asked for brisket for my birthday, and it was melting in their mouths. It had been hard, this year, to remember what I'd even liked before the Bill Gothard Seminar. I had meat to eat that they knew not of.

"I've been chosen to sing with Joyful Noise, a Youth for Christ choir, and I need to come for a dress fitting Tuesday. When Tuesday?" I said back into the receiver. "At 7:30 Tuesday."

"Joyful what?" Momma said. A familiar tension made its way around the table. People put down forks.

"Chosen? How were you chosen?" Daddy said. "Did they come door to door? How were you selected if they never heard you sing?" Open defiance after all this submission—this he could sink his teeth into. After weeks of living with a Stepford daughter, he knew how to behave. "You didn't try out for one of those YFC choirs did you? After we specifically told you not to?"

"Now, George, how could she have when we didn't take her over there," Momma said. "I don't understand, Kelly." She tried to come to my side, but none of us could move. The telephone cord was already stretched over a brother-in-law's head, pulling strands of his thinning hair. He made no attempt to remove it.

"Just a minute," I said to the woman at Youth for Christ.

"Is there a problem?" she said.

"No, I don't think so. Everything's all right."

"Why did this woman call you out of the blue for a dress fitting?" Daddy said. "I'm waiting."

My three sisters looked at each other and cringed. They had all, at one time or another, done a seemingly harmless thing that sent him into a rage. It didn't help now for Momma or anyone else to remind him that my arms weren't riddled with needle marks and that I hadn't gone into an alcoholic coma, fired a gun in the house, eaten glass, built a pipe bomb, shoplifted, spray painted my name on the Raytown water tower, harmed the upholstery, or painted my room black. I had not even come close to kissing a girl. I had auditioned for a Christian girl's choir.

"How did they get our phone number, honey?" Momma said, buttering a roll while she talked to reassure me that dinner would go on. "Kelly?"

"I went with Cheryl Tupper. When Cheryl tried out, the woman asked me to audition."

"Oh, and you couldn't just say, 'No thank you, my parents say no'?" Daddy said. "She dragged you up there on stage and forced you to sing? At gunpoint?"

I felt the woman's voice vibrate into the earpiece of the phone.

"Just a minute," I said to her. "I'll be right with you."

"How many times do I have to tell you you have a perfectly good church?"

"It's too liberal," I said, quoting Cheryl. "They don't talk enough about Jesus."

Mention of Jesus made everyone visibly nervous, even Karen.

"Oh, so the church your mother and I attend isn't good enough. So we aren't good enough. We don't know Jesus." Daddy referred to Momma as Mother only when he needed to threaten us with distance, with taking her away from us, as if that were somehow within his power.

"Just tell the lady no—tell her you can't, honey," Momma said.

First I grew very ashamed. I didn't see anyone's faces, only bits of sleeve, jaw lines, and greasy fingers.

And then, to my surprise, I felt a yell welling up and out of my swollen throat. My arms stiffened, and I dropped the phone on the floor. The real me pushed aside the obedient plastic one.

"I'm going to do this," I said. "You don't understand. God wants me to sing." It was a scene worthy of Loretta Lynn. I stiffened and forgot where I was in my dressy chinos and pirate-sleeved blouse, my belly full of brisket. Yelling felt so good. So would have falling down and flopping around if there had been enough room.

Momma asked Roger to pick up the phone because he was closest to where it had fallen. Several people passed it down to her like a bowl of mashed potatoes. She said into it, "I'm sorry. There's been a misunderstanding. Kelly can't sing in your choir. Her father and I . . . No, you don't need to talk with her again. She's fine. You'll just have to find someone else. I'm sorry, too."

I stopped yelling and returned to my seat. A tear fell into the pool of grease and barbecue sauce on my plate, revealing a pink flower on Momma's wedding china, which we ate off of only on special occasions.

"Kelly," Karen said from across the table. Several pilgrim candles stared through the glass door of the hutch over her shoulder, waiting for Thanksgiving. "Remember this is what God intends. No matter what, remember the umbrella of protection. Even when it doesn't make sense."

"Don't you start now," Daddy said to Karen.

"George," Momma gave him a look.

Wiping my eyes, I saw them all, my sisters and my brothers-in-law staring at me in my birthday chair. I leaned it back on two legs to move away the few inches I could from them all until I tapped the glass of the sliding glass door behind me.

"Put that down on four legs. How many times have I told you not to tip? Next time, you're going to glue the legs back in." Daddy finished me off. I ate and chewed and swallowed. Brisket slid down my throat that was now throbbing with not only infection but aborted rage. I tried to sniff but my nose was completely plugged.

"Now, see there," Momma said in a soft voice. "How could you sing all sick like this?"

✦ ✦ ✦

That December break, I spent two days in the hospital having my tonsils out. All the strep throat had left me with a heart murmur. The ear, nose, and throat doctor said if they did not remove my tonsils, which held *streptococcus* like wet sponges, I would never be myself again, even though whatever that had been was now in question. It would take a long time before I fully recovered from the submissiveness.

"See," Momma said to me one Friday night as we watched a Joyful Noise repeat on TV50. I lay on the couch in post-operative silence. "Just like Karen said, God knew best." She could make use of Bill Gothard herself now since Karen had more fully explained the parents' place in his diagrams. "It was His will that you didn't sing in Joyful Noise. But in August, you just couldn't have known that, could you?" Momma liked being an umbrella.

I couldn't have known either that by forbidding my YFC choir experience and full fundamentalist immersion, she and Daddy, mean though he was, had prevented me from becoming so entirely strange I would have no longer been able to relate to anyone anymore, maybe not even Imaginary Jesus.

"Raise up a child in the way she should go and when she is old, she will not depart from it." Momma happily quoted another verse she'd memorized and rarely had the opportunity to use. I grimaced at her. "That's a good sign." She patted my head. "That's my Kelly." She offered me cheese and a cracker to chew into a soft bolus I could barely swallow while we watched the soprano, whom I could never have, let her braces shine. Slowly, my appetite was returning. People recognized me again.

5

Tearing

My double, Alsace Nedresky, and I didn't look alike. On most days, Alsace looked like she'd just come from a protest. She wore an unbuttoned navy-blue pea coat and a Dr. Who scarf. Her teeth were small and beige and the corner of a front one was broken off. Two matching cowlicks rose from her head where horns would be. She had small olive-green circles around her eyes. She smelled like mothballs. We both looked like boys, but I looked like a Christian boy. I wore a gold cross necklace with a diamond chip, pastel oxford shirts, topsiders, and khakis. Our resemblance wasn't physical; it was spiritual. We shared the same Lord, and each of us was nigh on becoming the same rare hybrid for him: Christian-lesbian. We acknowledged this neither to each other nor to anyone else. According to the fundamentalist view, we both knew that right after the whore of Babylon, practicing lesbians would be rubbed out by the Four Horsemen of the Apocalypse.

We had met in eighth grade French class. I took French for five years after that solely because it guaranteed Alsace and I could spend at least an hour a day together, sharing the same thoughts, the same impulses. Otherwise, I wouldn't have continued. My mind was so impervious to language acquisition that in an interview for a scholarship from Andre's French Patisserie, I said I planned to attend college to become a murderer. Because of this one glaring difference between us, the scholarship went to Alsace, the only other person who had taken French as long as I had and thus, my only competitor. I didn't mind; when she won it, I felt like I had. She deserved it more anyway since, not only did she think in French, she even prayed in it.

Had it not been that Alsace and I looked nothing alike, one could have taken over the other's life, and no one would have noticed. We worked diligently for minimum wage at the Jones Store, a Midwest department store chain, to save money to attend the same commuter college. We lived in our childhood bedrooms in a kind of post-pubescent limbo, dating neither women nor men. Since we couldn't face becoming "young women," we transmogrified, changing back and forth from one sexless thing to the other—Boy Scout one minute, Puritan spinster the next. We also shared a fascination with the British royal family. The only man Alsace said she would marry was the Prince of Wales, and she claimed to resent the stunning Diana despite numerous pictures pinned to her bedroom walls. At the same time, I spent hours blow-drying and cutting the wild pieces out of my hair that kept it from looking like Diana's—my head a kind of bonsai—and I also imagined rescuing Diana from unappreciative Charles.

Alsace and I lacked intellectual as well as gender consistency. One minute we could be reading Carl Sagan and contemplating black holes and the next wondering aloud what the angel Gabriel sounded like coming into Mary's chamber. (We were both virgins, too, after all.) Other fundamentalists in our lives had led us to believe that college professors wouldn't be content to simply let Alsace learn the French and me the writing and literature we hungered for. They would pressure us to abandon our faith. We girded our loins like Shadrach, Meshach, and Abednego for the furnace that awaited us. Though good and eager learners, we would fight tooth and nail the education we had so looked forward to.

As I left for college that first morning, my parents waved enthusiastically from their individual square windows of the garage door they had just shut after I backed their huge Ford Granada out into the world. "Everything will be all right," they had said. Everything, as it turned out, would not be all right. In fact, I quickly made it impossible for Alsace and I even to leave Raytown for the University of Missouri-Kansas City, the bastion of secular lies.

Alsace lived in one of the only two houses along Raytown Road, a four-lane collector that everyone in town traveled at high rates of speed. She shared close quarters with her parents—a German mother and Polish father—who fought viciously in an indecipherable pidgin—and two older, obese sisters who occupied opposite ends of the attic. To leave Alsace's, I had to back the Granada into a slender wedge of front yard between a deep drainage ditch and a tool shed her father had painted with Wile E. Coyote, Foghorn Leghorn, and Pepe Le Pew. A sculptor, her father rode his bicycle twelve miles every day to Kansas City Vase and Lamp where he made ceramic molds of mermaids, dolphins, and other sea creatures, both real and imaginary. He was a lapsed Catholic who loved the Pope. Like Daddy, he was a World War II veteran and older, stranger, and stricter than everyone else's father. Alsace, her mother, and one of her sisters were nondenominational holy rollers. In the rearview mirror, I could see her mother in an enormous pink nightgown, praying in tongues from the doorway that we would survive pulling out onto Raytown Road. Alsace and I had both been raised by mothers who didn't want to let us out of their sight.

The Granada's trunk loomed so wide and long that I didn't even try to see beyond it into the Nedresky yard. I simply estimated. When I had finished backing, the car pointed into the sky like the space shuttle. All Alsace and I could see out its front window was its wide white hood dotted with bird droppings.

"Um," she said. "Houston, we have a problem." We. Even in the face of ridiculous disaster, she did not abandon me.

Just how firmly I had wedged the Granada on the hillside would not become apparent until the tow truck tried to remove it. Katrina Nedresky, her sister, who lived at the east end of the attic and worked at Woolf Brothers' Men's Store—which exacerbated her lifelong hatred of men—hurried through her sausage and eggs to drive us to UMKC. She dropped us off with just minutes to spare.

This wouldn't be the last time this driveway would better me. Every school day afterward, I would have to conquer my fear of it; every day Alsace would have to tell me when I had the right of way. I had so taken to heart many of Imaginary Jesus's parables—especially the one about sitting at the back of a room at a party until you're invited to come to the front—that in every instance I yielded to the other driver, making us late to class nearly every day.

Just as we had expected, college rocked us immediately. In the first session of her World Literature class, Alsace's professor encouraged everyone to read the Bible as metaphor. We reminded ourselves of what we'd poorly understood in high school Creative Writing class: metaphor meant a substitute for a real thing.

"In other words, read the Bible as lie," she said.

"That's so scary," I said. "What are you going to do?"

"Read it as Truth and keep my mouth shut, I guess."

In my required Intro to Philosophy class that same first morning, Professor Uffelmann, a childhood survivor of the Holocaust, had asked my classmates and me to write a paragraph about our expectations of the course. I wrote that I was a Christian, pressing hard with my new ballpoint pen, and that I planned to remain one. The next session, he made the following announcement: "If your faith doesn't withstand my little class, then it wasn't faith to begin with." I felt so much better after Alsace said she didn't think that she and I should be forced to listen to such rubbish from atheists, especially not to pay good money for it.

That we offered each other mutual support was only one of the reasons Alsace and I couldn't get enough of each other's company. Why bother trying to cultivate other friendships when we could always rest assured we would relish the same strange pastimes. On hot midnights, we laid on our backs on a farm road near my house, wagering who would be the first to sense a car. We took turns choosing classical music to listen to with our eyes closed and then described the pictures in our heads. Our rule said we listened to nothing composed after 1960, nothing formless or dissonant. One time, we snuck ticket-less into the second half of a student production of *Tartuffe*, and then whispered to each other that we could tell from their delivery that the student actors didn't understand the jokes. After the final curtain, we slipped into the dark bowels of the Helen F. Spencer Theater until just seconds before they locked up. We had flirted with the possibility of spending the night in the green room with only the light from the vending machine to see each other by, a handful of change between us for Coke and peanuts. In the end, we knew our mothers would call the police.

✦ ✦ ✦

Unlike the other salesclerks at the Jones Store who leaned on terminals looking bored or hid behind counters to read paperbacks or do their homework, Alsace and I viewed our jobs as a ministry. "Whatever your task, put yourselves into it, as done for the Lord," Colossians 3:23 told us. Old ladies began to confuse us as That Nice Salesclerk and to inquire about us in the same hushed tone. "You know the tomboyish one," they would say. We became spectacles. People brought their children to watch us. They stood off to the side and whispered things like, "You don't see that much anymore." Alsace worked in Coats. Her manager's favorite story told how Alsace had walked right up to help the woman who all the clerks in the department knew had been saving quarters in a Tupperware bowl until she could afford a London Fog. She told how Alsace had painstakingly arranged eighty-five little towers of coins across the counter and how sticky they had been and how they smelled. Alsace had helped the woman on with the coat as she did everyone, as if she had mistaken her for the Queen of Denmark.

I worked in Ladies Shoes where the other clerks looked like roller derby queens. For fun, they pulled shoe-fitting stools out from under each other, which did not stop me from hoping to reach them with my silent example. From the looks of the department, you would think Ladies Shoes was the only place in town that sold shoes. In this retail heyday of the early '80s, we had to use a number system, or the mobs would become enraged and throw shoehorns and display shoes at us and at each other. I scurried through its dark stockroom maze, balancing towers of shoeboxes between extended arms and chin. I tried not to read the obscene limericks and pictures scrawled on its plywood shelves: boobs and cracks with fart clouds coming out and disembodied penises coming in. I helped the customers the other Ladies Shoe clerks hid from—old ladies, people with disabilities, the dirty. Because it came in 12-wide, the largest shoe the department offered, the Easy Step offered the only option for transvestites. It had a patent leather upper, crepe sole, block heels, and a gold buckle over the instep: a pilgrim nightmare. Transvestites frightened me until I sensed that if Jesus had sold shoes, he would have knelt before them as he would have any other woman, shoehorn at the ready. To my surprise, I found them interesting and nice. I approached them and every other customer with a strange spirit of humility I haven't known since. Nothing turned me away. I straddled my shoe stool and touched sweaty bunions, nail fungus, a set of post-op toes with no bones that I had to guide into the shoe like thread into a needle. I listened to stories of careers long past, husbands buried, real and fictitious cruises to explain why they came back for yet another color of espadrilles. I didn't push. If a pair of shoes made someone happy, I wanted that for her. Otherwise, I laid them back in their paper-lined box, heel to toe, toe to heel, smiled, and took them away.

Though Alsace and I worked only a few evenings and weekends, for several months we each had our names engraved on department plaques as top salesperson. The spreadsheets didn't lie. About retail, Alsace and I would also remain in deep and complete agreement. Retail didn't pose difficult questions.

✦ ✦ ✦

I didn't tell Alsace when I began to find Intro to Philosophy interesting. Like Chang and Eng, one couldn't shift her weight too far in either direction without toppling the other. It worried me a little that I liked learning about Descartes and Camus and his vision of demystified hell—a word I loved being required to say—and Sartre and Kant. I loved the looks of them all, the curls, the black-rimmed glasses, and the cigarettes hanging from lips. I liked knowing their ideas, even though on most days they threatened the religious security I thought I needed to survive. One night in my Bible reading, I dwelt on the words "render unto Caesar the things that are Caesar's, and unto God, the things that are God's." As I understood it, God had given me permission to save one part of myself for my philosophy professor and another for my fundamentalist friends. I made a secret promise to myself that someday I might write a book like the ones I'd been reading in college—George Eliot was homely like me—and really make something of myself. Fundamentalists don't make things of themselves. It required too much critical thinking, self-esteem, and trust in the "wisdom of the world."

Professor Uffelmann assigned me a paper on moral relativism. He had further gained my trust by pointing out that Jesus's philosophy of nonviolent resistance revealed an emotional intelligence the world had never known. I'd braved a few cursory relativistic thoughts. Finally, I could hold them in no longer. "Just because I believe something," I said to Alsace, "doesn't mean everyone who doesn't is wrong." This day, we drove through the slushy remains of a freakish late spring snowstorm. The trees had already leafed out, and the branches bowed under great clumps of snow. Some had already broken under the strain.

"What about the way, the truth, and the life?" she said. "What about no one coming to the Father except by Him?"

"What if Jesus didn't mean what we think he did by that? He challenged religious authorities. He broke laws. He opened doors to everyone."

That day, Alsace had borne her own burdens. During a discussion of Genesis, her World Literature professor informed the class with incredulity that some people believed in a literal flood. "It was like he was talking about a tribe hidden away somewhere who still wear clothes made of bark or something," she said. "I believe in a literal flood. Be honest, don't I look like I could believe in a literal flood?"

I didn't answer her. As always, she looked like she'd just broken through the fence around a nuclear plant.

"But let's get back to you," Alsace said. "Basically, you're asking me if I think there are absolutes. Yes. Of course, there are absolutes." I had scared her and myself as well. *But wasn't college the time to test intellectual limits?* I thought. *How would we know what we didn't believe if we never encountered it? I had wandered out toward thin ice, but I could always turn around and come back, right? Imaginary Jesus loved me, this I knew.* I'd made Pascal's wager, taking comfort in the verse that said, "nothing could separate me from the love of God in Christ Jesus," even if I stopped believing.

"I'm just saying—I've never thought about it this way either— that just because we think something is wrong doesn't necessarily make it Wrong for everyone. I mean how do we know for sure anything we say that we do?"

"Because the Bible tells us so," she said. "Squirt your windshield. How can you see through all those drops?"

"Because I don't want to listen to this," I said. The decaying rubber scrubbed across the half-dry glass, smearing the spatters into a muddy swath. "Now I can't see anything," I said, raising and lowering dramatically to find a clear arc.

"You need new wipers," she said sighing. "They cost about two dollars." Malaise settled. For the rest of this day, we had trouble pretending we'd conquer this and other crises of faith. Not the least of these was that we knew we could never mean anything more to each other than we already did. Though neither one of us could imagine life without the other, we knew better even than to mention that some women made official arrangements to make sure friendships like ours went on forever. We were, after all, the age that humans begin thinking about a mate. Occasionally, I even found Alsace oddly beautiful. On Blue Ridge Cutoff, we looked in silence at the dirty snow retreating up the enormous lawn of Earp & Son's Funeral Home and then at the plaid-skirted girls flooding onto the wet-black parking lot of St. Bernadette's where each could be certain her parents waited in the family car for her to take her home to the blessing and a hot meal provided by God. And that St. Christopher glued to the dashboard would protect her on the ride home.

"I have to say these things," I said, tapping my temple. "They're in here."

"I'll pray for us both at church tonight," she said. "You're welcome to come. We're halfway through Daniel. King Nebuchadnezzar is growing long hair and claws for trusting in his own wisdom instead of God's." The one time I had visited her church, Alsace wore the first dress I'd ever seen her wear. After the service, she went to the prayer rail and howled. Her fists pounded the vinyl cushion, and her feet kicked up behind her. Seeing my face after the service, she apologized, then took it back. She said she'd made groans of prayer too deep for words. I'd never imagined such a thing could come out of her. What had she groaned to God that she couldn't say to me?

"I have to work," I said. I'd had enough of the far-fetched for one day.

That night in Ladies Shoes, Kierkegaard leapt past my mental gatekeeper when my back was turned. I had read about his idea that post-Enlightenment Christians have to pull an intellectual hamstring jumping across the void to belief. I had just found the shoe a woman wanted high up on a shelf in the stockroom, the Connie Avalon, a popular pump because it came in a double narrow, but whose heels fell off. The woman wore a 6½ double narrow, which we miraculously still had. But was it really a miracle? Hadn't the company simply shipped us the shoes and hadn't this small pair just failed to sell? Not that many people have double-narrow heels anyway. As I looked up at the black empty hole I had just made removing the box from the shelf, I felt lightheaded.

I heard the Muzak version of "Eye of the Tiger" in the stockroom speakers. What if there was no God? What if the idea was just an opiate, an elaborate game of pretend? What evidence did I have otherwise?

I quickly stopped thinking. I returned to the sales floor and the woman—with the pair of 6½ double narrows that any other night I could have convinced myself that God had arranged for her to have. I felt ashamed at my relief to have finally thought the worst thought I could imagine. The boulder had fallen; I had not been crushed. I quickly checked in; Imaginary Jesus was still there in the little room in my head, being the best kind of a friend. But something indeed had changed. Before this moment, I'd always had an easy sense that everything would turn out all right, because Jesus would make it so. There would always be meatloaf and glazed carrots. I had a drawer of clean socks. No one had to know I was gay if I didn't want her to. But now, every other heartbeat for the next hour or so, I felt a queasy uncertainty. I was on a raft; chaos licked at its edges.

After my shift, I sat in Momma's gold recliner to tell her and Daddy that I'd decided to quit college. It would not have surprised me to know that at precisely the same moment, Alsace had made the same announcement to her parents.

"What brought this on?" Daddy said.

For once, his bluster felt reassuring. Some part of me wanted him to snap me out of it.

"Some of my professors say there isn't a God."

At this, I was sure he would relent.

"Well, if somebody told you to drive off a bridge, would you do it?" Daddy said. Always hot, even in winter, he spent most nights stripped to his undershirt like a boxer.

"No," I said.

"Well then, just because someone tells you there isn't a God when you know darned good and well there is, you start believing them? You're going to face this all your life. You might as well start learning to take the bull by the horns."

"But I'm supposed to take notes on what my professors say and then write that on the tests."

"I'm telling you right now you don't have to write on a piece of paper that there isn't a God. You just have to learn what you can and stick to your guns. Call a spade a spade." Under stress, my parents spoke in idioms.

Momma chimed in, "That's what we've told your sister Karen about home schooling." My parents worried about her son Luke, who had no friends. He may as well have lived in a soddy in the middle of the prairie, they said. "If a person doesn't ever face a challenge, she'll never know how to think for herself. Do you see what a pickle that puts someone in? I know you feel like you're in over your head, but nothing ventured nothing gained. You have to bloom where you're planted. We're not saying this to punish you."

For a while, they sat and watched me cry. Finally, both of them said I'd feel different about things in the morning. I had better; college wasn't negotiable. When I went to bed, I looked in at Daddy in the light of the lamp bolted to the wall over his shoulder, his side of the bed, a heavy book open over his chest, one side thin with pages; I could not tell whether he'd just begun or almost finished it. The stack of books on the shelf he'd built into the wall above their heads seemed ready to teeter. Though certainly not the most loving man, he made sure none of his daughters settled for stupidity.

My parents were right; I did feel better in the morning. God was in his heaven where he would remain until the next crisis. I never again felt naïve ease, though. Childhood was over.

After their talk, Alsace's parents made her switch her major from French literature to accounting. Simple columns of numbers didn't erode your faith. Plus, they said, she could get a real job with an accounting degree.

Thus began the painful tearing, the hemorrhage. I continued to ask questions that Alsace could not. Finally unable to live with the tension of the contradictions raised by her remaining liberal arts requirements and by spending most of her days with me, she quit college with half an accounting degree. I continued to drive the Granada to college alone, while she worked in the customer complaint division of a bank. She kept a mirror at her desk to remind her to smile. "People can hear if you aren't smiling," she said in one of the last telephone conversations we ever had. It was true; I could hear that she wasn't. She bowled everyone over by marrying her pastor's son. He thought we were closer than two Christian "sisters" should be. As she told me about her new job, I could hear a third person on the line, breathing, shifting his weight. He pushed apart the shredded remains of our similarity.

Alsace and I gave each other plenty of difference to gape at in the years to come. I insisted on remaining conflicted, switching churches, moving away and then back in with my parents again, doubting, returning, questioning. Before she knew it, all Alsace's clothes were made out of flower prints. She had no outside job at all, three babies with olive circles around their eyes just like hers, and 150 pounds she could not lose. I pitied her for dancing too close to the fire in her attempts to become what our kind cannot. Thanks to her, I would stop myself from finishing the very same dance just in the nick of time. As our parting gift, each let the other see what could have happened to her.

6

A Hair's Breadth

Despite my best efforts to destroy them all, every so often a copy of my engagement picture surfaces from a family member's old wallet or a junk drawer, and I have a lot of explaining to do. Someone usually says, "That's not really you, is it?" "It is and it isn't," I say, which fails to satisfy. Often, the long answer fails as well.

I tell them that in the mid-'80s, single fundamentalist young women were hard to come by. Many people my age had been raised by hippies. Black-and-white thinking and blind obedience hadn't yet come entirely into fashion. Faced with this dearth of virginal female partners, suitors couldn't allow even a plain-faced tomboy like me to remain in the sanctity of my childhood bedroom. Neither could they waste time reading signals. At this tender age, I lacked the confidence and clarity to fend them off. Also, like so many other gay people, I felt increasingly pressured to be or at least to appear "normal." Just as Alsace had, I had to quit dawdling and start exhibiting heterosexual behavior. The first and only boy who had ever taken interest in me was thrilled to learn that while he had been away in the Army becoming an addict and having hallucinations that drove him to Jesus, I had, in my own less dramatic way, become a Christian as well. He took this as a sign. Kurt had been dishonorably discharged for shooting a hole in the roof of his barracks. He'd been trying to clean his rifle and drink a case of beer at the same time.

When I said I wished I had a more dramatic conversion story than a Youth for Christ altar call, he put his hand with its bitten nails over my mouth.

"Be glad you found the Lord easily. You don't want to go through what I did." Then he told his story again. Satan had chased him through a Jeep maintenance facility. After running and running, he somehow wound up in the room of a fellow private who was watching *Jesus of Nazareth*. God was offering Kurt one last chance. "It was awful. I was so close to hell it melted the rubber on my boots. I could show you the places where, and that's when the Lord saved me." The fellow private watching *Jesus of Nazareth* helped him pray the Sinner's Prayer, and then Kurt went back home to his bunk. "I woke up feeling so clean, you know, so new?"

I sat at the opposite end of the twin bed in my childhood bedroom from him blinking like a cow. Trying to connect, I said, "Yeah, I felt better the morning after I became a Christian, too."

"Yeah, but you never did drugs. You can't know how good you feel after not taking them. Well, a little while after not taking them you feel like crap again—oh shit, I have to stop swearing— but you're on the right track at least, little by little."

When Kurt decided we were meant for each other, I went along with it. I could have stopped the whole thing. I could have taken myself off the market, but dating meant I could stop peppering my conversations with things like, "Oh, now *he's* cute." Coming from me, these things didn't sound right, quite true anyway, but I needed to see the small looks of relief on people's faces when I said them.

"You're not ugly," Kurt used to say, even though I had never given him any indication that I thought I was. On the third date, we saw *Octopussy*. Kurt had always loved James Bond and still struggled with cutting secular entertainment from his life as his new church friends at Englewood Assembly of God seemed to have done easily. (Trinity Presbyterian, the church we had grown up in together and where I still went, couldn't satisfy his appetite for the Lord.) At the top of the stairs of my parents' house, Kurt ran his tongue around inside my mouth and then dashed back out the door to his idling Vega. I went to the hall bathroom and vomited. I wondered, as I fell asleep that night, how I could prevent him from ever doing it again. Because she heard me vomit after every date, Momma worried I had bulimia. I concocted a story about Kurt's smelly car heater, which she believed when I didn't lose weight or obsess about the way I looked. I had never obsessed about the way I looked.

On a semiconscious level, I wondered how many times I would have to date Kurt before I had bought enough time to stop dating men for a while. I cast about for a conflict we could not surmount, a religious reason why the two of us should not be together.

My reprieve from Kurt came in the form of another religious man-boy, who, because of his respectable family and Christian principles, would court me in a protracted and pleasantly nonphysical fashion. Since I felt I needed a heterosexual charade, I thought I might just as well play it out with a better kisser. As far as the real me I worked so hard to repress, this relationship was over before it ever started. I pretended to like these man-boys now watching me, hoping that in doing so, a real affection would materialize. I would "fake it 'til I make it." I just had to wait for the frightened fundamentalist inside me to stop toying with the idea that I could marry this man or any other one to do the right and normal thing. Before they know it, many gay people find themselves between this very same rock and a hard place. Innocent children often wind up pinched between it with them.

Kurt introduced me to Royall at Strike and Spare at 40 Highway and Noland Road in, ironically, Independence, Missouri, where the singles group had gathered after Sunday evening services at Englewood Assembly. Royall presided beside Kurt and me, holding his pool cue like a shepherd's staff. After a measured silence, he began the interview. "What do you do?"

"I sell shoes," I said. "And I'm a student."

"What are you studying?" he asked.

"English."

"I took an English class at Evangel," he said. "English 230: Christian Fantasy Writers. We read George MacDonald, C.S. Lewis, and Madeleine L'Engle. Except for a few of her ideas, I liked L'Engle. She did write some iffy things about hell."

"Iffy?" I said.

"She doesn't think it will be permanent," he said, one eyebrow arched. At surrounding pool tables stood freaks from my high school days. The idea that the doors of hell double-bolt from the outside is important to fundamentalists. They say they want the unsaved to feel a sense of urgency, but more likely they can't imagine an eternity in their company.

"She thinks even Satan will wind up in heaven," Royall screamed over the cracks of a powerful break. His declaration startled everyone in the room but for different reasons. Like Royall, I thought heaven and hell were so real that I could taste them, and I didn't like the idea of Satan or any of these people from my high school in heaven with me either. To hope Imaginary Jesus would divide us all up into companionable groups didn't make me feel any better. I felt ashamed for being unable to love the freaks as Jesus did. At Royall's declaration, a whole row of freaks screamed, "Satan in heaven? Partay!" It had been too long since high school when they had had someone to bully. A couple of them approached Royall and me, "Do you like Satan? We do. Can you tell us how to get to heaven so we can be with Satan?" Royall ushered me behind him and took the brunt of it. This shared moment of persecution cemented our relationship.

Shortly after, Kurt brought Royall to Ladies Shoes. When the two of them appeared near the clearance rack of odd sizes of dark winter boots, loafers, and pumps, I had just sold three pairs of shoes to a quadriplegic. They watched me put her socks and shoes back on. Royall quoted Jesus, "If you've done it unto the least of these, you've done it unto me.'" My humility turned him on.

I couldn't really blame Royall and Kurt for taking so long to perceive they were barking up the wrong tree for a mate. In the confusing waltz of religious courtship, frigidity can masquerade as chastity. All a girl had to do was remind him she wanted to offer him the dowry of her virginity to keep everything buttoned and zipped. I could go only so far in my heterosexual imaginings before the screen went black. In his polo shirt, his forehead beaded with sweat, Royall looked like a dad just in from mowing a small lawn, with sex the farthest thing from his mind. For our first in a series of long-standing dates, he asked me to Englewood Assembly for Sunday evening services. After Kurt had told him how "dead" Trinity Presbyterian was, Royall tried to get me to stop going there altogether. But I wasn't ready to immerse myself in the strange new world of the Pentecostals. I told him that because I was still living with my parents, I thought I should respect their wishes and go to church with them and do as Bill Gothard had instructed. Bill Gothard sounded strict to Royall. He liked spiritual discipline, so he conceded defeat in this area. Sterile, proboscises drawn, Royall and I drank deeply of nothing and, for our individual reasons, found it satisfying for a time. Partly, I stayed with him longer than I should have for the meals that as the man, the head of our relationship, he insisted on paying for. It was the twentieth-century equivalent of slinging down a kill, only I didn't have to clean it for him. Feeding myself was the first of many personal responsibilities Royall would try to find biblical support for unburdening me of.

Kurt quickly moved to the fringes. As a fresh and inconsistent Christian male, he ranked far lower than Royall. He returned to sitting next to the latest in a string of backsliders whose time in the Englewood singles group was usually short-lived. Gerri had accepted Jesus during a counseling session at a rehab clinic. Even in the depths of winter, she wore revealing shirts despite several attempts of the other more spiritually mature girls to "speak the truth in love." She and Kurt, unable to set an example for each other, left several times during each service to sit in his car and smoke a cigarette the Lord hadn't healed them of craving. If cigarette smoke hadn't made me sick to my stomach, I would have rather sat in Kurt's car with them. I wasn't ready to stop being

Presbyterian. Daily doses of college left me wondering if I might not want to return to a more metaphorical religion some day. Also, I could never quite conquer my fear of Sunday night service at Englewood Assembly.

Sunday nights were designed to help people like me stop resisting the Holy Spirit's anointing. But they also gave me a spiritual thrill, like playing with Pentecostal matches. Each Sunday, God looked down and chose people at Englewood. Some night, he might choose me. For what, I wasn't sure. Maybe to become a completely heterosexual church lady. Maybe such a peaceful life without intellectual challenge or unwanted sexual desires awaited me if I were open to a personality overhaul, if I were willing to admit that my "old man" Kelly, the former unsaved self the Apostle Paul speaks of, was crappy and evil. All of us were crap, and—if we were willing—happy, Holy Spirit-filled crap. But to be chosen, you had to be willing to lose control. I'd been raised never to lose control.

Going to Sunday night services was something Royall and I could do together. Outside of church, he didn't have many other date ideas. It gave us both a sense of accomplishment. Sunday night after Sunday night, while I was supposed to have been seeking the Spirit, I gawked at people losing control of themselves. All around me they stiffened and fell over without hurting themselves. They laughed long and loud at nothing in particular and leapt over pews. All of these were dispensations of the Holy Spirit, free to those open to them. When not otherwise occupied, all the men held their hands up high and wide as if bringing in an aircraft. The women kept theirs lower with upturned palms as if holding out two halves of something broken for Daddy to glue back together. Only all the unanointed teenage boys and I could keep our hands hanging at our sides. During tinkling piano interludes—spiritual cool-downs—someone would murmur a long series of "Thank you Jesuses" and "Praise the Lords" into a microphone to prime the spiritual pump. From this initial voice would issue a collective torrent of murmuring. With my eyes closed, I could imagine an international airport terminal during a bomb scare. Finally, one voice would again rise above the din speaking loudly, tearfully in a foreign tongue. When the foreign tongue had finished, another loud voice would interpret just as the scripture prescribed. Then, after closing prayer, we would all collect our things and ourselves and have a Styrofoam cup of decaf coffee and maybe a stick of gum to freshen our breath, and then, Hallelujah, Royall and I and the rest of the singles group could go to dinner. We did all this as if the Spirit of God hadn't just commandeered the building and most bodies and tongues and had his way with them. We didn't bother to ask what that meant. No wonder Royall wasn't much of a reader. He didn't need to be. You couldn't make this stuff up.

Royall was right; I was resisting the Holy Spirit and him as well. Both of them charged at me too hard and too fast, so much so that I couldn't even hear myself think. After weeks of Sunday services, I had not evidenced even the most rudimentary of manifestations of baptism in the Holy Spirit: speaking in tongues. Royall had doubts about my spiritual fitness. I did have to pray for the infilling of the Spirit, he reminded me. I did have to want it.

+ + +

After supper on Sundays, Royall always drove me in his silver Cutlass to the parking lot of the funeral home across from Independence Center shopping mall. It was still sitting in the middle of a fallow field surrounded by vulnerable countryside with a sign that said "For Sale—Zoned Commercial." Royall would turn off the engine and make a sucking sound between his teeth, a sound he made when he wanted us to say and do something meaningful. After a little talking, he would ask me to stretch out across the bucket seats, straddling the gearshift. Then he would lie on top of me. Always fully clothed, groin pressed downward, he would gently touch my face and say, "You're so pretty," and, "I love you." He kissed me as softly as anyone could have. Waiting to feel something, I lay stiffened beneath him. I looked up at him with mild curiosity like someone watching TV and about to change the channel.

Once he said, "Why don't you ever look at me like I look at you? Why don't you say you love me?"

"I love you," I said.

"No, not after I tell you to. On your own."

The longer we were together, the closer I came to slipping into a religious coma, where I would lose myself entirely and would never have to worry about anything unacceptable ever again.

"I'll try to do better."

He sighed and lifted off me, a cloud of the aftershave I didn't like filling the warm space just left between us.

I could go for days without thinking about Royall. Sometimes in the middle of the week, he would telephone, which always surprised and annoyed me. By the middle of each week, I would have recovered a sense of myself again. I tried to finish my homework and talk to him at the same time. Suspicious, Kathy said to Momma, "That's just not normal. I just about died when I couldn't see Sam."

Everyone in the family eventually soured on Royall except Karen, who praised me for sticking with the relationship. "You've become so much more submissive," she said. This was the goal of every fundamentalist Christian woman. I felt both proud and irritated; not just anyone can be an appealing doormat.

Royall continued trying to change me into the woman of his dreams. For example, he didn't like my coat, a forest green Pendleton all-weather that I'd saved up to buy with my 15 percent discount from the Jones Store. He asked me one Sunday night not to wear it anymore over my dresses. It wasn't a Sunday coat. He was right; they didn't go together, just like the two embattled halves of me. When Momma found out why I didn't wear my new coat anymore, she began to nurse an irritation that would, by November, flower into full-fledged hatred. If she had to lose me to someone, it had to be someone who genuinely liked me. It didn't help that he pressured me into spending Thanksgiving lunch, my family's traditional mealtime, at his parents' house. Still, I defended him. Still, I added flourish after convincing relationship flourish. Still, we ate sumptuous meals out with no price limit imposed, which, for the hour I ate them, made me appreciate Royall. The longer I let things go on, the more anesthetized I felt. "Mustn't withdraw too soon and destroy months spent on the heterosexual performance of my lifetime," said one part of me. This one would have to serve as proof for years; I wasn't going through anything like it again. "Mustn't stop before I gave heterosexuality a fighting chance," said the other side of me, even with Royall, a full-figured accountant who tucked his sweaters into his jeans.

✦ ✦ ✦

By January, my failure to speak in tongues had become a problem. Royall wanted an anointed wife. My charade had reached a climax. In November, I had accepted his proposal in a steak-, caramelized onion-, and chocolate-induced euphoria, greedily pulling the shiny ring off the paw of a stuffed animal. That night, a year seemed too far off to ever come anyway. But by January, I knew differently. I should have seen my inability to speak in tongues as a means to an end. But I had developed what can best be described as performance anxiety. During the week I wanted to be the best scholar possible; on Sunday nights I wanted to be the best Christian. I worried that it wasn't in fact enough that Jesus loved me as the Bible told me so. This was Royall's trump card. His doubts about my ability to measure up to his religious standards cut me to the quick, and he knew it. "You have to want the Spirit," he said, after yet another unproductive Sunday service. I began to feel barren.

"Why do I have to do anything at all? If God wants me to speak in tongues then he'll see to that, won't he?"

"Yes, but the Holy Spirit's a gentleman. He won't force himself on someone."

"So I'm not good enough for you," I said. "I don't speak in tongues."

"No—" he paused. "Tongues are just evidence of your salvation, an outward proof of its authenticity."

This infuriated me. "Are you saying I'm not a Christian? I've *accepted* Christ." With Royall, I developed the terrible habit of talking about Jesus by his last name and in the third person, as if he weren't there, which he may just as well not have been. Admittedly, I'd let my relationship with Imaginary Jesus slip. I certainly wasn't encouraged to check in with him at college. My relationship with him was one more thing Royall told me he needed to be in charge of. That was the Man's spiritual role as spelled out in the scriptures. In the future, I would be a receptacle of Royall's spiritual knowledge and experience and, heaven forbid, of his children.

"No, I'm not saying you aren't Christian, but I am saying you seem not to want the full blessing. You're just like Bevee."

Bevee Robeson didn't wear makeup and had one long, thick, and always-damp gray braid dragging back and forth across her back. Once when her son spilled her purse, several bottles of herbal supplements rolled into the aisle.

"She's never spoken in tongues, either. She has a massage table in their basement."

We were only half-watching *The Brain That Wouldn't Die* at Royall's place. Because the main character's head couldn't leave the pan it sat in, you could easily pick up the action, even if you missed a few lines of her dialogue.

"All I'm saying is just look at her. Ron has no control over her. She does whatever weird thing she wants. And she's never spoken in tongues." With that declaration, he drummed his fingers on the back of my hand.

✦ ✦ ✦

We had my solitaire sized at Montgomery Ward's jewelry department where Royall's friend Gil, who was also engaged, worked. The two of them were in something of a nuptial race. Chubby Gil had glass-blue eyes and long lashes, which his anointed girlfriend, Tammy, thought were his strongest physical asset. It amazed me that she seemed to really love him without trying.

When my hands were cold, which was most of the time, my engagement ring flew off my finger at the slightest movement. I also jammed my hands in my pockets, a manly habit no amount of determination could break me of. Each time, the diamond's sharp edges made an ever-widening sore on my ring finger. In the course of one long shift in Ladies Shoes, one prong in the four-prong setting moved to the side and the stone pitter-pattered across the stockroom. We took the ring back to Gil to have it reset only to have it disappear again. Only after much searching did I find the little diamond nestled in a pluck of lint at the bottom of a pocket of chinos. At that point, Gil soldered on two additional prongs and admonished me, "Stop being so rough, sister."

Finally, at a Sunday night service in December designed to woo the holdouts, I felt determined to ask for the full blessing, if for no other reason than to prove to myself that the Holy Spirit could inhabit someone like me. Danny, the unanointed boyfriend of another girl in the singles group, and I moved with a herd to the first carpeted step of the stage. Pastor Mike perched on the edge of the second step, dangling his short leg, which he and others had periodically laid hands on again and again with the expectation that God would grow it out to a proper length once he had learned whatever lesson a short leg had to teach him. Pastor Mike's wife, Constance, stood next to him, holding a cruet of holy vegetable oil. He moved across the stage from one supplicant to another, throwing the microphone cord ahead of him like a lariat and then tucking the mic back into his armpit upon arrival. He wanted it there so the congregation could hear as each person received his or her very own tongue.

I felt not only Royall's warm hands on my back but his mother's as well. I tried to pray and concentrate on everything Royall had told me about the Holy Spirit, how I had nothing to fear from a gentleman. On the step next to me, Danny finally yielded. His girlfriend had told him she would break off the engagement if he didn't receive the anointing before New Year's Eve. Riding a wave of Hallelujahs, Pastor Mike sidestepped to teeter in front of me. For an eternity, he pressed his oily thumbs into my forehead and murmured. Nothing happened. I tried to pray but found myself far from any person of the Trinity. I tried to distract myself from my failure by reviewing my times tables and the 23rd Psalm, but I found I couldn't remember them either. In a panic, I opened my eyes wide, which Pastor Mike took as some kind of sign and shouted, "Glory." I opened my mouth and said the first thing that occurred to me. "Shi blah, bli blah." From then on out, it was easy. I let out a flood of gibberish and peeked again at Pastor Mike to see if he'd caught on. I didn't want him to peg me for a liar and push his thumbs through my forehead. Instead, he said, "Listen to this sister bless the Lord." The hot hands on my back began to shake. I jabbered as long as I guessed might be appropriate for the first time. "Aren't you glad?" Royall said. "You're my sister in Christ now. Now there's nothing between us. We're equally yoked." He gripped me in a long Pentecostal hug, hoping that, like he and everyone else watching, I'd eventually break down in tears. The relief I felt fooling them quickly dissolved into shame. What, after all, had I accomplished? How many others under similar duress had done the same thing? As Royall hugged me, over his right shoulder I could see Bevee Robeson. She wasn't smiling the sweet Holy Spirit-filled smile I saw on every other face. Her knowing grin assured me that the approval would wear off. I'd eventually tire of faking.

During my second slice of deep-dish pizza that Royall bought in celebration, Imaginary Jesus's voice broke through my confusion with a series of short declarative English sentences. "This must end. It's wrong for both of you. Everything's going to be all right. I have come that you might have life and have it more abundantly." After years of living together, slowly but surely this steady trustworthy voice would become indistinguishable from my own. In time, I would realize it had been my own voice all along, the voice of my best self who had studied its inflections from one of the truest humans who had ever lived.

✦ ✦ ✦

Luckily, Royall turned mean, and put an easier end to my stalling. "What if I were to come home sometime and tell you we had to move to Alaska?" he said as we drove to the photographer for our engagement photo shoot.

"Did you get a job in Alaska?" I said, my residual panic rising and then falling again.

"I'm speaking hypothetically."

"I didn't know you liked Alaska. You're always cold."

"It's just that you're obviously too close to your family. You overdo everything—birthdays, Christmas, the Fourth. I mean what would your mother do if I came to her and said, 'We're moving to Alaska'? It would do you good to move away. It would make you grow up."

He pulled into a parking place in front of the photographer's. I instinctively locked my door, which he'd come around to open for me. He wanted me to want him to do this. He tapped on the glass of my locked door peering in at me, biting his large lower lip and then putting his hands on his hips. I sat quietly, forgetting to move, enjoying the separation.

"Open the door, sister," came his muffled voice. "This isn't funny."

We'd decided on sweaters for the photo weeks before when Royall had looked through my closet so he'd know what to wear. A Woolrich I'd been able to afford only because it had been on the clearance rack met with his approval. It was navy blue with an alternating zigzag of beige, gray, and light blue yarn. The navy blue in Royall's crew neck matched mine so well it looked like they'd come from the same dye lot. He loved that from the neck down it was hard to see where one of us left off and the other began.

The photographer pulled down a window shade with a marbleized blue surface and then dragged out two wooden blocks stapled with white fur, one slightly higher than the other. At his instruction, I sat on the lower one, and Royall knelt on the higher one, putting both hands on my shoulders, as if to push me into the ground like a "Contract Pending" sign. I smiled when told.

✦ ✦ ✦

The day the Challenger blew up, Royall called to tell me he was booking our flight to Colorado.

"Colorado?"

"The honeymoon . . ."

I gave myself a deadline after he tried to suckle a breast he pulled through a wide neckline. When I pushed him away like a cat weaning her kitten, claws out, he thanked me for being the strong one.

✦ ✦ ✦

Valentine's Day morning, he sent me a dozen purple roses. I put them in a vase of water and set them on the center of my parents' television set where I would let them wither to give some semblance of mourning. I had bought him a card with a rabbit on the cover. Inside it read, "Hoppy Valentine's Day." Beneath, I wrote, "Kelly." I didn't feel anything more than that and, because of what I had to do after supper, I didn't want to offer one additional shred of encouragement.

I waited until after the arrival of the finger bowls at V's Italian Restaurante on 40 Highway, where I had savored a plate of chicken tetrazzini, to begin frowning. With four children to feed, my parents had never been able to afford V's.

Royall put me safely back in my seat of the Cutlass. As he rounded the hood, I practiced my first line aloud. When he opened his door, he heard the tail end of my practice speech, ". . . so sorry."

"I'm sorry, were you praying?" he said.

✦ ✦ ✦

Royall drove every road he knew and many he did not. His fury accelerated at freeway entrance ramps.

"Who talked you into this?" he said. As we passed through the sulfurous cloud from Sugar Creek (no one knows where the smell is coming from), I said, "I just know. I didn't have to ask anyone else."

"Have you prayed about it? Now, there's someone you actually should ask."

"I've been praying. And I've been feeling really guilty."

"Then maybe you aren't doing the right thing."

"No, I mean guilty about letting it go on this long."

With that, he pulled into the sprawling parking lot of the Adam's Mark, a hotel that overlooked Royals Stadium. Its logo looked like a huge red fig leaf.

"If this is the right thing, the Lord will give you a great sense of relief," he said.

"Oh, he has," I said, exhaling, trying not to smile.

✦ ✦ ✦

In silence, Royall drove past the Blue Ridge Mall, the Jones Store, the Big Boy Burger where I wished I could ask him to stop and let me buy a sack of onion rings for old time's sake. At Norfleet, I knew I was close enough to walk to my house. On trips home from the kennel, our basset hound always waited until Norfleet to howl over being returned where he belonged.

Royall pulled in the driveway and peered at me through the blessed shadow my house cast over our tattered engagement. I would hide there in its safety for a few more years, first window to the right of the door, the sexless sprite of East 53rd Terrace.

"I want the ring," he said.

A week later, the sore it had created on my finger would begin to heal.

7

Witnessing

With a convincing heterosexual engagement behind me, I had bought some necessary time until people, like my Aunt Lucy, started worrying about my sexuality again. A cake decorator, she had made all of my sisters' wedding cakes. "I have arthritis," she said. "I can't wait forever. Are you even dating?" I could finish college, get a job, and take half-hearted runs at adulthood. At my daddy's encouragement, I took a job as the Assistant Editor at an engineering firm where I wrote the interoffice newsletter. I got off my parents' insurance and bought a baby-blue Ford hatchback. Momma helped me paper over the clowns on my childhood bedroom wall with lavender flowers so that I would live with her longer, which I was more than happy to do. I knew that once I left there would be no turning back; I would have to face my sexuality head-on. A puritanical college friend invited me to Southwest Bible Church, which would, sadly, become the first church of my own choosing. Momma still paid my membership fee to the local Presbytery every year in the hopes, I'm sure, that I'd return to my senses, although she tried not to criticize my choices. I couldn't have found a more regressive church than Southwest Bible; they even criticized charismatic churches like

Royall's for distracting from the truth of the gospel with their emotional outbursts. The Bible—and their interpretation of it—was the sole source of truth. My new high-haired pastor pointed toward a nearby Presbyterian church and clucked at how sad it was that the minister was leading people straight to hell with his mealy-mouthed, Jesus-less gospel. It was a church just like Trinity Presbyterian where people were indeed squeamish about saying Jesus. They believed Jesus was a word—and a person—that had become diluted through overuse. By embracing the monstrously rigid people at Southwest Bible Church, I made fundamentalists like them my friends rather than my enemies.

Southwest encouraged us to witness to members of Presbyterian churches, and for that matter, to everyone else. The Great Commission to go into all the world and preach the gospel chewed at the backs of our brains. We mustn't go to the grocery store simply to buy food or to the post office just to buy stamps; "the fields were white unto harvest." Every idle moment meant a soul lost. The teacher of the Singles Sunday school helped us write down the verses we could quickly turn to in explaining the plan of salvation: "For God so loved the world that he gave his only begotten Son that whoever believes in him should not perish, but have eternal life." . . . "For all have sinned and fall short of the glory of God." . . . "Therefore having been justified by faith, we have peace with God through our Lord Jesus Christ." . . . "And when I came to you, brethren, I did not come with superiority of speech or of wisdom, proclaiming to you the testimony of God. For I determined to know nothing among you except Jesus Christ, and him crucified."

The few times I worked up the nerve to try it, I witnessed badly. What I said was too elliptical. For example, I asked an old friend from Trinity youth group if she "knew" Jesus. "Well, yes," she said. She seemed confused that someone who she'd gone to church with would ask such a question. I couldn't bear to use the words I knew my fundamentalist friends would want me to, "Are you saved?" Deep down I wouldn't have been able to explain what I meant by saved. Using such a phrase made me feel rude and embarrassed. How dare I tell someone who is doing their best, that their best isn't good enough? I witnessed out of pure obligation. It had nothing to do with my love for Jesus. People at Southwest said that if you don't try to help someone be saved and that person dies, you have to answer for why she will spend eternity in hell. Not *an* eternity, not a long line at the Department of Motor Vehicles, but eternity. Their whole never-ending torment will be your fault. Despite Imaginary Jesus's lack of concern about hell, I continued to worry about others' salvation, an appealing distraction for the repressed.

I made a mental list of the unsaved around me. A lapsed Baptist punk rocker coworker and her Catholic roommate expressed an interest in Revelation. Though the book's wacky prophecies put me in way over my theological head, I took their interest as a sign. They were practically begging me to witness to them. On a family trip to Colorado, it occurred to me that my brother-in-law Sam seemed too unhappy to be saved. Forced to go to Sunday school as a child, he refused to go to any church with Kathy. I lay in the top bunk of our rented condo stewing about his salvation. I tossed and turned, frightened by thoughts of Sam in hell, my insomnia punctuated by the bolts of static cracking between my socks and the sheets in the dry Georgetown air. In the end, I decided it would cause too much family awkwardness to witness to him and hoped that Karen had already made sure he'd heard about his need for Jesus.

Distracted by my discomfort, I always forgot to care primarily about the potential convert. Instead, I worried how I would look to them, how uncomfortable I would make both of us, and whether or not they would like me anymore after I told them how awful they were. Stripped of all the extraneous talk of love, witnessing is very antisocial. It tells people something is wrong with them. Not something cosmetic, not a spot of mustard on their cheek, not even a tumor that can be removed, but something Wrong. It tells them that they came from the manufacturer defective, destined to fail. It announces a mandatory personality recall and a forthcoming cosmic replacement. Few warm to the message; most, in their God-given hearts, know it can't be true.

Another problem I had was when I told a person how he or she could be born again, I offered a living, breathing example of how it didn't work. The verses I read to lead people through the plan of salvation were dangerously close to others like, "For they exchanged the truth of God for a lie, and worshiped and served the creature rather than the Creator, who is blessed forever. Amen. For this reason God gave them over to degrading passions; for their women exchanged the natural function for that which is unnatural."

"You need to live the truly alternative lifestyle," my Sunday school teacher said, "by following Jesus, not by being tattooed or addicted to something or homosexual. You need to show that there's no need to be perverse to set yourselves apart from others, to be cutting edge." I squirmed in my chair. So did my friend Jane, who, though she hadn't said so, I could tell wasn't heterosexual either. An athlete, she only owned a few dresses and wore them over and over. Her hair was cut like Billie Jean King's. I watched Jane write "alternative lifestyle" in capital letters in her Bible and then underline it, the sweat from her nervous fingers pulling the thin pages up as she slid them and the pen along.

If people like Jane and I believed that every word of the Bible was God's word, as Southwest demanded that we do, then we were poorly concealed abominations, saved or not. It didn't matter that the voice inside me that I believed was Imaginary Jesus's had never once mentioned that being a lesbian was a problem. To my fundamentalist friends, persistent deviance proved a person didn't know him. Another problem was that the secret horrible something they said was Wrong with me wasn't something I could simply confess and be done with. The real me to whom my sexuality was attached always floated back up from the fathoms where I'd tried to sink her. I may as well have confessed my digestive system.

In the Southwest Singles group, a disproportionately large number of us were secretly trying not to be the same kind of abomination. We went through the motions of dating each other properly, boy with girl and girl with boy, thus avoiding the risk of any real attraction. We witnessed as a recreational activity. Coming out of our sullen mouths, the gospel didn't sound like good news. Our "good news" emphasized hell. Not surprisingly, our efforts rarely bore fruit.

A group of twelve of us organized by Doug G. (the Singles group had two Dougs) climbed into his mother's station wagon and headed for the American Royal Parade in downtown Kansas City to pass out tracts. The parade is always in early November, and it always rains. No one wants a soggy piece of paper from socially awkward, wet people. Besides, people don't want to be distracted from pretending for their children's sake that they are having a good time at the parade.

Even I wouldn't even have wanted one of the hackneyed tracts I peddled, and I supposedly believed what it said. In a grotesque rendering of rough-looking people printed in the pamphlet, a gang war developed, and someone got stabbed. Right at the last possible minute before they bled to death, several characters, whom the reader had neither the time nor motivation to develop a concern for, got saved. I extended my copy halfheartedly to mothers pushing their strollers in wide arcs around me. The long-unaccepted tract went limp; I may as well have offered a bit of soggy toilet paper.

When I finally acknowledged that I was being a nuisance, I wandered out of sight of my group, apologized to the trees the tracts had been made from, and threw them into a trashcan. I found an empty spot on the wet sidewalk and crouched down to watch. Clydesdales, sheep, ponies pulling carts jingling with bells, goats, hogs, stallions, and mares all splashed toward the American Royal building where they would spend the next two weeks either waiting to perform or to be herded onto a truck for slaughter. A clown with a sad face tossed me a Tootsie Roll. It fell into a puddle, but I unwrapped and ate it anyway. Out of the corner of my eye, I watched for my evangelism team's energy to wane. When it did, we all filed back to the station wagon and rode for a long while engulfed by silence and the smell of wet hair and wool. A single new to our group finally spoke, "Don't you think that was wrong?"

"Wrong?" said Doug G. into the rearview mirror.

"What we did, bothering people, handing out cheap, badly written pieces of . . . I mean, Jesus is more important than this, don't you think? We don't know a thing about the people we handed them to. What if someone they loved had just died? What if they have had such a hard time in life, they don't see how Jesus could love them? What if we were just bugging them while they tried to watch the parade?"

The beauty of tracts was that they prevented you from having to interact with the unsaved. They worked just as well to wash the blood of the unsaved from your hands as did talking to someone and taking the risk he or she would ask a question you couldn't answer.

"Don't you think Jesus bothered people?" Doug G. said. He had paid good money for the tracts.

"Well, yes, of course, what he said bothered some—made them think—but they came to him. He didn't follow them around shoving cheap little . . ." and he shook a wet tract, flinging water all over the singles in the first two seats. "He would have talked to them. He would have listened to them."

"You think they'll care about a parade when they're in hell?" Doug G. said. Everything was clear to Doug G.

"You know what I think? I think Jesus would have watched the parade with them. And he would have arranged to meet with them later. He would have tried to establish a rapport."

"A what?" Doug G. said, eyebrow raised.

✦ ✦ ✦

Besides being closeted, another thing many Southwest Singles had in common was that they worked at jobs they didn't like and had difficult, unsaved bosses. Rather than complain, they went the extra mile in the hopes of converting their bosses through excessive agreeability. Every single longed to hear something like, "You're different—why do you work so hard? What's your secret?" They wanted their bosses to know their secret.

Here I diverged from the group. I loved my unsaved boss. My enjoyment of my job as Assistant Editor at the Burns & McDonnell depended almost entirely on her presence. Before I worked for Gretchen, I had never met a Jew, that I knew of. Overnight, Judaism fascinated me: the guilt, the uniqueness, the persecution. Most interesting of all, the Jews were related to Jesus, not by adoption, like me, but by blood. Gretchen looked a little like Barbara Streisand, whom I also tried not to find attractive.

Gretchen took it upon herself to teach me to use the computer we shared in my double-wide cubicle. She sat on the desk with her legs snug against my arm and with her hair brushing my face as she leaned forward to see what was happening on the screen. Our computer, one of the first desktop models ever sold, looked big enough to roast a twenty-pound turkey. It had a key next to backspace called "break" that, without warning, when pressed, erased everything you had typed. I loved that break key. When Gretchen hit it, she needed to type the text of her article all over again. I wondered if sometimes she didn't push it on purpose. I bought her Chanukah, Rosh Hashanah, and Passover cards, and, at her suggestion, I read Rabbi Kushner. I didn't share any of this with my Singles group friends who believed Jesus could finally come again when every last Jew converted to Christianity and made her way back to Jerusalem. They wouldn't have wanted me to encourage Gretchen to remain a Jew. It never occurred to me to witness to her: I wanted her to like me. Besides, I didn't want her to leave Kansas City for the Holy Land.

✦ ✦ ✦

In my Single Ladies' Bible Study, we were all encouraged to establish a "regular quiet time," which was lingo for scripture reading and prayer. It was one of the regimens I was supposed to suggest to all the new souls I was not winning. Each night, I sat in a rocking chair in my bedroom. When I got stuck on something, like the parable about the worker who got paid the same for working five minutes as those who had worked all day, Imaginary Jesus always helped me understand. He reminded me that when you love as hard as you can, the results don't always seem fair.

Because that was the only way fundamentalism understood Christianity, I thought of Imaginary Jesus as living inside me like a parasite or one half of a split personality. Over time, I would spend so much time reading about him, how he stopped and looked when someone else was missing or in trouble and thought twice about judging someone without knowing the full story, that Imaginary Jesus's life became a part of mine. He wasn't a supernatural invader as I thought of him then, but a way of thinking, a way of being, a Way.

Because my Single Ladies' Bible Study leader wasn't there to supervise, Imaginary Jesus turned my little bedtime vespers into something else altogether, offering insights that would have stung my leader's sensibilities. One night, Psalm 51 pinned me to my chair: "You desire truth in my innermost being and in the hidden part you will make me know wisdom." I could hear my father in the bedroom turning pages, my mother out listening to the nightly news, just like always. They hadn't felt the shift of a tectonic plate in my bedroom. "What do you mean by "truth"? I said aloud. I read further; I had been "knit together in my mother's womb." God had watched and been pleased. "But I've been this way for as long as I can remember," I whispered. Hobbled by fundamentalism, my mind could only contain this large thought for a few moments. Accepting myself would be heresy.

✦ ✦ ✦

When my Single Ladies' Bible Study leader suggested we begin thinking about which unsaved person we could invite to an impending Christmas coffee at her home, I immediately thought of Brenda, the typesetter. She wasn't a good typesetter; she also seemed lonely and unhappy. At the sight of such a person, Southwest Singles reached for their Bibles. Lonely, unhappy people were the only ones vulnerable enough to listen. Jesus came to save the sick not the well, we were reminded.

Before I moved into my cubicle at Burns & McDonnell to write the employee newsletter, I had never seen a typesetter, the person or the machine. I guess I thought that books, newspapers, and other printed things emerged from paper cocoons perfect and flight worthy as butterflies, that nothing as fallible as human fingers had been involved. I quickly learned just how much room for inconsistency and variation that typesetting, like life, allowed. Inconsistencies hadn't always been seen as errors. So respected were fifteenth-century typesetters that they could even take the liberty of spelling words their own way. They reigned before writers of dictionaries and style manuals informed them that they were wrong. When I met Brenda the typesetter, time and patience had all but run out for this once noble profession.

I returned proofreading sheets as many times as necessary to Brenda without reporting to my boss or hers that her mistakes were slowing my production schedule. In fact, I became part of an underground railroad of writers and paste-up artists who tried to protect her. Unfortunately, though, we could never find Brenda an adequate hiding place. Each time she fixed one error in the ever-increasing amount of type she needed to set, she made three or more new errors. Unlike today's forgiving spell and grammar check features and design programs that allow you to see numerous pages of text at once, the Linotronic 2000 demanded perfection. When you made a mistake you started over. It displayed only the last eighteen characters that had been typed in a little glass slot the length and width of a church pew pencil. Once an error moved out of range, the typesetter had no way of knowing this one bad apple had spoiled a whole bushel of type until she finished the column and pulled it from the film canister dripping with developing fluid.

Brenda's optometrist concluded that she had one eye that focused higher than the other. Most of the time, she saw two of everything, one hanging slightly above the other. The quarter-inch-thick lenses of her eyeglasses would have helped if the bridge of her nose hadn't been perpetually wet with nervous sweat and tears, giving the pink plastic frames nothing to grip.

Day after day, Brenda reported to work with good intentions she couldn't realize. After the daily report of mangled type, Walt, the manager of the Art Department, would puff down the hallway to Typesetting in shoes that sounded like they were going flat. He leaned red-faced around the door, beckoning with a curled pointer finger. Brenda knew the drill. Walt would spend an hour of precious eyesight she could have used to typeset scouring away whatever residue of self-confidence had built up since the day before. It should have occurred to me that Brenda couldn't be saved with warnings about hell; she was already there.

I got a brief taste of Brenda's predicament when Gretchen pulled her chair next to mine to tell me I'd made a significant error in a newsletter headline. She had been called up to the President's office to take a drubbing for it. It read, "Power Division Performs Second Rate Study," which, as I pointed out, wasn't a true mistake since I hadn't hyphenated *second rate*. I spent the morning facing the orange burlap-covered shelf of my cubicle reading the dictionary and picking off my cuticles until my fingers bled, a habit even Imaginary Jesus had been unable to break me of. I spoke to no one. Had I had scissors in my desk, I might have cut off all my hair. The worst part of it was that Gretchen had absorbed the reprimand intended for me. I couldn't help thinking about Imaginary Jesus, who, fundamentalist doctrine told me, had been killed for me. I set out to make no more mistakes, to take on whatever shape necessary to fit perfectly into any situation I found myself in. I believed such things were possible. I believed imperfections were wrong. No matter how many ways Imaginary Jesus tried to explain grace during my "quiet times," I couldn't seem to understand. I couldn't quite take in that there was no perfection, only brave fleshy experiments. Grace didn't mean I must be shredded to pieces and put together again to be a fully human being. It meant that I was loved, regardless of imperfections, maybe even because of them.

Brenda had no one to take the shock for her. Had my ears not been filled with Bible Study chatter about her eternal salvation, it might have occurred to me Jesus wanted her to be fired, that her salvation lay in a finding a better future than one spent staring up at the Linotronic 2000 with tears in her myopic eyes. If I had been any kind of a friend, I would have bought her a copy of the career guide *What Color Is Your Parachute?*, rather than invite her to the Christmas coffee.

✦ ✦ ✦

Across the mantel of a fireplace with no fire in it, my Bible Study leader had spelled out "Jesus Is the Reason for the Season" with nursery blocks painted Christmassy colors. She thought she had bought enough bags of blocks for everyone to paint the same decoration, but then she realized she was short on *s*'s. Brenda offered to paint only Jesus.

"Jesus is enough," Brenda said. "I'd probably spell anything more than that wrong." She made sure I saw her clonk her knuckle against her head.

After crafts, I ate my lemon poppy-seed muffin (which didn't feel Christmassy) in a panoply of guilt and insecurity that saved people aren't supposed to feel. I suddenly knew that the last thing Brenda needed to hear after a particularly long session in Walt's office that day was that she wasn't living up to God's standards either. I considered knocking over a scented candle and starting a fire that would put a stop to the evening, but Southwest Singles didn't start fires. Instead, I selected a large, deep chair I couldn't see Brenda from. When she sat on the hearth so others could have the chairs—something Imaginary Jesus would have done—I began to wonder whether the two of them might already know each other. She finally agreed to sit on a pillow someone offered.

The Bible Study leader played a record of "Sweet Little Jesus Boy" while we passed around a Christmas present she had wrapped multiple times. When she lifted the needle, whoever held the package took off a layer of wrapping. Brenda won the privilege of removing the last piece and opened the box. Inside was a crocheted cross.

"Why did I wrap a cross for Brenda to have for Christmas?" The leader posed several rhetorical questions to the unsaved. I won the prize, I guess, for bringing the person most in need of saving. "Because Jesus's death on the cross is the greatest gift you will ever receive." That night, like many nights before, we were asked to enfold the fundamentalist *reductio ad absurdum* that if Jesus hadn't been killed, his omniscient, loving Father who made him and the rest of us wouldn't have been able to stand the sight of us. "I need all the help I can get," Brenda said, looking embarrassed. My Bible Study leader had left me no way to avoid further witnessing. Here I had the opportunity for "follow-up" with a potential convert to make sure she understood "the plan of salvation," and I didn't want it. Brenda had enough problems. I didn't want to tell her that no matter how hard she tried, it would never be good enough for God or for Walt.

On the way out to our cars, an apology stuck in my throat. I couldn't find the words to say that I hoped I hadn't put Brenda off ever wanting to meet my imaginary friend at all. Withered with fear and self-preoccupation, I reassured myself that I had done what Southwest Bible asked before whatever was bound to happen did and I would no longer see Brenda again. Before we said goodbye, she squinted, straining to see me in the dimness of the Study leader's porch. For my pitiful sake, Brenda called herself a bad Lutheran. "I need to start going to church again," she said. "Thanks for reminding me." I'd never bothered to really get to know her, a mistake Imaginary Jesus gently pointed out later. I realized in the privacy of my car that night that I didn't want to get to know Brenda. I didn't want to be associated with her failure, didn't want to hear why she wore pilly sweaters and always brought her lunch instead of going out with the rest of us. I didn't want to know that this job in Typesetting came as close to journalism as she could get without going back to school, something she'd always wanted to do but couldn't afford. I couldn't bear to hear that getting hired had been a dream come true for her.

The next morning, I heard Brenda pack her spider plant, deodorant (which she had had to reapply several times daily), eye drops, and Kleenex into a box. Instead of torturing her that morning before Christmas vacation, Walt had decided simply to fire her. I invented a reason to plant myself in Gretchen's office when I sensed Brenda was nearly ready to leave. As I crept by, I noticed Typesetting smelled like foundation mixed with tears. From my hiding place, I heard her walk up and down the hall calling my name.

8

Are You My Mother?

All young animals eventually feel an urge to leave their parents. Exceptions to this rule are chased off. Some even get injured in the process. Television shows about this unavoidable passage made Momma change the channel. (Among other things, we watched far too much television together.) With the early, deep awareness that I would not want or need a husband and babies of my own, Momma defied nature and groomed me to remain a woman-child who would keep her company the rest of her life. Throughout my childhood, she had sat me down at the dining room table—odder still because we rarely did anything there—and read me the story of Ruth and Naomi. "Where you die, I will die—there will I be buried," she would read, then read again. She always stopped before Boaz complicated things.

Momma wasn't entirely to blame for my arrested development. My lingering at home after college suited Daddy, as well; I allowed him to remain emotionally irrelevant. Staying at home instinctively felt safe and simple. A term has even been coined for people of my ilk: house homo. Though this subspecies is rarer today than it was even twenty years ago, mothers and offspring still go to perverse lengths to make their arrangements seem normal.

Basements and attics are converted into apartments. Life skills such as cooking and laundry aren't passed down. Great quantities of money are saved for degrees never earned, for the realization of dreams that never materialize.

I could have remained forever unperturbed had representatives from the real world not come inside looking for me. I encountered a series of women who, their own maternal dreams unfulfilled, saw in my twenty-two-year-old self an unfinished project. They could see that I did not yet know what kind of person I wanted to become. And, in them, I saw surrogate mothers.

First, a forty-something friend, Janet, who liked my poetry in a college class, took me under her rough and insensitive wing. She loved how eagerly I accepted her unsolicited advice. She quickly ascertained that I liked Momma's company too much. She said everyone but I could see that. Janet had helped me get a short story about a spinster who lived with her mother published in an anthology, and she liked to think she had discovered a fresh talent. I nervously belonged to a writing group made up of people she had handpicked from a college writing class. The writing group clashed with the rest of my life. Before one of our meetings, a member called Janet to say she had stuck a knife between two of her ribs while her husband watched, just to spite him. She had punctured a lung and so wouldn't be able to make it that night. Another member had left her husband for a woman in my nine-teenth-century British novel class. They lived together in a bun-galow beneath the KCTV5 transmission tower, flouting Janet's concern about their daily exposure to electromagnetic waves. An-other member was an apprentice witch. Encouraged by South-west Bible to do so, I worried about her and everyone else's eternal salvation. After my failed attempt with Brenda the typesetter, I had vowed never to proselytize again. So, before I could tell mem-bers of the writers group about the plan of salvation, I had to wait for them to ask how I could still be happy when they saw no out-ward explanation for it. I spent meetings quietly smiling in the background, thinking of witty things to say and then not saying them. Imaginary Jesus's reach extended my grasp. He found writers group stimulating and encouraged me to take a more active part, to swim a little closer to the deep end, with the adults.

The summer before we had all been in writing class together, Janet had been run over by a pickup in North Kansas City and dragged a few blocks. She had kept from being killed by hanging onto an axle so the driver wouldn't run over her again. At the first writers group meeting, she passed around pictures her husband had taken of her in the emergency room. Because she had been wearing only a halter and tiny track shorts, much of her body was mottled with bloody ovals. Though I felt embarrassed to rifle through the private moments of someone I barely knew, I felt honored. Being near Janet also made me feel somehow safer. In those days, I believed lightning didn't strike the same place twice.

Janet telephoned me at home one night ("a little late," Momma said) to read me a poem she'd written about survivors of the Titanic, with whom she identified. "You know, at least something *happened* to me," Janet said. I sat in the dark kitchen writing down things she said that I wanted to memorize. I also pretended not to be Christian; I didn't want to seem simple. Janet's mother had pulled her out of Baptist Sunday school because, she said, "they did too much 'cutting and pasting.' Come on, the resurrection?" I felt for a split second as if I should say I believed that, though once dead, Jesus was still very much alive, because I sensed him with me in the dark kitchen trying to make me a little less nervous about talking to her. Imaginary Jesus liked Janet. Meeting them both halfway, I unscrewed the lid from the saltshaker on the Lazy Susan and poured little hills of salt into my palm and licked them off, a bad thing I hadn't done since I was about six. At 11:00, I saw Momma silhouetted in the kitchen door. She flicked on the light and mouthed "long distance?" When I shook my head no, she tapped her watch and frowned. I had to go to work in the morning. I lowered my voice so I wouldn't keep her or Daddy awake but remained defiantly on the phone. That night, as I did any evening I spent with Janet, I went to bed without reading my Bible, washing my face, or brushing my teeth. They felt like trivial things you'd put off after just surviving an accident.

Writers group met at alternating locations with everyone but me sharing hosting responsibilities. "Remember, I live at my parents' house," I said at yet another meeting, rolling my eyes as if to shift the blame for my life onto them. "In Raytown," I added, when I didn't get the proper sympathy. People from Kansas City used to make fun of its suburb Raytown because it had so many bowling alleys and pizza parlors. Now they make fun of it because it's a good place to get shot.

Even though my stories were more interesting than the witch's—Janet said mine were full of virgin whores—the witch got more respect than I did. We could meet at her grown-up apartment and sit on her secondhand furniture covered with Arabic sheets and balance drinks on her milk crate coffee table.

After the conversation left our writing, it often degenerated into alcohol-soaked games of truth or dare. One night Janet said, "Okay, let's tell when we lost our virginity. I'll start."

In my panicked brain, I tossed around several alternatives, hoping the group would become so drunkenly discursive that they'd never make it around to me. I could choose not to answer at all, but the dares frightened me even more. I could take the moral high ground and say that I was still a virgin, and, technically speaking, probably always would be. After hiding my true self for twenty years, lying had become the easiest way out of any sexual pickle. When they did finally get around to me, I said, without the softening effect of alcohol, "A year ago."

"Really?" they all said, shocked.

"Well?" Janet said. "Who?"

"My fiancé, Royall."

Janet squinted but did not challenge.

"Well," the witch said. "Give."

"It wasn't great," I said, as I knew it would not have been.

"Pity," said the bisexual. "I hope you try again. Maybe you just need to try a woman next time."

"That's it?" Janet said. "That's all you have to say?" She became more confrontational with every swallow of beer.

"Not much to report," I said.

I consoled myself that I didn't have to come back to writers group anymore if I didn't want to, even though I knew I would.

+ + +

Delores Hyde, a Southwest Bible Church friend who could never have children because of endometriosis, saw potential in me as well. On Thursday nights, I went to a Bible study at her house and then stayed overnight, ostensibly so I wouldn't have to drive back to my parents' house in the dark. Really, I stayed because it allowed her time to disciple me. (Safety, Momma could endorse. Discipleship, she would not have understood. It would have made her feel I didn't need her.) Older and more spiritually mature people made disciples of less mature brothers and sisters, men of boys and women of girls. Many people waited years to become someone's disciple. Some were never asked at all, remaining religious wallflowers. Herself an English major, Dolores thought it was wonderful that I was involved in the arts instead of automatically labeling them suspect and ungodly as so many fundamentalists did, although she did lament that so many artists and writers felt they had to be homosexuals.

So grateful was I to be Dolores's disciple that I bought an elaborate stitching project to make into a pillow in time for Christmas. I had never undertaken something so foreign to my nature. Filling a foot-square piece of heavy white canvas with uniform little knots tested the limits of both my manual dexterity and sanity. When finished, you could detect, if you looked hard, only one drop of blood. "That's sweet," Momma said. What she did not need to say was that I had never made *her* a pillow. I went back to Hobby Lobby and tried to find another candlewicking kit like it, but couldn't. The first one had been on closeout.

The Thursday after I lied about my virginity, I helped Dolores prepare a coffee tray for Bible Study. "Oooo," she said opening her eyes, so that I could see the whites both above and beneath, her look of moral concern. "What did you say, when it came around to you?"

Undermining weeks of work on my integrity, I answered in the way I knew Dolores would have wanted. "I told them I was still a virgin."

"Good," she said. "Good, Kelly. And what did they say?"

"They think it's abnormal," I said, which in my imagined disaster of truth-telling they did. "It was wrong to even have had such a conversation, don't you think?"

"Well, not necessarily, I guess. It gave you the opportunity to say you're a virgin, to explain why that's important to you. Did you tell them why you're still a virgin?" I imagined Janet laughing her dirty laugh. Such things wouldn't fly at writers group.

I reviewed possible scriptural reasons I could have given and said, "My body is a temple of the Holy Spirit."

"Good, Kelly, excellent. I think you said just the right thing."

"I think I should stop going. They're not a very good influence."

"Kelly, the Lord never told us to withdraw from the world. We're to live his life in its midst. We're to be salt and light. Not everybody is going to be Christian. That's why it's so great you're in the group."

◆ ◆ ◆

I didn't know how much longer I could keep the plates spinning. During a discussion at Bible Study concerning the verse in Philippians about remaining pure and blameless until the day of Christ, I thought about the last story I had taken to writers group. In it, there was a girl who enjoyed looking under an amusement park bathroom door at her friend's red toenails. In my memory, I heard Janet's voice saying in front of the entire group, "This narrator's gay." And my own saying, "She is?" And Janet's saying, "Oh, come on."

The same week I received a letter from Dolores praising me for being a virgin and a writer, Janet mailed me an index card with one sentence written on it: "Why do you still live with your parents?" She set a goal for me to be out of their house by my birthday, as good a date as any. Raw with humiliation for feeling content in one place for too long, I began to listen for new opportunities.

Almost immediately, I fell prey to another maternal forty-something. Peggy was in the Southwest Bible Church Singles group. She needed a roommate to help pay her half of a two-bedroom duplex about a mile from my parents' house. I didn't find it strange that she planned for the two of us to do everything together as I had done with Momma. How naïve, malleable, and pleasantly uninterested in men I must have seemed. As an older model on the singles lot, Peggy no longer had many dates. Rather than ask Imaginary Jesus what he thought about living with her, I took the lazy way out and assumed that whenever a religious option presented itself, it was always the right one. Ultimately, he and I made the best of a difficult situation. If I learned anything from Imaginary Jesus, it's that few decisions are irretrievably wrong.

It took five minutes to drive to my parents' house from the duplex, not nearly far enough to help me automatically remember that I had moved. More often than not, I missed my new turn. Momma had resisted my move as she would have a divorce. "Why do you feel you have to get away from me?" she asked. "If Mother were still alive—I didn't have her as long as you've had me, she died at fifty-one, too young—I'd be living with her right now." After my grandfather drained the bank account and left them, mother-daughter was the only relationship that made sense to them and that they trusted. My grandmother died of kidney failure before I was born. With curly hair like my grandmother's and her unprecedented love of classical music and the arts, I reminded Momma of the intense relationship they had and of the reason she wanted our relationship to go on forever unchanged.

In the face of her complaints, my explanations seemed flimsy. I had broken our unspoken agreement to remain inseparable. "Is it *that*, Janet?" Momma used "that" to refer to people she didn't like, which was anyone who took my time away from the family. I didn't tell her I was moving out because Janet felt I should at my age. Had I revealed any cracks in my resolve—such as my motivation being entirely external—she'd have lured me back under her spell, which was what the inertia of living at home really felt like.

Only one balm soothed Momma: Peggy's failure to replace her. After trying to spend one weekend in the duplex alone with Peggy, Momma's house seemed even easier to live in. Peggy questioned my writing: "Are your stories Christian?" She thought people didn't have enough time to read the Bible as it was and didn't need secular writing to distract them. She also thought I just read too much. She wanted me to stay home with her in the evenings and weave wheat wreaths and angels, a craft she'd recently learned. While we pulled wheat fronds from a bucket of water, we listened to a record album of her award-winning high school choir. It made me feel so lonely and purposeless I felt sick to my stomach. After discovering all Momma hadn't taught me, Peggy established herself as the spiritual alpha. We would share food as the early Christians had, most of which she ate. After politely critiquing the desiccated fish I served my first night on supper duty, she promised to teach me to make simple and affordable newlywed meals: sloppy Joes, tuna casserole, and porcupine meatballs.

Very quickly, it became hard to hide a major un-Christian dislike for her. I hated her split skirts, which she said allowed an active woman the modesty of pants without looking masculine. As a physical therapist, Peggy had to put her body in awkward positions. "I feel a responsibility to look like a Christian woman," she said. "It's hard, you know, to be both attractive and decent." Though never before had I disliked any animal, I resented her cat, Hagi Baba, because his hair was exactly the same color as hers, light red mixed with gray.

Every Friday night, like a college freshman, I packed a duffel bag and went home to Momma's. There I could be assured not only a video and a Friday night hot dog from the Sites gas station rotisserie, but also Saturday visits from both of the in-town sisters, Karen and Kathy, and a day of outings and takeout from Jeong's Canton or Big Boy Burgers. We flocked to Momma like homing pigeons, mixed messages of love, dependency, and guilt strapped to our ankles.

Alone at the duplex on weekends, Peggy tried to embrace her free time. She lovingly mowed the scanty lawn around our half of the duplex. She planted petunias. She sat cross-legged on her twin bed playing hymns on her recorder to arthritic Hagi Baba. To keep down the smell of his litter, something Peggy suspected might be driving me away, she moved it to the basement. Hagi Baba decided to urinate in my shoes rather than make the arduous walk down the basement steps.

Unintentionally, I found Peggy's Achilles' heel. I didn't watch television, but not because I thought it was evil. I just had found better things to do with my time since I had moved out of Momma's house. Peggy wanted me to watch television with her so badly I could feel an electric yearning coming through my bedroom wall. Not even limiting herself to an eight-inch screen could dampen her craving. "You've worked all day," she said in the same tone Momma used to when she called me to watch *Murder, She Wrote*. Peggy did not even allow herself the comfort of sitting on the couch but sat on our toxic new duplex carpet with her back pressed up against its hard base. "You need a break now, Kelly. Come on." Just out of curiosity, she had tried two programs, *MacGyver* and *Scarecrow and Mrs. King*, to see if "there was anything on television that was not completely ungodly."

"See these two people?" she called from the living room. I had just settled under the covers with Chekhov. "This man and this woman are friends. They solve mysteries together, and you can tell they like each other. He is a complete gentleman though." In the middle of reading "The Duel," I heard her praying that a perpetrator wouldn't hurt Mrs. King. I stopped short of asking why she thought watching television was okay but reading wasn't. I just didn't have the energy for another theological argument.

In a fit of passive aggression, I brought home a stray black kitten from Karen's backyard that spent his time dropping off the back of furniture onto Hagi Baba's ancient back. Peggy had encouraged me to get him, assuming that if I did, I would stay home on weekends to take care of him. Instead I packed him up, litter box and all, and shuttled him to Momma's with me. I didn't have the courage to tell Peggy she drove me crazy, so I used Singer as the excuse that I had to move back with my parents. The car rides traumatized him.

Under the guise of saving for a house, I moved into my old bedroom for the final act of a protracted childhood. At Janet's warning that I leave Raytown altogether or risk permanent social disfigurement, I began quietly applying to graduate school. "If you won't save yourself," Janet said. "Let your writing save you. You need to grow up, move away, fall in love." Dolores agreed. "Don't hide your light under a bushel. Trust God. Step out." During the lunch hour at Burns & McDonnell, I typed one of my short stories into the computer and mailed it to a contest. Several months later, I received a registered letter from the Missouri Arts Council saying I had won $5,000. Because I couldn't find any-place else to do so, I went outside to my car and whooped with joy. I came back inside, the letter still in my hands. No one in my family had ever received a registered letter, let alone prize money. Daddy found his glasses and took it from me. "Are you sure it doesn't say $50.00?" he said. About a month later, the phone rang in my cubicle at work. The director of the Writing Program at the University of Montana wanted to know if I wanted to accept one of ten new student positions within it. I sealed Momma's fate as well as my own by accepting. My body could think of no better reason to develop irritable bowel syndrome. I lost several pounds that summer from having diarrhea over my fear of leaving.

My graduate advisor could not meet Momma and me the week she insisted on flying with me to Missoula to find me an apart-ment. Though she didn't exactly say so, Momma had planned to hand the baton to this woman, and it made her angry that my advisor did not understand the importance of her duty. Instead of picking me up at the airport, as she would have other visiting dignitaries, my advisor said that Missoula had a nice bus system.

During the standard, hair-raising descent between mountain ranges, Missoula looked more like home than any place I had ever seen before. I yearned to get out and begin trying to survive there as soon as possible. As we stepped through the gate at Missoula

International, Momma and I both spied the stuffed mountain lion poised to spring on new arrivals from a log he was fastened to over the security doors. She added big cats to her list of things that would do me in. Unable to figure out the bus schedule, we walked all over town, even though Momma had worn strappy leather sandals. She limped on blistered feet to the Butterfly Herb Coffee House, where the new roommate we had interviewed suggested we get mocha lattes. Neither of us had ever heard of one. It took the stoned help quite a while to notice that two bodies sat in one of the booths. A girl with half-open eyes handed our order to a boy with dreadlocks, something neither of us had ever seen. "What do you suppose happened to his head?" Momma said. Cat Stevens sang into the silence between us, "I'll always remember you like a child."

Back in Raytown, Momma sat down near the telephone, propped her still injured feet up on a stool and let ferocious love combined with fear get the better of her. She made a phone call to my advisor that she planned never to tell me about. According to my advisor, who finally, just weeks before I graduated, told me about their conversation, Momma tried to convey that I was a fragile genius who needed much more careful tending than I had gotten thus far. Knowing this would have explained why my advisor would complain, in front of everybody in my first writing workshop, that she needed my new phone number but then said, "Or should I just call your mommy?" It would take me a year to win her over, racking my brain to figure out how I might have offended.

Momma hoarded our last days together before my move, telling herself and others that we'd still have a week together even after she and Daddy drove with me across five states in their ramshackle truck, Old Blue. Rather than drive the truck, which always had something wrong with it, Daddy had used it as storage for chair legs and scrap wood to refurbish antique furniture, his new hobby. The truck had slowly become encased in aphid droppings, scientifically known as honeydew, parked as it was under the oak tree where the aphids and the ants who "farmed" them lived. Shortly before I left, Momma and I watched a program about the relationship on PBS. In exchange for protection from other insects, the aphids agree to be kept as slaves and to squirt a bead of honeydew whenever ants stroked their bellies. "Isn't that nice," she said. I felt nauseous for the aphids.

By some miracle, my brother-in-law got Old Blue running, and we set out for Montana. I followed behind in my aging Escort hatchback crammed with boxes of books, clothes, a new computer, and a pot of Swedish ivy, whose precipitous decline during the journey mirrored Momma's. In a motel in South Dakota, road-delirious Daddy threw off the scratchy sheets at 2:30 in the morning and shouted that we'd better get back on the road. When Momma woke him, he sat in the dark, rubbing his head, and said, "I'll be seventy when you come home," he said. "I'll be an old man." It amounted to his goodbye.

My Escort, itself in the final stages of deterioration, tried but failed to make it across the Divide at Butte. "Vapor lock," a highway patrol officer told Daddy at the scenic outlook we had babied it to. I had already flattened down on a picnic bench in despair. Just the previous day, we'd had to take the Escort to a mechanic in Wyoming to see if the part that had caught fire and fallen off was necessary. From the bench, I watched a woman pull a cat from her RV and drag it behind her by a leash. I took the vapor lock as a sign I'd had no business leaving home. Forgetting I had just won a contest, Janet had said at my final writers group meeting, "I've judged contests. The winner usually isn't that good. We just don't have that much to choose from. Real writers don't enter contests." I'd taken her words straight to heart like a shot of cobra venom.

"Maybe it's not meant to be," I said to Daddy's knees.

"It better be," he said, "or I've driven way too far."

"I guess I'd better call a tow truck," I said.

Momma's face appeared upside down. "Honey, Missoula's 150 miles from here."

"Then I guess I'll just have to stay in my car." They didn't appreciate my helplessness, but it certainly shouldn't have surprised them.

"We're not staying at the Divide," he said.

"Not we," I said. "Me."

"Now you get yourself up off that bench and go talk to that ranger about your car," he said.

"He's not a ranger."

"Listen, now you're starting to make Daddy angry." He spoke of himself in the third person when he didn't want to be held responsible for what he was about to do.

"Now, honey," Momma said, "you should say a little prayer of thanks that vapor lock is all it is. Get up now. Come on."

"Thank you, Jesus," I said sarcastically.

Imaginary Jesus chuckled.

I wanted to heed omens. *Look at Oedipus*, I thought. *Even with the Sphinx, the Sybil, all the death and disaster, he still couldn't see any of it coming.*

"I should never have done this," I said.

"Now, George, she's just disappointed," Momma said. "Go over there and simmer down." And then, to me, she said, "Well, I wish we'd have known you didn't really want to go a few months ago."

I heard it, the unmistakable sound of hope in her voice. My fear of losing hold of my first kernel of independence rose to my throat and formed words.

"Let's see if it will start." It did.

◆ ◆ ◆

While sitting on my new roommate's futon watching an episode of *Big Valley* that evening, I learned that classes started the very next day, not a week away like I'd written on my calendar, subconsciously putting the whole thing off. Four or five evenings later, standing beside Flathead Lake with my parents who were trying to salvage some sort of vacation, I said, "Now *this* is a lake."

"So the Lake of the Ozarks isn't good enough for you, huh?" Daddy said. In one sentence I'd nullified the summers my family had been able to afford at a lakeside cabin there because it belonged to his uncle.

"This isn't manmade," I said. "It's a lake that always has been."

"I know what you meant. You didn't need to tell me what you meant. And it hasn't always been. You'd better take a geology class."

Momma bought a jar of huckleberry jam from the Indian Trading Post, and we all bought Buster Bars at the Flathead Lake Dairy Queen, peeling back the paper, slowly eating a last sweet thing together.

The day before they left my apartment, Momma said, "I'm hot."

"Open one of those windows," I said, with too much clip in my voice.

"I guess Daddy and Momma had better leave when we've become this much of a bother," he said, threatening me with a departure that was already imminent. To me they already had left, detached like booster rockets and broken up on reentry. It seemed strange to hear their voices in this new place among foreign things I'd already begun to adapt to: temperature inversion, the dry crust in my nostrils each morning, the pine and the sweet green smell of the Clark Fork River, the burble of red-winged blackbirds.

The trumped up hostility in those final days helped only a little to complete the final weaning. Nothing could have assuaged Momma's grief in the wee hour that they loaded the truck. Saying she was afraid to wake my roommate, Momma insisted I not turn on a light. I could not see, but I felt her soaked face pressed against the dryness of my own. No words could have explained her stifled sobs, the reluctant release of her fingers, my own nausea. I had simply meant more to her than I had ever have been able to bear. In return, all I could offer was sleepy confusion and an affectionate murmur of farewell. With the sound of Old Blue finally disappearing, all I felt was relief. The diarrhea I'd had for the three months I'd anticipated leaving Momma resolved that day. I returned to the still warm sheets of my new bed and slept her away. When I woke in the morning, I had all the things I needed: a bank account, a new set of kitchen towels, a metal spatula that my roommate didn't already have, and my name on class rosters.

9
Reconciliation

My grandfather had tried to leave the part of himself that couldn't stop drinking along the shoulder of a western road after he abandoned his wife and his two daughters—my mother and her sister, Norma. We know little of what happened after he emptied his side of the closet and Momma's college savings account other than that in California he ran out of ground to cover. Years later, in rehab, he finally stopped running. There, he vomited and shook and felt what counselors helped him identify as regret. Once sober, he married a nurse who mopped his veiny red face no longer hiding lies. Several years after he stopped drinking, he died of cirrhosis of the liver, but that's beside the point. He had finally listened to his shadow side. The two parts of him made a tenuous peace. I had similar reconciling to do.

How easy it would be, I imagined, to become a lesbian around strangers. I didn't yet understand that other people weren't entirely to blame for my self-loathing. For nearly a decade I had waited for my inner lesbian to shrivel in the heat of fundamentalism. But she hadn't; she was me. Now that the tables were turned, my fundamentalist, my religious addict, who had protected me from the pain of being different, had no intentions of leaving me either. The battles these two waged in my psyche prevented me from falling into the very love that Janet from writers group had encouraged me to leave home to find.

If Janet hadn't convinced me she didn't believe in God, I would have sworn she had prayed that the fall quarter of my second year in graduate school would happen to me. Drained of prize money, I accepted a graduate assistantship and attended two weeks of training that, though it failed to prepare me to teach college composition, led me to her. In my small group where we did writing exercises we would teach our students, I first heard the raspy voice I would learn to filter from the din at great distances like a dog does a certain whistle. Rachel's first freewrite had something to do with an overwhelming urge to move her bowels during childhood trips to Toys "R" Us. "I wanted so many things there that I guess my body needed to make room," she read and then stopped to apologize. "I don't even know why I shared that." The fluorescent lights made a halo on her yellow hair.

"The same thing used to happen to me in the children's department of the library," I said later, after class.

"Really?" she said. "I've never met anyone willing to own up to this."

I thought this made us soul mates. Lots of people wanted to be Rachel's soul mate.

Hoping to be near her compelled me to go to MFA mixers at my advisor's home. I always wound up in the same corner studying the same wood block print of a buffalo. At one, I found myself hemmed into this corner with her and a Boston fern. I had become so obsessed that my mind failed in her presence. I strove for the same emotional congruity as our first encounter. I brought up teaching, hoping she did it as badly as I did. I told her the story of how a student had pointed out a yellow chalk handprint on my breast. Rachel's loud dirty laugh made my palms throb, a lifelong, bloodless, emotional stigmata to distract me from wanting something I shouldn't have. I imagined being allowed to touch a palm to her cheek just once and only for a little while.

"Do you have tics?" I said, still fishing for deeper connection with a person my inner fundamentalist constantly murmured that I could never have.

"Do I what?"

"Have tics . . ."

"Oh, my God," she said, "Where?" She swatted at her neck and slapped her head.

"No. Gosh no. I mean t-i-c-s in the classroom—like saying 'Um' or pulling at your clothes."

"So you don't see a tick on me?" Rachel said.

"I have a tic," I said. "I jam my hands in my pockets over and over."

Silence ensued. She began to look around as I figured out people did at parties when they needed to abandon a dying conversation.

"Well, I need another one of these," Rachel said, waggling her empty.

I remained in the corner with the fern, pressing ever closer until the fronds sprang in front of me. I understood what she must have felt, trapped there with me, when a man told me his novel from start to finish. After several mini seizures in my legs, I finally ask to be excused. In my hurry to get away, I crunched through the shards of a ceramic jar that a drunken poet had just staggered into. I waited for him to bash into each side of the doorjamb and stagger outside before I walked into the night myself. On the way home, the dark hump of Mt. Sentinel over my shoulder reminded me of something more permanent than my own awkwardness.

Another time, I listened to landscape painter Russell Chatham read a passage from a book of essays about fly fishing, a topic I couldn't have been less interested in. I sat behind Rachel and the two close friends she had inevitably made. I couldn't stop my internal warfare long enough to offer reliable companionship. As Chatham droned on, I studied her neck. For a split second, it looked like something I wanted to spread with jam. Horrified, I tried to get control of myself by keeping count of the number of times Chatham said fish. I considered checking myself into a mental health facility. Thinking they couldn't ever apply to someone like me, I refused the balm of the passages from Song of Solomon. The narrator compares the beloved to wine, dates, pomegranates, and honey, fit for eating and drinking without a plate, a cup, or shame.

People trailed Rachel in large groups to plays, to pool halls, to watch her try brains and eggs at the Ox, a bright, twenty-four-hour lunch counter with grimy linoleum and Keno machines. Usually, I lingered long past the time when the others left, saying they had papers to grade or books to read. I always wanted to be the last person left but then panicked when I got my wish. I painted myself into conversational corners. One thing led to another, and I wound up telling Rachel things she couldn't have wanted to hear, about my parents' overprotectiveness, my childhood insomnia. She listened carefully, kindly, her long white fingers stitched through her yellow hair.

I invited her to see *Angel at My Table*, a movie based on the cryptic, depressing autobiography of Janet Frame, who, after a series of very bad days, was misdiagnosed as a schizophrenic and administered more than 200 shock treatments. Winning New Zealand's Hubert Church Award helped Frame narrowly avoid a leucotomy. I identified with her debilitating self-consciousness and unmanageable hair. I'd already seen the movie six times. I bought a large sack of popcorn and balanced it on my palm between us. It took me about the first third of this viewing to forget that Rachel was sitting beside me, sharing the same wooden armrest rubbed golden from countless affectionate forearms.

"I'm tired of stories about tormented writers," Rachel said afterward at the counter of Hansen's Ice Cream. "I don't think you have to be disturbed. Like you, for example, you're not disturbed."

I looked up, surprised, egg cream dribbling down my chin.

"Well, I mean you're not an addict, are you?"

"I think I know what you mean," I said, scrambling to agree with her. "Madeleine L'Engle thinks that, too. She writes out of a place of health and sanity, about health and sanity."

"Isn't she Christian?"

"Yeah," I said. "*Wrinkle in Time . . .*"

"Are you Christian? If you don't mind me asking?"

I'd ruined even a pretend date.

"Sort of," I said. "I guess so." My inner fundamentalist kicked loudly on her closet door.

"That's nice that you find meaning in it. I didn't. God knows I tried."

My persistent faith in the face of all evidence to the contrary intrigued her. "Well, there's liberation theology?" Rachel said. "Jesus's solidarity with the poor and oppressed. That seems reasonable. But Jesus born of a virgin, the resurrection? What do you make of all that?" She asked me a host of such questions I couldn't answer. How could I explain that this man she thought of as a dead Jewish prophet had walked out of scriptures into my head? "I guess if I believe God made the world then I don't have a hard time believing he could bring Jesus back to life," I said.

"Literally?" she said. I couldn't yet make such distinctions. All of my beliefs were literal.

Rachel backed away, probably seeing the blank look on my face. "I just can't believe that," she said smiling.

"That's okay," I said. Religious people can seem strangely charming, our unfounded hopefulness offering a momentary relief from catastrophes, malaise, and dark nights of the soul.

"Thank you," she said to me when Hansen's owner finally asked us to leave. "Nobody else will let me talk about this." I felt the faintest old pull that I should say something compelling about the gospel, but my hunger for further contact led me to think better of it.

Back on our bicycles for home, I pulled out in front of a car that I hadn't seen because I hadn't checked over my shoulder. The driver swerved and called me a name. He yelled that he hoped I'd never do that again. Riding away from Rachel, I couldn't imagine an after. I hoped my dangerous maneuver would be perceived as devil-may-care.

When her feet appeared near me in the university bookstore, I continued to kneel at the cubbyhole where I'd just stuffed my book bag, trying as always to recover from the delicious shock of seeing her. She bent over, and put her pretty face upside down in front of mine.

"You're charmed. A car almost hit you the other night." She held two fingers an inch apart. You want to go contra dancing? A bunch of us are going."

"Contra dancing?" I said. I knew before she even answered that I could never dance with her. "Isn't there jumping?"

"Oh, come on. Don't you want to jump with me?"

She'd see me stunned with internal conflict, teeth bared, arms dangling.

"I just can't," I said, fleeing. "If you do something that requires inhibition, you be sure to let me know."

"Wait, your book bag," she shouted after me.

✦ ✦ ✦

I tried starving my inner fundamentalist since she wouldn't go away. I had stayed away from church altogether, which neither she nor my gay self appreciated. Both wanted to continue a life in the church, to live a life of faith. Finally, I lost my resolve and tore a phone number off the bottom of a flier that invited college students to an "exciting, contemporary worship service" in the hopes that contemporary meant they welcomed gays. I sat next to Nita and Burt in a folding chair in the free-throw lane of a basketball court that doubled as a sanctuary. After a run-of-the-mill fundamentalist service disguised with drums, we ate dinner in the hot double-wide belonging to Burt's shut-in mother. It was full of chiming clocks. Nita and Burt praised me for standing up for Jesus at the university. Did I want to go with them to the basketball court again? No, thank you, I told them.

Sunday morning after Sunday morning, I trudged through more snow than I had ever seen, hoping to find a church that could welcome the warring halves of me. I crossed them off in the phone book as they failed to do so. I tried the Wesleyans, lazily assuming they might have some affiliation with Wellesley, where a fellow student had studied with the wildly theological Annie

Dillard. I would never make such a spelling mistake again. Hoping to return to my progressive religious roots, I tried Evangelical Presbyterian, but Presbyterian doesn't mean the same thing with evangelical in front of it. For fun, at the Sunday evening service, they were learning steps and hand motions of a dance to help them remember the major events of the Old Testament. The night I visited, they paused and froze for a few beats to become pillars of salt like Lot's wife had when she turned to look at the homosexuals she had left behind in the ashes of her former town.

I felt least uncomfortable at Missoula Free Methodist. My Southwest Bible Church friends back home would have disparaged Pastor Andy as touchy-feely and accused him of watering down the gospel with his talk about the importance of his and other people's inner children. It did make me little nervous to learn that Andy felt he had the gift of discernment, a kind of religious ESP. After one Sunday service he stopped me to say, "Okay, this is weird, but I think I hear the Lord saying this," he paused and tipped his head to one side as if tuning in a faint radio signal. "He wants you in the game. I'm not sure what that means. Does that mean anything to you?"

After a few months of attending Missoula Free Methodist, I'd never brought or even mentioned a boyfriend. Pastor Andy and his wife arranged a blind date with a musical instrument repairman.

"I should warn you," Pastor Andy said. "He's Finnish, and apparently, they don't talk. I saw this *60 Minutes* about them. Husbands don't tell wives they love them until one of them is dying. That's some pretty heavy-duty silence. But he's a really solid Christian guy." They thought we'd be perfect for each other. Writing and musical instruments were both artistic.

Tuba—the name I came uncharitably to call this man—would become my next casualty, the next in a string of relationships I could point to that just didn't work out. I hoped Pastor Andy would hear another "word" or just figure out I was gay and needed help.

For our date, Tuba decided the two of us would watch the Twins play the third game of the World Series in the basement apartment his widowed landlord rented only to quiet Christians.

His television took up most of the living room. We sat at either end of a long flowery couch eating egg rolls he dumped from a box and baked on a new cookie sheet.

During a commercial, he said, "Family?"

"Three sisters, parents," I said, in shorthand, like he did.

"I've never gotten along with Daddy," I said, scattering hints of psychological struggle so that he wouldn't blame himself when I said I didn't want to see him anymore.

"Girls should love their fathers," he said and withdrew into silence again at the bottom of the seventh. During another commercial, he showed me the scar where a hockey puck had hit his face. One date would be all I could manage.

When I got home, the answering machine was blinking. Rachel had asked me to please get her out of her tiny dorm room to do something, anything. I felt enraged, first at Tuba, then at myself, because I went places I didn't want to with people I didn't like. I did all of this to keep from telling the truth.

I called her immediately and got her machine. Instead of searching for this woman I now realized I loved and confirming my fear that she could never like me the way I did her, I went to the Quik Shop behind my apartment carport for a bag of chips and called for a takeout falafel sandwich. I assembled my food on the floor around me. Swishing away my roommate's two cats, I watched a marathon of the original *Mickey Mouse Club*.

Tuba sent flowers. At my desk, the bouquet looming over me, I wrote him a letter excusing myself from ever seeing him again. I left the flowers at the door of an old lady across the hall. I felt as if I'd done exactly the right thing, a rare thing.

✦ ✦ ✦

Despite all his talk about emotional healing, Pastor Andy still referred me to the same exacting God that fundamentalists invented to contain their own anger, discomfort, and self-loathing. I still roamed most of my days in a confessional fog, regretting every wrong turn of my head. When I tried to pray, God closed his eyes and pointed to the cross. I faced a terrible disconnect; loving, Imaginary Jesus, the cross behind him, and his prudish, whip-cracking father didn't seem like they could be in the same family. I thought maybe I should be more intentional about spending time with Imaginary Jesus in case I hadn't given him adequate opportunity to speak his mind. With difficulty, I found a wrinkled five-year-old prayer list I had brought west with me. On it were stale worries and names of people I couldn't remember. I'd had a suspicious-looking patch of skin that had turned out to be nothing. I'd also listed missionaries I had never met with needs I never understood. Clearly, I needed to start over from scratch. Every evening, I suited up and assumed a reverent position. As I broached the subject of my sexuality, Imaginary Jesus remained consistently reassuring as he did about most other people's sexuality if no one was getting hurt. "Why fix something if it isn't broken?" I thought I heard him say. How could this be? In a muffled voice, my inner fundamentalist said, *This isn't Jesus. Be careful.* You just want your ears tickled: "For the time is coming when people will not put up with sound doctrine, but having itching ears, they will accumulate for themselves teachers to suit their own desires." Despite my inner fundamentalist's rantings, Imaginary Jesus and I reached a quiet ecclesiastical plateau where I, as I had as a child, felt naked and unashamed. For too short a time, I lingered there. I couldn't stop myself from loving this woman, and he didn't seem to care.

◆ ◆ ◆

Over Christmas break I renewed my family's hope that I was heterosexual. I occasionally had to fan the flame of their belief that I might eventually wind up with Brad, an old friend from the Southwest Singles group. Many times he and I had used each other as stunt dates at official functions, each of us instinctively relieved that the other wanted nothing more than friendship. Thrilled, Momma called everyone else in the family when I told her I was going to hear jazz in midtown Kansas City with him. That night we spent driving from club to club, leaving after only a few songs. Nothing sounded like the jazz Brad needed. At our last stop of the night, he leaned forward and shouted over a horn solo, "I've learned something. My father didn't spend enough time with me. My mother and I weren't on good terms either," he said, his jaw tightening with the effort of telling his new story right. "She kept me away from my dad. She is beautiful though. I know that. I can see that now." After her divorce, Brad's mother had moved him and his brother from Kansas City to a house in the desert outside of Las Vegas. As soon as he graduated from high school, Brad enrolled at the University of Kansas to be closer to his dad, who still couldn't rearrange his schedule to see him. Now, since he didn't see his mother anymore either and thought he should, Brad tuned into a late-night jazz show broadcast on NPR from a club in Vegas she frequented. During breaks between songs, he could sometimes hear bursts of her laughter. That was as much of her as he could stand.

"If my Dad had ever just said, 'You know Brad, you're a good boy,' that would have been enough," he said. "Kids need to be told that once in a while. If he had just patted me on the head, you know."

A beautiful man, Brad belonged on the cover of magazines kept behind counters with the cigarettes. Women in the club turned to look at us, jealous of me, I suppose. Though Christian women found him irresistible, he had managed to date none of them longer than a month. The only exception told him she'd be leaving in three months for Romania as a missionary. Everyone had warned him not to become too attached to her, but I understood perfectly the security of such an end.

"I think maybe I'm ready to tell you something that might help you because it's beginning to help me." He studied the sodden coaster left behind when the waiter took away his empty glass. He phrased this as a question like a young woman who lacked confidence.

As I watched him struggling to put together his pitch, I interrupted, "Are you gay? Because I think maybe I am."

I'd finally said it, the thing I thought I'd take with me to the grave.

"That's Satan's word," Brad said. "That's what one of the counselors said at this place I've been going. It's something you have to find a key to unlock yourself from. It's like shackles or something. I just try to think of myself as a man who has this problem, this unmet childhood need for my father that has lingered and that makes me attracted to men. I don't have to accept the lie and say, 'I'm gay.' That's Satan talking."

It had been a while since I'd heard the word "Satan." It snapped me like a wet towel. "Well, I'm the word you don't want to use anymore," I said. "And maybe I don't want to be because of the conflicts with Christianity and God, not that I have conflicts with God—except that maybe he doesn't like this thing about me, this problem—but I don't know what to do about it. " Talking didn't help.

"I thought maybe you were someone with the same problem as me," Brad said. "I knew I could talk to you. I think you would like this group I go to, Living Waters. You go through this program to learn why you feel the way you do and how to keep from feeling that way. It's helped me learn how to deal with it and not feel ashamed. It's not our fault, really, that we are the way we are."

"Then whose is it?" I said, drowned out by a crescendo of cymbals. I hadn't expected the solution to my life's oldest and most complicated problem to sound so simple.

Brad picked up his glass and strained the dregs from the ice with bared teeth. He and I had been the only two people in the Southwest Bible Church Singles group who felt Christians could drink without compromising their testimony.

"Could you give me their phone number," I said. "This group?"

"They don't have one. The director runs it out of her home, and she started getting threatening messages." He wrote the address on the back of a chipboard coaster that I slipped into my shirt pocket.

"Send her a letter. She won't respond unless you tell her how you found out about the program. You'd better mention my name."

For a moment, I realized there were people out there who wanted to hurt me for who I was and, for that matter, anyone who tried to make me someone else. After our conversation, I collapsed back onto the fundamentalist bed of nails. I found myself pinned there again like a collected moth. Maybe it had just taken God time to get all the dominoes in place. I could hear the dominoes clickety clacking, my reorientation already underway. Finally, I had not only a diagnosis, but also the address of a doctor.

While I was unpacking back in Missoula, I found the coaster. I set a perspiring glass of pop on top of it, half wishing the ink would bleed, but it didn't. I lost it anyway under the winter's debris of papers to grade and my own stories whose narrators reminded me of myself. Despite my attempts to alter or disguise them, they taunted me with their absolute refusal to be characters they were not.

I spent lots of time in my GTA office down the hall from Rachel's in the hopes I would see her. Instead of writing, I listened to my office mate tell stories about his days at a New Zealand boy's school. He'd even been chased by sharks and caned by one of his teachers. While I listened, I wished Rachel would come down the hallway and into our office. Just to be close to her, I went for coffee with her, along with my office mate and another MFA student who had won an obscenely large Swiss writing grant. Wanting not to seem ordinary, I ordered a double espresso. The barista handed me a doll cup. I drank the tar water inside without flinching. While I rocketed into caffeinated mania, the three of them talked about politics, drugs, and other things I had spent my twenties avoiding.

"You're brave to drink that," Rachel said.

"Oh, I need it," I said, "to stay awake," which I would do all afternoon, evening, night, and the following day. I was so keyed-up on my way home that I skipped across the Higgins Street Bridge over the Clark Fork whistling "You Made Me Love You."

◆ ◆ ◆

A visiting writer from South Africa made it her goal to carry out Flannery O'Connor's edict and discourage as many writers as she could. She made us produce new material so that everyone would be on a level playing field.

I brought in a recollection of an amusing singles canoe trip. I had just gotten to the part when the characters sang "Amazing Grace" into a cave full of sleeping bats when she held one hand up like a traffic cop.

"Stop. This sounds like a young adult novel that isn't working."

Whether out of self-loathing or unfounded self-confidence, I couldn't tell which, I joined ranks with those who vowed to remain enrolled in her workshop. Like dance marathon participants with collapsed partners, we in the dwindling remnant whispered about our individual points of no return after each session.

In this workshop, I wrote one of few stories of my entire tenure in writing school that worked. I learned to speak of stories like this, as if I'd pieced them together out of balsa, glue, string, and rubber bands. When I let this one go, it flew. On it, the professor allowed herself to pencil a double negative, "Not uninteresting." Even Peter S., a hypercritical troll with upturned fingernails, liked the story. In the margin, he wrote, "Though deeply flawed, this has potential." Unfortunately, he and my professor weren't the only people who liked the story. A writer who would later become famous and rich for something else.

The night of the 1992 Winter Olympics opening ceremonies in Albertville, France, I ordered pizza as trade for this man's help resolving a problem I'd been having revising another story. As I was telling him how I thought the problem had something to do with the father, who was like my father, he put his finger to my lips in a shush and kissed my closed mouth. I stiffened and turned my head toward the television to see French children dancing around the screen dressed in inflated plastic bags. I literally had no idea how we had wound up in this predicament. I didn't realize how close we'd been sitting, how close he'd been putting his face to mine. I apologized. He apologized. I dragged out unconvincing excuses. He said he just wanted to have sex without making a big deal out of it. I said I wanted him to be my friend. I couldn't believe he'd thought this was a date. He couldn't believe I hadn't. He left whistling. I put the hardly touched pizza in the refrigerator and then laid on my bed, face down, holding my breath. I hoped I would black out and then regain consciousness as a different person, filled with resolve, my own true self, even though I didn't know who that was.

I couldn't tolerate the pain in my lungs and so had to start breathing again, unchanged. As I saw it, I had two options. I pursued the first, lifting books and papers from my desk in search of the coaster Brad had given me. I couldn't find it. I took this as a sign and permission to move to option two. I put on my coat and boots and walked to the GTA offices. I stood beneath Rachel's window in the yellow square of light her lamp made in the blue expanse of snow. I saw her cross in front of the window many times. It took every ounce of my strength to shame myself out of calling her name and saying that I loved her whether or not she could ever love me back. At 10:30, when she turned out her lamp, I scurried away, stepping in the footprints I'd already made through the crust in the snow so that it would look like whoever made them had simply vanished. Back home, I found the coaster on the floor in front of the desk as if someone had laid it there for me. In a superstitious trance, I closed a letter to Living Waters with the following: "If God doesn't want me to be a homosexual, then you're my last chance to obey Him. Please write back to the enclosed address about your program." When I tried to print the letter out, my printer malfunctioned, which I took as another sign that I needn't bother trying to change. But the next day, my roommate smacked the printer lid when I asked her to look at it, and it and my capricious God started working again. I mailed the letter and waited.

Unexpressed love and repressed desire don't go away when we tell them to. They sour and ferment and work their way out as something else like intestinal problems, joint aches, or insomnia. The last three weeks before I returned to my bedroom in Raytown—where Momma encouraged me to live rent-free until I

could figure out what else to do or forever, whichever came first—
I couldn't sleep more than about forty-five minutes at a stretch.
I tried everyone's remedies: warm baths, sleeping with my head
at the foot of the bed, reading *The Decline and Fall of the Roman
Empire*, strenuous exercise.

I defended my thesis of short stories with repressed narrators
trying to be heard and then I made plans to leave Missoula with
as little presence of mind as possible. I rented a truck. I filled holes
left by nails I had pounded in walls. I envied a magpie in the lawn
of my apartment complex for not having to leave.

The letter I'd sent to Living Waters came back stamped
Address Unknown, which I took as another sign, but one I
couldn't interpret. It seemed like Imaginary Jesus didn't care I
was gay. Maybe God didn't either, or maybe he simply saw me as
a lost cause.

My awakened sexuality sealed in a cardboard box I would
quickly misplace, I drove from town like I had finished everything. I waved at friends, frost-heaved sidewalks, restaurant stools,
red-winged blackbirds in the cattails, blue foothills where I'd left
strands of hair and skin cells and other pieces of myself. I waved
at Rachel. But instead of actually leaving things, I drug them all
along behind, awkwardly bundled together. Every night, they
all appeared in my dreams, haunting me in their disarray. Every
morning, I had to put them all back. Everything had a proper
place 1,000 miles away except the authentic person I had just
started to become. Waking or sleeping, I could find no place to
put the unreconciled pieces of myself.

10
Living Waters

Now in Jerusalem by the Sheep Gate there is a pool called in Hebrew Bethzatha, which has five porticoes. In these lay many invalids—blind, lame and paralyzed, waiting for the stirring of the water; for an angel of the Lord went down at certain seasons into the pool and stirred up the water; whoever stepped in first after the stirring of the water was made well from whatever disease that person had. One man was there who had been ill for thirty-eight years. When Jesus saw him lying there and knew that he had been there a long time, he said to him, "Do you want to be made well?" The sick man answered him, "Sir, I have no one to put me into the pool when the water is stirred up . . ." Jesus said to him, "Rise, take up your bed and walk."
— John 5: 1-4

A man wearing a trace of blue eye shadow stole up behind the folding chair that may as well have been a block of ice when I sat my bare legs on it seconds earlier. He asked if I remembered him from a long-ago Sunday school class at Southwest Bible. I didn't want to remember him. I didn't want anyone to recognize me, much less know me. I had come here for treatment. I didn't want to chitchat with other participants who shared my "condition," which I believed the supernatural monster I now viewed as God had moved heaven and earth through an elaborate series of coincidences and phone calls to cure me of. Where I'd always imagined myself mostly alone in a world of heterosexuals, now in the catacombs of a borrowed Nazarene church we all were here—this queeny man and I and fifty or so skittish others. He and I had been the first to arrive in the fluorescent-lit basement where a sizeable group of us would spend one evening a week for the next nine excruciating months, hoping to be cured. Though it was August outside, my teeth chattered.

"How did you find out about the meeting?" the blue eye shadow man said. I could understand why he'd asked. Enrolling in Living Waters, ex-gay ministry for Midwest homosexuals, was like joining the Resistance. (People want to hurt homosexuals, even the ones who were trying not to be anymore, said the clandestine brochure, so you couldn't be too private.) Privacy, I understood all too well.

"Brad," I said, discreetly leaving out his last name.

"Oh, my God, Brad from Sunday school? He's the last person I would have suspected. Oh, my God, he's so good-looking. Is he coming?" After three full years of Living Waters, Brad wasn't coming. He wanted to take a hiatus to see if he could put into practice some of the heterosexual thinking and behaviors he had learned in the program.

A towering blonde in a pink-and-white plaid suit stepped to the mic to convene the first session. She terrified me, but I've always been afraid of people dispensing treatment. "I'm Colleen," she said. "Though I've never struggled with my sexuality, my heart goes out to all of you who do. I'd like to introduce my co-teacher and son-in-law, Ron." She welled up, and Ron stood with her shoulder to shoulder. This wasn't the last time he would make her cry. Two years later, she would oust him from his position as Sexual Healing Director after her daughter found him in bed with another woman. With this peccadillo, he would join a host of people who have become religious sexual clichés. One infamous one is the Director of NARTH (National Association for Research and Therapy of Homosexuals), the biggest organization promising to help gays and lesbians change their sexuality. This man was caught renting a boy who, he said, always stopped massaging before actual "sexual release."

"So, you might be asking me, 'Colleen, why is a straight woman like you leading a ministry like this?'" She scratched deep in her fluffy hair with one long purple fingernail and began. Years earlier, she'd been looking at greeting cards in her neighborhood Christian bookstore and saw what she assumed to be a young woman browsing in Marriage and Sexuality. But then she heard a man's voice asking the clerk if she knew of any Christian books on homosexuality. "The clerk said, 'No, we don't have anything like that,' and just walked away. My heart broke for him because the clerk seemed so afraid. Now, I'm not a shy woman, so I took him aside and asked him what kind of book he wanted." Here, Colleen's tears flowed again. In short, this man wanted a book about what do next if you knew you shouldn't be a homosexual, a book that, she lamented, she could not yet help him find. "But what he really wanted," she sobbed, "was someone to tell him that God loved him. If you know you're loved truly, that heals everything. The lie of homosexuality just falls away." The Lord told Colleen things about homosexuals that he didn't bother to tell homosexuals themselves. This often happens to prophets. God skipped the Ninevites and talked to Jonah about them instead. It's a religious game of telephone that leaves so much room for errors in translation.

Colleen made it her mission to help people "out of homosexuality," which made me picture her pulling people from a burning vehicle or a flooded mine shaft. I didn't like the helpless feeling it gave me. But when one is being rescued, one mustn't struggle or resist or try to help. It only makes matters worse for you and your rescuer.

The phrase *fox in the chicken house* looped in my brain like a bad song. I prayed that it would go away, but it didn't. I was a fox in the chicken house. We all were. "You are helpless to change without deep, drastic healing from the touch of the Father Almighty," Colleen said. "Your sexuality is beyond your control. You must give it to God." I basked for a moment at the end of this meeting in the pleasure of deep agreement.

"Keep them, these children of yours and help them change," Colleen said in her closing prayer, telling God what she wanted to have happen to us. I could tell she dreaded ending the meeting and letting any of us out of her sight.

Her prayers for me that evening did just what she had asked them to—they left me dangerously capable of change. Imaginary Jesus would use her misguided ministry to jostle me from decades of sexual inertia brought on by the condemnation of people like her. He didn't want me to keep pretending I was sexless as a gum eraser, neither this nor that, here nor there. Imaginary Jesus and Colleen were both concerned about the need for a cure; they just didn't have the same outcome in mind.

After the closing prayer, Colleen invited us to have foam cups of punch already poured and slices of dessert bread cut in half and laid on a napkin for us so we wouldn't have to touch anything.

Eager to finally understand my condition and its causes and treatment, I purchased every last one of the books on the table at the back of the room, including *Pursuing Sexual Wholeness* and its accompanying workbook; *Healthy Friendships*; and *Homosexuality: a New Christian Ethic*. On the drive home, all of these books, their covers still shiny with newness, slid off the neat pile I had made of them onto the floor of the car I'd borrowed from my parents. There, they scratched over road salt, gum wrappers, and plastic cup lids.

As I mentally ticked off the once familiar freeway exits toward what no longer felt like home—Roe, State Line, Wornall, Gregory—I reviewed what I had learned: 1) God could reverse a lifetime of sexual maturation in only eight months; 2) if I stayed out of his way, I would no longer want to act on my feelings for other women even if I still had them; 3) I might even feel attracted to someone of the opposite sex; 4) in another eight months, I might look like Colleen with long purple nails and a plaid suit. (Outside of the spell of her presence, her predictions about my future made far less sense.) As I remembered this specific prediction, I hit the brakes and only accelerated again when I saw headlights of the car behind me approaching fast. Though I could not yet envision such a thing, if Colleen was right and God wanted me to look like her, then I guessed I could learn to want that, too. He was the potter; I was the clay.

Internal conflict made even walking difficult. I stumbled up several stairs of my parents' split-level, dropping the brightly colored ex-gay books as I went. This wouldn't be the last time that I, like Dostoevsky's Raskolnikov, would parade my crime in front of the dull-witted authorities, subconsciously hoping to be apprehended. That night, I went to bed with a splitting headache, the first of a series of Tuesday night sexual healing barnburners.

My homework for the next class was to read the first chapter in *Pursuing Sexual Wholeness*. In it, I learned how an early separation from Momma had impaired my ability to become a heterosexual. I had developed a psychic wound that left me completely unable to give or receive heterosexual love. There it was, finally, in black and white: the root cause of what I'd hidden about myself all these years. My workbook exercise said to pinpoint the time of early separation and then write it down. "If you have difficulty remembering, ask God to help you," it said.

After listening to Mozart's "Requiem" three times—it was the most cathartic piece of music I could find—I finally drummed up the following: when I was four, Momma left me for three weeks to stay in Cleveland with Daddy while he had open-heart surgery. My Aunt Lucy and Uncle Sam came to live with my three sisters and me. They ate all our food and ground up silverware in the garbage disposal by accident. They'd never had a garbage disposal. They'd never had children either, and so they did not understand how either thing worked. Aunt Lucy wouldn't let my oldest sister, Karen, stay by my bed until I fell asleep. When Daddy was well enough to come home, I had a cold, and Daddy could not be exposed to colds. The doctor suggested I stay at Aunt Lucy's and Uncle Sam's until I recovered. Then someone talked to Momma about how I had said I didn't believe she would ever come home again, and it was decided that Daddy, and not I, should stay at

Aunt Lucy's until I got better. I felt mean and bad for having caught a cold and keeping Daddy from everyone.

Because the workbook didn't leave me enough space, what I did not write was that before Momma and Daddy ever knew they would need to go to Cleveland, I had made a habit of wearing his Romeo slippers and practiced kissing imaginary girls in the hall bathroom mirror. Nevertheless, there. Assignment done. I had my separation story, the first of many written assignments no one would ever check to see if I was doing correctly.

Colleen's *modus operandi* was to get us into spiritual states that would allow Jesus and us to return to the scene of the crime. She didn't want us to just remember it; she wanted us to literally walk into that place of primal separation so he could heal us once and for all. There, he would love us enough that we would no longer want to meet our need for the love of the same-sex parent by having sex with our own sex. Sex was something my Christian training had prevented me from even imagining anyway except in wild, REM episodes just before waking. At the next Living Waters meeting, I curled up in the memory of my childhood, and Imaginary Jesus sat down on the edge of the bed and petted my head until I dozed off. This is what Karen would have done if Aunt Lucy had let her. After this and many other sessions like it, I felt still entirely loved by Imaginary Jesus and entirely attracted to women—the woman offering free hand massages at the Clinique counter, a gas station attendant, and one of the women at Living Waters who Colleen had promoted to small group leader because she wasn't a lesbian anymore. Colleen had warned us that our condition would initially "flare up" after beginning treatment. Nevertheless, discouragement with my lack of progress settled in.

♦ ♦ ♦

Every night except Tuesday—I told Momma Living Waters was a church singles group, which, of course, it was—I went home from work and watched reruns of *Murder, She Wrote* and *Father Dowling* with her while Daddy watched the same thing or something similar in the basement. Singer, the black cat I had left to entertain Momma in my place when I went to graduate school, stretched on the back of her chair. Sometimes he pawed the top of her head. While we watched our programs, Momma and I drank powdered cappuccino, which may as well have been a barbiturate. "It's just as if you never left," she said smiling. It was. That was the terrifying thing: I could pick up becoming an old maid so easily where I'd left off.

I realized, by the middle of my first week there, that I felt trapped and I blamed it on Raytown and my new job as a legal secretary. I looked like a legal secretary in the new suit and skirts I had bought myself, but I wasn't one. One afternoon after a long look at my face in the cracked law office bathroom mirror—the same face I had seen on caged animals—I knew I must quickly put on and do something that came more naturally.

One week after I had started there, I turned in my resignation. The lawyers predicted problems for me if I ever pulled such a stunt again. I worried Momma, too. Imaginary Jesus reminded me I couldn't allow myself to care what they thought. I couldn't continue to just lie on the ground after I had fallen down and hope someone else would notice. This is a lesson I would have to be taught over and over.

✦ ✦ ✦

I finally confessed to a friend I'd known since high school that I thought I might be gay but was going to some meetings to get it "taken care of." A week after I bared my soul, she sent me a letter saying the woman she lived with wasn't just a roommate. Even though they were in the process of breaking up, she thought I should know the truth. Finding this out both disgusted and thrilled me. Rather than simply rejoice that I finally had a friend who could truly know and understand me, I had to make sure she knew she could be as miserable as I was. I asked her if she wanted to borrow my copy of *Healthy Friendships*. It never occurred to me that this loan might offend. "I don't want to stop being gay,"

Carole said. "I like being gay." *How could she,* I wondered, *knowing how most people felt about her?*

Colleen would have fought Carole tooth and nail had she had a way to monitor things that occurred outside her watch. Carole invited me to Broadway Baptist, a church whose senior pastor encouraged people to be gay as God had made them, and Imaginary Jesus encouraged me to take her up on it. The Southern Baptist Convention had recently voted to excommunicate Broadway Baptist for its senior pastor's heresy. I hadn't dared to hope to find a church where I could be entirely myself; weekly meetings with Colleen told me that being entirely myself wasn't a good idea. Thankfully, during the service at Broadway Baptist, no one asked me why I was crying. Lots of people cried there. Every Sunday, Topeka pastor Fred Phelps and his minions from Westboro Baptist stood in front of Broadway Baptist, holding up signs and singing about how much God hated fags. Phelps's message differed from Colleen's only in approach. She loved the sinner only so far as that sinner was willing to change. At prayer time, the senior pastor had the entire congregation turn and face the back of the sanctuary and the gantlet of picketers we'd all just run past. "God, please help them see all the other things they could be doing with their time," he prayed. During greeting time, I spotted a fellow student from Living Waters, who ducked her head and disappeared down one of the naves. We caught each other red-handed.

At the next Living Waters meeting, I found Broadway Baptist on a list of local churches Colleen forbade us to attend. I hoped I hadn't derailed my reorientation. "You don't want those messages in your head," she said. "The Bible clearly says homosexuality is wrong." Broadway's senior pastor said certain verses taken out of context said homosexuality was wrong but so was wearing clothing woven from different fibers. Colleen had a closet full of poly-cotton blends. Broadway's senior pastor also challenged us to find anything Jesus had said about homosexuality. I couldn't. Behind my back, Imaginary Jesus clapped his hands with delight at the spiritual confusion this left me in. Little did I know that, to him, confusion signified progress.

◆ ◆ ◆

With the hope of eternal life, fundamentalists aren't supposed to suffer from depression. Mine sort of snuck up on me. When former Bible Church friends Dolores and Joe Hyde offered me a job as a technical writer in his sanitary sewer rehabilitation firm, I thought, *that's what I need, a change of location.*

After weeks of looking for a place to live in Lawrence, Kansas, I finally found the perfect hovel for my growing spiritual disarray. If a cave had been good enough for John the Baptist, this tiny apartment should be good enough for me. Again, I fell victim to the small, the affordable, the unimaginative, the familiar. The apartment had one small window, a sliding glass door looking out onto a balcony with a dead pigeon being eviscerated by maggots, and a thin metal railing about to rust through. Someone had gone to the trouble to change the wooden lettering on the old brick sign in the complex lawn from University Terrace to University Terror. "That happens a lot," the very pregnant manager's wife said. She squinted at me as she handed me the key, as though unaccustomed to light.

Though the refrigerator freezer and oven didn't work, at least I had intact plumbing and an HVAC system, even though it spewed fine grit from the main duct each time it kicked on. A previous tenant had left thick bamboo shades that I couldn't figure how to open. The blinds always came shattering back down, heavy, brown, and foreign. Inside my apartment, it was always midnight. Depression muted the anger needed to tear them from the window or to pry down the five randomly arranged painted mirror tiles someone had glued to the wall beside the front door. Every day as I left for work, I could see only bits and pieces of myself coming down the hallway in the various mirrors. "You are not yet whole, but broken," Colleen weekly reminded me. Only the Lord could put me together again, she said. Imaginary Jesus must not have been the Lord. He didn't seem to like Colleen and remained thin-lipped about Living Waters. But he remained respectfully silent for a time. I took my crushing unhappiness as a sign that I needed to work harder at becoming heterosexual. I didn't want to feel good until I should. Living Waters thrived on unhappy gay people.

The lion's share of each small group session we devoted to confession. In my group, a librarian with a little gold cross pinned to her turtleneck owned up to joining a weekly knitting class to be close to a coworker. "I'm no good at knitting," she said. "It took me weeks to learn to even cast on, but I get to sit right next to her. Isn't that sick?" We'd been told not to offer pat consolations like "that's okay," which I wanted to say to this woman. How many times had I done something like it. But, then again, perhaps that was why I was in the shape I was; I thought bad little things were harmless. Colleen said that if the person's conscience had been bothered her enough to confess a behavior then it wasn't okay. Unable to come up with anything more tangible, I confessed an over-attachment to *thirtysomething* reruns. "I know I need to make more friends," I said. "But right now, this is easier." At the Kool-Aid and cookie table after one meeting, a not-unattractive woman tried to strike up a conversation. I couldn't participate. I had practiced asexual-ity for so long, it took me a while to recognize its opposite. For people like this woman who had already admitted that the ex-gay thing wasn't working, Living Waters was a meat market.

One week Colleen assigned the lesbian half of the room the task of building friendships with straight women so that we could fill up on our same-sex deficit in a healthy way. I couldn't have looked for meaningful heterosexual female companionship at Hyde & Associates, even if I wanted to. I spent most of my waking hours there, but I worked with eleven men. The nubile secretary had gotten herself fired for being too assertive within a week of my starting. Instead of hiring another woman as I hoped he would, Joe trained me to do both my own job and hers. When Joe wasn't looking, my coworkers played together, throwing their keys over exposed ceiling beams and holding the methane gas-de-tecting wand near each other's buttholes. At lunch, they brought back boxes of fried chicken gizzards from the gas station up the street and played Hearts with a greasy deck. I ate a sandwich and carrot sticks at my desk while I watched the phone.

When I wasn't answering the phone or processing job receipts or producing invoices, all the things the secretary used to do back then, I immersed myself in sanitary sewers. I edited Joe's technical papers about the nation's decaying sanitary sewer infrastructure. I wrote the computer manual for Pipedream, the aptly named buggy computer modeling software Hyde & Associates offered along with their services to a county or municipality. Also, I organized the company's slide library of sanitary sewer degradation, including many dramatic shots of "pissers," or streams of sewer water shooting from a surcharging manhole. And, when I had absolutely nothing else to do, I went to the company conference room, closed the blinds, turned off all the lights, and watched videos taken by cameras fastened aboard tiny tractors that crawled through sewer pipes. While I watched, I made notations of the following problems: root intrusion, grease accumulation (near fast food establishments), cracks, crumbling, or dents. I also indicated in which quadrant of the pipe I had noted the defect and where on the videotape that defect could be viewed. Moving briefly across the screen and then off again would be stubborn clots of toilet paper, hung-up tampons, and albino cockroaches. Most problem pipes looked beyond repair.

That's the thing about sanitary sewers; you can't just dig a little hole, do a little patching, and call it good. Great gaping trenches have to be dug, pipes removed and replaced, and the soil replaced and reseeded before anyone will be able to stop thinking about sanitary sewers in a neighborhood again. No one thinks about sewers until they stop working.

Watching sewer footage usually reminded me I hadn't done my Living Waters homework. It had become so pointless and degrading that I put it off until the last possible minute. At my performance review, my boss suggested I find a local church fellowship to improve my attitude. My exposed unhappiness was an eyesore.

✦ ✦ ✦

One Tuesday at Living Waters, we pushed all the chairs out of the way so people could safely collapse as they gave up their same-sex lovers during healing prayer time. After she found out why I was sitting bolt upright, Colleen said the fact that I was the only person in the room with no one to give up was something to be proud of rather than ashamed of. "Remember," she said, "acting on homosexual feelings is far worse than simply having them."

In our large group session after healing time, she issued a warning about a new book. "I need to tell you about a book based on the false claim that some animals are homosexuals," she said. "God does not make homosexuals. Just look in your backyard. There are boy robins and girl robins, boy rabbits and girl rabbits. Clearly, this is junk science. This man obviously jumped to conclusions about behavior he didn't understand." As an antidote to this book, Colleen gave us handouts of a newspaper article that said research proved homosexuals could become the heterosexuals they were intended to be if they were "highly motivated to do so." It took several months for my name to come to the top of the long list of people waiting to check out a copy of this forbidden book at the Lawrence Public Library. As much as I tried not to, I found it compelling, especially the passage about female grizzly bears that formed pair bonds for cooperative child rearing.

✦ ✦ ✦

One week, my homework assignment was to reveal my "sexual brokenness" to a family member.

"What do you mean gay?" Kathy said.

"What do you mean, what do I mean?"

"Give me evidence," she said.

"I mean I like women, not men. Sexually, I'm attracted to them. And emotionally."

"I mean how do you know for sure?" Kathy was the family di-agnostician. She pinpointed all ailments either because she her-self had had them or knew someone who had.

"I've always felt this way," I said.

"What way?"

"Attracted to women."

"What do you mean attracted? Give me an example."

"I have dreams." I'd just had one about Rachel the night before. I'd ripped her clothes off and didn't know what to do next.

"That doesn't prove anything to me. Dreams."

Neither one of us said anything for a while.

"Remember how I always wanted to be a cowboy instead of a cowgirl, how you made fun of me? I played with trucks and Army men. Everybody thought I was a little boy. Remember how you thought it was so weird that I didn't care if I saw Royall?"

"Well, I wouldn't have wanted to see him either," she said. "I don't want you to take this wrong, but you're impressionable. You met church people, and you became religious. You met hippies, and you started wearing those awful hemp pants. My guess is you've been around someone who's gay, so now you think you're gay. Just stop worrying about it. You're not."

"I am, too," I said.

My family prided itself on never having to ask for prayer for anything but accident or sickness. With my sisters and me grown, my parents assumed they had piloted the family craft into the dol-drums. Nothing really good happened to us, but nothing really bad happened either. They preferred starvation to shipwreck. As far as they could tell, every last one of us had turned out normal. I'd thought Kathy would be happy I was trying to correct myself, but the worst thing any of us had ever thought a person could become other than a criminal was gay.

❖ ❖ ❖

By winter, whatever tiny shoots of independence and authenticity had taken root in graduate school had finally withered. I retreated to the safe and familiar, driving from my hovel in Lawrence to Raytown to sleep in my childhood bedroom every weekend. Every Sunday morning, Momma and Daddy left for church in a cloud of Final Net and English Leather. "You just rest, honey," Momma called on their way out the door. Worried about my growing malaise, she reached for the easiest solution: I didn't want to get out of bed to go to church with them because I worked too hard during the week. For the first time in my life, I had stopped going to church altogether. Why bother if the only church that had ever welcomed me was evil? If Imaginary Jesus chose to remain stubbornly silent about all I was trying to reverse for him at Living Waters, then why should I go out of my way to attend church? Wasn't this what most people who claimed to know him insisted that he wanted? His standard doses of encouragement about everything else—voiceless murmurs of "Everything's going to be all right; I'm right here"—had become irritating as high school cheers. Why couldn't he just come out and tell me what he thought about my sexuality? Why couldn't he explain why most of his followers couldn't rest until I changed?

Every Sunday morning, I would eventually make it as far as my parents' couch, where I lay in my pajamas until they came home bringing lunch in a paper sack from somewhere. While they worshipped, I took pleasure in doing self-destructive things. I slouched. For breakfast, I ate boiled hot dogs, stale cashews, Daddy's stash of beef jerky—any other strange thing I could find—slathered with onion dip. I longed for unintentionally kinky television. The scene from *The Moon-Spinners* with Hayley Mills bound and gagged in the bowels of a rickety windmill had me so enraptured one Sunday that I didn't hear the garage door open and my parents climb the stairs until much too late for me to reassume the hangdog look I'd had on my face when they left several hours earlier. Weekends could have gone on like that forever.

One Friday night, it snowed. I like to think Imaginary Jesus had something to do with how much snow fell. Forecasters said unless you had an emergency you should stay off the road.

Though I couldn't have explained this to a state trooper, staying at home surrounded by all that silence felt like an emergency. I'd already spent all week not having a meaningful conversation. It had been the worst week I could remember, not because something had happened, but because, by the end of it, nothing had. I realized that probably nothing would happen for a long, long time. I could feel my life culminating, settling over me. I had returned to the Midwest and taken the same kind of a dead-end editing job I'd worked before I went to school to become a writer. Every week I went to a class to learn how not to be the self I'd been since I was a child. I had no place left to hide, nothing left to distract me from things as they were, which is exactly the moment Imaginary Jesus had been waiting for.

Every time the furnace came on this bitter evening, I felt guilty for consuming so much energy. I couldn't justify heating an ugly apartment for just one person who had so little to offer. I turned the thermostat down to 50 degrees. Desperate for any kind of distraction, I turned on my garage-sale television. I could tune in nothing but a PBS concert of spirituals sung perfectly by a woman with coffee-and-cream-colored skin surrounded by dozens of shiny brass instruments that had been polished so that they sparked across the screen like fires starting.

I can't remember when I first put the afghan over my head. It was Momma's practice afghan, an experimental zigzag made from quick-sale acrylic yarns in brown, orange, gold, and black. The holes in it were so big I could still see everything I needed to, until I started crying—not sobbing or sniffing, just tears rolling from my eyes. A knee-jerk religious fear kept me from fantasizing about suicide and specific means to an end, but I did allow myself to think what a relief it would be not to live until I reached the other side of whatever this was.

I lost track of how many hours and inches of snow later it was until my cheeks were dry. When I took the afghan off and tried to sit in the blood-red lounger Daddy bought me for $5 from a man down the street, it threw me over backward. For about a half an hour, I sat behind it, overturned, wondering what in the world I could trust if not the furniture. Finally, I wedged it into the corner of the room partially reclined and climbed aboard over the armrest. I said aloud into the silence. "I could use a little help here. What is it, exactly, that you want from me?" I heard nothing right away and felt nothing except the smallest bit of relief over having finally asked the right person the right question. "Help, please," I said again. Imaginary Jesus happily played along when I tried an old religious trick to force him into showing his cards by randomly opening the Bible. "You know when I sit down and when I rise up; You discern my thoughts from far away. You search out my path and my lying down, and are intimately acquainted with all my ways. . . . I am fearfully and wonderfully made; wonderful are your works; that I know very well. My frame was not hidden from you when I was made in secret, intricately woven in the depths of the earth."

"Have you ever considered," Imaginary Jesus said, "that nothing is wrong with you?" These people I had been listening to had cloaked their own fears and prejudices in a few ancient scriptures torn out of context. Lest I provoke them, I languished in the shadows of my own life hoping to be healed of something as permanent as my fingerprints. Colleen had been right about one thing; I had been very sick indeed. Lying inert, crippled by shame, had left me that way. "Rise, take up your bed and walk," Imaginary Jesus whispered from the New Testament. I watched the snow fall as if I'd never seen it before. Stunned with relief, I took the healing news that I'd been misdiagnosed. I put the Bible away and nudged the thermostat up a few degrees.

The next morning, on my way out the door, I decided the mirror tiles didn't belong there on the wall by the door, splitting me into pieces. I pried all of them off the wall, pulling some drywall with them. They were the first in a long series of things I decided would torment me no longer.

✦ ✦ ✦

In April, a week before Easter and the resurrection from the dead, Colleen held graduation. I endured the final few months of Living Waters so that I could prove I had emerged from a full round of treatment as gay as the day I was born.

As a treat, Colleen let us watch a video hosted by a Christian psychologist who compared us to the pioneers. "Just like them, you will continue to face obstacles and uncertainty during your long and arduous journey, dumping many heavy things you no longer need along the way."

An androgynous woman who couldn't look directly at the camera said, "It wasn't natural or of God what Lyla and I did with each other. I formed an unnatural bond, and those are harder than iron to break. I had to let Jesus fill the empty place she left. I had to invite him into that hurt. I had to want that. No one else could want it for me. I had to do it over and over until she was gone." I cringed. Like a graduation day bolt of lightning, it hit me that this woman could have just as easily been talking about a bad heterosexual relationship. It also occurred to me that probably the vast majority of people enrolled in Living Waters and the rash of other ex-gay ministries springing up around the country, were people fresh off a bad relationship, either with the church or with another human being. Contented people—gay, straight, or anywhere in between—do not seek out spiritual and emotional cleansing. The film also featured several couples that had met each other at ex-gay meetings. One woman sat with her effeminate husband on a wrought-iron bench. "I used to feel like a vampire," she said. "It wasn't enough for me just to be with women. I wanted to consume them. All the women I was with had some aspect of myself I thought I was lacking, like beauty. But, as you can see, God doesn't make junk." Her beautiful husband squeezed her ample shoulder with his slender white fingers. I had seen enough.

Before we left, Colleen gave us two things, a diploma and a helium balloon. "I want you to find a place where you feel safe and comfortable and then release that balloon and, with it, whoever you need to let go," she said. "Only you have to know exactly who that is."

I thought briefly about how satisfying it would be to watch Colleen carried quickly up and away by the wind, but I had read that balloons released in fervor all around the country often wound up in the crops of geese that mistook them for food and eventually starved to death. Sacrificing her last metaphor, I took the balloon to my car and popped it.

11
Practice

Pié Jesu, donna aes requiem.

The therapist I had finally admitted I needed to see suggested that, as other people practice the piano or tai chi, I needed to practice taking care of myself. As a youngest child, I had always sat patiently waiting for others to attend to my physical and emotional needs, and my therapist showed me all the help I didn't need. I needn't equate being gay with a life-threatening emergency. I didn't need the love and approval of those who did. I realized that though I had once interpreted the gospel solely as rescue, I didn't anymore. I didn't need a fundamentalist caricature of Jesus to snatch my life away from me like a bossy older sister and say, "here, let me do that for you." My therapist and Imaginary Jesus encouraged me to do my level best with the raw materials I had.

She suggested I make a list of things I could do to take care of myself. At the top, I wrote: find a new apartment. In addition to having working appliances, the one I found was in the same complex as Hyde & Associates, so I could take a forty-five-second, non-polluting stroll across the parking lot to work. Even though my new place was dark brown and only a little wider than a hallway, it was snug. It had thick walls and excellent blinds. Fast out-growing my shell, I didn't want anyone observing what could be a strange and messy transformation.

On my to-do list, I also wrote: take in a stray cat. The first ap-plicant, a calico I named Ellen, appeared outside my sliding glass door on Halloween, her whole rail-thin body a smile. In exchange for a warm bed and a bowl of food, she allowed me to love her. It was the first reciprocal relationship of my life. I learned from the maintenance man that before I took her in she'd lived in the en-tryway of a unit across the complex, surviving on things someone put in a dirty china saucer and on house sparrows she caught in the yew bushes. From my work cubicle, I could see her sleeping on the end of my bed, striped with sunlight through the blinds. By tolerating her many neurotic fears of electrical storms, men, crying babies, and having her tail touched, I began to see my own insecurities in a kinder light.

I also found myself good things to eat. In particular, I foraged sacks of black walnuts no one wanted from a tree across the com-plex. It dropped its abundance on the sidewalk and the lawn that the apartment manager tried in vain to keep manicured. Because I didn't know any better, I shucked their spicy green hulls bare-handed and dyed myself the color of old pennies. I then cured the walnuts in my water heater closet and cracked each one with a hammer. I picked the brown, vein-covered nuts into empty pea-nut butter jars I'd saved to put them in for Christmas gifts. No one likes black walnuts. Though I'd suspected this, I didn't care; *I* liked them. I correctly suspected a fussy brother-in-law would chip a tooth on an invisible pink rock of inner shell, but I couldn't help but offer them anyway as proof of autumn, a season I had processed and eaten.

I'd also written "settle" on the list of things I could do to take care of myself. I tucked in the pocket of a jacket the little map a coworker had drawn for me and rode my bike to the levee trail that edged the Kaw River one spring night after supper. I hadn't known I lived in a river valley. I pedaled from sunset into blue dusk and finally rolled to a stop beside a wetlands rustling with life, some creatures settling to sleep, some stirring awake as they did every evening, a mile from me, without my notice. After, I pedaled back up the long hill toward home, winded, legs burning. Then I took a long soak in a bathtub with candles in the corners. That night, I knew my proper size, what state I was in, and where on earth I was.

Week after week, I checked things off my list and reported back to my therapist. "I'm embarrassed that I have so little to show for all of this," I said.

"*Au contraire*," she said. She thought I'd made great strides. She made me stop and praise myself, mid-session.

"It feels stupid, sort of selfish given the state of the world," I said, "to take this much time paying attention to myself. Remind me again. Why am I doing this?"

"So someone else doesn't have to," she said. "That's the most unselfish thing you could do."

Before long, I had the breakthrough she'd predicted. One lunch hour I sat watching a downpour out my sliding glass window. Balanced in my lap was a plate of leftover curry I had learned to make myself. Suddenly I was overwhelmed with what felt like contentment. I realized, as I watched rain wash down the glass, that I was grateful for my life. Instead of a drag on the world's limited resources, on someone else's time, I saw it as a gift. I might have continued that way, happily alone and grateful, unchallenged and uncontaminated.

After a year of concerted effort, I had devoured a library of self-help books that taught me about separateness and autonomy. I enjoyed holding barely articulated opinions. I could go whole days without saying a word to anyone but Ellen or the spiders in the corners, which I had also named. I saw my life unfurling slowly before me with no risk of challenge or contamination. Then one evening after watching two small, identical birds fly in tandem up and over the pitch of a neighboring roof, I found myself feeling utterly lonely. I feared I would never do anything like that with anyone. What does a person do when she develops an allergy to her own species?

After all that work, there I was right back where I'd started. I needed others, a weakness I thought I'd finally conquered. When an antidote arrived, it came in a form I hardly expected and so didn't have time to run away. I'd just settled down in front of *MacNeil-Lehrer* and put a bite of supper in my mouth when an unsolicited mental image began to form.

I'd only heard of such things. At Broadway Baptist, people came to microphones stationed around the sanctuary to describe "God pictures" that they had seen during guided meditations. During the same meditations, I would have mustered up only one of the following things: 1) nothing, 2) pink and green swirls, which anyone can see if she presses on her closed eyes long enough, or 3) meany fundamentalist nightmares, "I'll give you something to cry about." My God was terrifying because I had needed him to be. I had needed him to remind me I was a deviant, how fundamentally wrong I was, and how unlike everyone else.

In this mental picture I had not asked for, a pair of hands held my own in the way first-aid guides recommend treating frostbite, warm flesh holding cold. A familiar voice said, "When this starts to hurt, you let me know, and we'll stop. Then when you're ready, we'll start again. Remember, I'm right here." Figment or not, Imaginary Jesus's hands were enough of God for me to picture anyway. I forgot to feel terrified. I'd simply been frozen and I'd been found. Finally thawed, I felt as ready as I ever would to emerge from my brown apartment as my real self, sexuality included. I felt ready to join a world of humans who had great potential to delight and to hurt anyone brave enough to approach.

12
Meeting O'Keeffe

During a sermon on homosexuality, Broadway Baptist's senior pastor reminded us that as far as we knew, Jesus said nothing on the subject. Not one word. That Sunday afternoon, I threw all but one of my ex-gay books in the dumpster in the parking lot outside my apartment, something I'd never done to a book in my life. The *Pursuing Sexual Wholeness* workbook, where I'd written answers to questions about my own particular deviance from the norm, I shredded into Ellen's litter. I had one lingering worry; I didn't want the man who rumbled up weekly in his blue truck heaped with college apartment detritus to try to sell these toxic books to someone else. I stood in my doorway and prayed for a sign whether I should go back to retrieve them. Before I said amen, I heard big raindrops hitting cement.

At my next therapy session, I said, "I think it's time for me to move on. Sexually, I mean."

"It's about time," my therapist said.

"You mean you've been waiting for this?" I said. Despite all the useful time we'd spent together, I still had a lingering fear of the "Christian" in Christian Psychological Services. Her eagerness unsettled me.

"This doesn't mean I'm going to rush right out there." I didn't even know where *there* was. Then I remembered a clean, smart-looking woman in the balcony of Broadway Baptist. She wore a white linen shirt, jeans, and chukka boots.

"You're thinking of someone, aren't you?" my therapist said. "You're smiling."

Betty, one of the other church balcony lesbians, told Carole and me that this woman had a painting in a group show. Betty called her O'Keeffe because she took painting trips alone, sleeping in the back of her pickup with her canvases. Ever mindful of appropriate boundaries, I felt healthier now that I had something to go on besides mere curiosity about O'Keeffe's arms hidden under her white linen shirt. I liked art. As someone who could happily spend hours by myself, I also had an interest in what Betty described as this woman's "hermetic lifestyle."

"Remember," Carole leaned over Betty to chime in, "she's not gay." Carole had this on good authority. I had no reason to doubt Carole, but it made the woman in a black leather jacket, a persistent thundercloud at O'Keeffe's elbow, hard to explain.

"What would it hurt to introduce yourself?" my therapist said.

I hadn't introduced myself for a very long time. "I don't have enough context."

"Don't be self-conscious," she said. "That's old behavior. You say something; the other person says something. Why don't we role play?"

At one of the after-church coffees in the bright, fluorescent-lit basement, I hid behind a cement pillar to rehearse. "If I might borrow a moment of your time." *You're not taking a survey.* "I hear you have a painting in a show." *That's it. Simple, straightforward.* When the Thundercloud left O'Keeffe's side for more coffee, I sidled over, dry-mouthed for our first conversation. O'Keeffe's name was Lisa.

"I hear you have a painting in a show," I said.

She nodded.

"I'm Kelly—second row balcony," Lisa nodded again and brightened, trying to chew and swallow her cookie to respond.

"I have always loved—Turner," I said. I was so out of practice. I added, "So, you're another Georgia O'Keeffe, huh?"

She stepped back a little, and so I did, too.

"No. No," she said. "Where did you hear that?"

"Betty—second row balcony," I said. It took everything I could remember of my therapy not to run away.

"Ah, Betty."

All I knew about Georgia O'Keeffe was what a college friend had said about a poster of one of her poppies. I'd said what everyone says, "Is that really a flower?" My friend told me that O'Keeffe said, "Have you ever really looked at a flower?"

"Do you paint flowers ever?" I said.

I saw it, the slightest turn of Lisa's body toward the coffee urn. I had used up my time. I felt my eyes roll back in my head. On my way back to the safety of the pillar, I finally remembered to go back and get what I'd come for. "Where can I see your painting? The one in the show?"

On our way out to the parking lot, I stopped her again to try to repair the conversation. "Say hello to the cows," I said, "in the pasture."

"Prairie," Lisa said. "Wait," she added, as I ran for my car. Why she engaged me further I couldn't imagine. "I have a story about the cows. They licked the grill of my truck once. . . . I felt the truck rocking." The Thundercloud elbowed her and snorted, looking embarrassed.

"What did they want?" I said racing through my mental flip cards of animals. "Salt?" I'd forgotten that one of the things about conversations is they don't give you enough time to keep from sounding like an idiot.

"I don't know," she said. "Just one of those mysteries, I guess."

❖ ❖ ❖

I found her small landscape in a poorly lit corner of the gallery. It was deceptively simple, just a yellow line of a hill with a single small tree that looked like it wouldn't be there very much longer.

It made me homesick for a place I had never been to. That night, I wrote a simple letter of appreciation. I misspelled my name and then tried to make it look like I hadn't. Adding to the general illegibility of it all, I wrote it on recycled map stationery over the contours of a particularly steep mountain. I added a P.S. in a lake near something marked Poop-Out Pass, "You've won a convert to Kansas." On a warm early summer day filled with the smell of peonies, I mailed the letter. Once ants have done their work on a peony, coaxed open its tight green casings with gentle ant jaws, it can't hold anything back. By the time I had second thoughts about sending the letter and snuck away from my cubicle to retrieve it from the clip on the mailbox, it was already gone.

The Thundercloud understood my motives better than I did. "She likes you," she said. Though Lisa didn't like being pursued, I couldn't have chosen more evocative stationery. Lisa loved maps, so it was hard to resist. As were the stories I told at a group lunch Lisa invited me to after church about an ill-fated Western vacation with Kathy and my niece and nephew. Dashboard Metamucil spills, a ponytail caught in a tent zipper, a groin pull and dramatic rescue on horseback, a family Armageddon at Old Faithful. After each story she asked for another. From then on, Lisa took up the pursuit, and I would remain oblivious to it. Admitting I was gay was one thing; being gay in broad daylight was quite another. What if someone saw me? Since I'd met Lisa, my internal protests were easier to ignore, especially as Lisa was equal parts real and harmless. As Carole reminded me, Lisa was not gay.

◆ ◆ ◆

Lisa had to leave a message for me when she called to invite me to the Shakespeare Festival in Kansas City because I was already on my way there. Carole, who was stage managing the show, had asked me to referee two of her relatives—her nervous evangelical sister, Sally, and her Sufi lesbian cousin, Judy, who preferred to be called Sophia—on their blanket.

I had no difficulty finding the sad sacks Carole wanted me to mind. Whichever of them had brought the blanket had chosen wool smelling of mothballs. They didn't need mediating. Not only were they not arguing, they weren't speaking.

I sat next to Sophia, the easiest to engage, and asked what she did. My voice crackled with infection. Joe Hyde had brought back an upper respiratory infection from a business trip and given it to the whole office.

"More importantly, what am I," she said. "I'm a Sufi. I'm a Sufi who works with computers. You sound sick," she said without concern. "Echinacea, goldenseal tincture, two drops in water twice a day for a week. Call me Sophia. That's my Sufi name."

"Oh. How about you, Sally?" I said. Carole's sister smiled politely and blinked. She looked as though she had a migraine.

"It's hot," they said in unison. Carole came down from her light board scaffolding and called them lackluster. Carole told me she was trying to use new vocabulary words to make herself more interesting.

"But you, you look great," Carole said.

"Sophia is the goddess of wisdom," Sophia said. "That's why I picked it as my Sufi name."

Across the sea of blankets behind Sophia, I saw Lisa and the Thundercloud. Suddenly, seeing *Romeo and Juliet* for the third time that summer seemed infinitely more interesting. They were seated close to the stage, the late afternoon sun beating down on them.

"Hey, there's the painter from church," I said.

"Where?" Carole said. It seemed as if it frustrated her that I'd spotted Lisa first, that I'd spotted her at all. She knew as well as anyone else that sooner or later most people pair off, even shy, clueless friends like me, and leave you. She had hoped, I'm sure, to be the one leaving.

"They have fried chicken," I said, looking through Sally's binoculars. "And, I don't see a bucket. It looks like homemade."

"Oh," Carole said. "I wish someone had made *me* fried chicken."

"And pie," I said.

✦ ✦ ✦

The sun finally slipped behind the stand of oaks to the west. The play started. Darkness inched in, ameliorating the misery. Finally, it grew too dark for me to see anything but Lisa's silhouette, then nothing of her at all. During intermission, I propped up on my elbows to try to catch glimpses of her through the parade of people stumbling over roots and electrical cords, spilling grog. As if drawn to Sally, a roving juggler had accidentally dropped a bowling pin on her head before the play began. Through the first two acts, she had remained on her side curled up, still listening, she said. Sophia read a computer magazine with the flashlight on her keychain.

I sat upright and swallowed suddenly, half to moisten my raw throat, half out of surprise to find Lisa squatting at the edge of the wool blanket. Sally called out a thin greeting. Sophia extended her hand. Despite what Carole repeatedly reminded me about Lisa, I saw Sophia give her the secret handshake.

Introductions over, we all waited for Lisa to speak. When she didn't, I started to fill the void.

"Sophie lives in Kansas City, too," I said. "Don't you?"

"Sophia," she said. "And yes, I do."

"And you live in Kansas City," I said to Lisa. In an act of self-sabotage that made my therapist cringe when I told her about it, I spent the last few seconds of intermission trying to set them up.

Carole blinked the lights. Two minutes to the second half and to the desperate, wailing Juliet. She would be burdened with Elizabethan layers, and bugs would encircle her sweat-drenched head like a streetlamp. I made a sucking sound between my teeth and raised my eyebrows. "It's about to start," I said. "You don't want to get stuck here. We're a boring bunch."

In what looked like distress, Lisa squinted, her cheeks pulled taut. Finally, she rocked back on her heels and spoke, "I'm going to Lawrence to see some galleries. There's a student show at KU. I applied there, at the University of Kansas. I thought since you already live there that maybe you might want to go to some galleries with me, and then maybe we could get a bite to eat after. Maybe Sunday?"

"After church?"

"Let's meet on the front steps." We didn't yet even sit on the same side of the balcony at church. She rose to her feet just as Carole dimmed the house lights for the last time. I watched Lisa's dark shape pick its way noiselessly between camp chairs and blankets, around coolers, ducking in and out like a coyote, a creature I had never really gotten a good look at. They can be perfectly in a place but not of it.

When I could no longer see her, I laid full out again. I wanted to see if the moon looked different like everything else seemed to. Not even Romeo and Juliet's impending deaths, some of the most infuriatingly avoidable deaths in all of literature, could sour my rising hope. Even as Juliet shouted out her "O happy dagger" speech, drowned out by a helicopter landing on the roof of nearby St. Luke's Hospital, I wondered at how full of possibility the world suddenly seemed. If Carole was right, why had Lisa been so nervous? Maybe she had social anxiety disorder, a condition I'd seen a commercial about. Or maybe she didn't.

"Was that a date I was just asked on?" I wondered aloud.

"Yes," whispered Sophia.

"Are you sure she's straight?" I asked Carole as we picked up cups, plates, balled napkins, and stripped turkey bones from the matted lawn after the show.

"Positive," she said.

✦ ✦ ✦

After church, Lisa followed me to Lawrence for our afternoon together. Even though the speed limit was 70, I drove 55 because I believed I wouldn't hit animals at a slower speed and because someone told me that lowering the speed limit to 55 was the best thing Carter ever did in his presidency, so dramatic were the energy savings. I believed I was saving fuel, and—no matter how hot—I always rode with the windows rolled up and the air conditioning off because I'd read that its emissions were destroying the ozone layer.

Lisa followed behind me politely as if she'd never been to Lawrence before. She adjusted her speed to mine. As they always did, other drivers whizzed and jerked around us, many of them giving us the finger and most just shaking their heads.

"These were supposed to be landscapes," Lisa said stopping in front of a self-portrait of a junior high school student at the last and only gallery on her list that hadn't been locked Sunday afternoon. "They were all supposed to be open, I looked them all up, I swear."

Several erasures showed how hard this student had tried to understand her face. She had drawn her nose in the middle of her forehead. "The eyes are in the right place," I said trying to stay upbeat.

"You must think I'm nuts, dragging you all the way out here," Lisa looked at her watch.

"You didn't drag me all the way out here," I said. "I live here."

"Maybe I should just go," she said. "I just want you to know I did have a real reason for coming here, besides seeing you. . . ." She stopped herself.

Thankfully, I convinced her to salvage the afternoon. At Terra Nova Bookstore, a haunt of Williams S. Burroughs that wouldn't survive the opening of a Borders two years later, I apologized that we didn't see Burroughs in the flesh, only a life-sized cardboard cutout of his head behind a shelf of his books. I pointed out Eudora Welty and May Sarton and Annie Dillard to her. She pointed out Anne Lamott and Fran Lebowitz and Lucy Lippard to me. In the three long years since graduate school, I hadn't met anyone who still read.

At cluttered Ernst Hardware, the oldest continually operating hardware store in Kansas, I was delighted to see she felt completely at home.

"Oh look," I said, picking up a piece of metal she'd unearthed, "a meat grinder. My mom used to grind meat and potato patties with one of these. You put everything in here and it comes out here. It makes this great crunching sound."

"Meat and potato patties?" she said.

"My father's German mother taught her to make them. They're great with ketchup." Nothing I said made them sound any better.

"Hungry?" she said, smiling. She reminded me of a few things: my sister Kim, a gust front before a thunderstorm on a sweltering day. Before we left Ernst's, she bought a blue toolbox to hold her paint tubes. I liked her almost more than I could stand when, at the Free State Brewery, she knocked it off the balcony, caught it in midair, and turned purple with embarrassment.

"Do you want to come in?" I said, back at my apartment. The thought made me nervous, but I didn't want to stop looking at her, at the cornflower blue of her eyes, her sun-browned fingers, the little square of turquoise on the ring on her pinky. I invited her into my usual clutter, a jumble of newspapers on the kitchen table, the floor strewn with cat toys. The couch was covered with the pilly polyester green blanket I'd covered up with the night before, books lying on top of it open, spines up. A half-eaten cream cheese and peanut bagel sat on my coffee table with the flimsy legs. Lisa sat on the floor by a dying Swedish ivy I hadn't yet had the heart to take to the dumpster. Like a child dragging out her new toys to show visitors, I played a song I thought she might like from my new Dar Williams CD, "I Was a Boy, Too," about a woman lamenting the days when she could be both little girl and little boy, both and neither. "I feel just like that," Lisa said. She asked to see Ellen and Mary Todd, the other stray cat I'd adopted. I called them both by blowing an open C on the recorder I'd played in elementary school. Both of them came loping across the manicured lawn of the apartment complex.

Lisa stared in amazement. "I've never met someone whose cats came when she called."

We sat on my couch for hours talking about our mothers who annoyed us but for entirely different reasons, about how we wished we could do our own work and be paid for it. A greeting-card artist, Lisa had just given her notice at Hallmark to start life as a full-time freelance artist and landscape painter. In a little black spiral notebook with replaceable pages, she wrote down books she wanted to read, quotes she wanted to remember. She also had made a list of reasons to stay at Hallmark and reasons to go. Her supervisors liked her. She did her work well and in the proper amount of time. She had a great benefits package and access to a gym. She had one of the best cubicles in the building. But from this high corner cubicle with glass windows looking out over downtown Kansas City, she had watched the monarch butterfly migration, hundreds of brilliant orange flakes fly toward her and, when they couldn't get through, batted their way up the glass windows around her and on their way again. "They helped me make my final decision—all the things I could see out there living their lives. Even plastic bags were out there, catching the wind. I knew if I didn't leave soon, I would kill the painter left inside me."

I told her that from my own cubicle, when I didn't have enough work to do, I wrote letters to my congresswoman about environmental problems that only a year ago I wouldn't have thought I had any say about. I wrote essays, too, hoping that I might someday be able to do my own work without hiding it.

I stood on the doorstep of my apartment, burning the soles of my bare feet while she fiddled with the seat belt in her truck to leave, hours later. Her ordinary red Ford Ranger would come to look like the Publishers Clearing House van. I would win over and over.

◆ ◆ ◆

"So you looked at things. You ate," Carole said.

"Yes, and we talked. I have never talked so much in my whole life."

"Hey, you talk to me," she said. I have to give Carole credit; it can be revolting to watch someone fall in love.

"So, what do you think?" Carole said, trying to sound interested.

"I'll tell you what. If she were inclined, I would be inclined." I'd never used that strange, unmistakable word before in my life.

Throughout August, Lisa and I scoffed at the heat, but if she had asked me to, I would have sat on fresh asphalt with her. That last summer in her Hallmark cubicle before taking the leap as a full-time painter, Lisa made cards of boats on lakes, flowers in vases, and Christmas scenes. On one card, she invited me on yet another outing. A committee had rejected it because it featured what looked too much like a wolf; Hallmark's target market, sixty-year-old white women from Kansas, didn't buy cards with predators. I would have. She knew just that summer I'd gotten up at 3:00 in the morning in the hopes of seeing reintroduced wolves in Yellowstone. I opened the card over and over again like a lab rat that keeps pushing a lever for that little tiny shock of pleasure.

I called Carole to read the card to her. "It says, 'We need to go outside again.'"

"It's a good thing she isn't trying so hard to be *my* friend," Carole said. "I don't like being outside. Especially not now. It's so damn hot."

It was so hot, I burned my hand on the handle of Lisa's pickup the day we hiked the woods behind the Burr Oak Woods Nature Center in Blue Springs, Missouri, one of those imperiled natural areas annexed before the rest gives way to subdivisions.

After our hike, she impressed me by identifying butterflies in a display case in the interpretive center. She said that when she was a little girl, she didn't have mesh to make a net, but this hadn't discouraged her. She made her own out of a coat hanger and a sandwich baggy and caught plenty of butterflies in the hay meadow behind her house. She whispered as if into a confessional how, like so many collectors, she gave it all up when she found one still trying to walk, pinned through the thorax into a piece of florist's foam in an empty chocolate box.

I told her that when I was ten, a Presbyterian camp counselor on her way to becoming Buddhist taught us the cup-and-card method of insect removal and release. Since then, I hadn't been able to kill anything. I used the method even with flies. When I opened the door to let them out, three more would come in. Soon enough, she would witness this firsthand.

That day, I didn't have a bra on. I had stopped wearing them several years earlier because my breasts were so small no one could tell I wasn't wearing one anyway. Bras were hot and uncomfortable. I had no important political reason. No one could tell, that is, unless I had on a thin T-shirt like the one I had on this day, a thin, pink and purple tie-dyed one. When we stopped to rest on an outcrop in the shade, I saw Lisa looking at my breasts and quickly looking away.

Imaginary Jesus whispered that if I could keep from overplaying my hand, I might just put an end to years of indefatigable loneliness. Yes, I could conceivably survive another winter alone finding little things to do in my brown apartment, but I was already on the lee side of solstice, the days growing shorter. "But she's not gay," I reminded him. He smiled.

Our time together that hot day was far from over. Even though Lisa's air conditioner had given out the night before, she still wanted to cook me dinner. She left a pan of sizzling onions to bring me an appetizer. "Sorry it's so hot," she said. It must have been 145 degrees in the kitchen. Even in the dining room, I could smell the varnish on the chairs.

"You don't have to go to all this trouble," I said.

"I want to." *But why?* I thought. No one I liked had ever liked me back. Never had I had so much trouble understanding simple, declarative sentences. When she breezed into the room with two plates of something nestled atop a bed of linguini, it was almost 8:30. A lit candle sat between us. Sweat had curled the hair at her temples. Her eyes each had a flame in them. Suddenly, I imagined the dead bodies of Romeo and Juliet and then Carole, surveying a lawn covered with trash. I had promised Carole I would help her pick up trash that night.

I excused myself to go to the bathroom, my stomach churning. "Remember, idiot. She's just being nice," my inner fundamentalist shouted. And then Imaginary Jesus held his finger to my lips. He and I had continued to work on better mental pictures. This time he reminded me of the time I found a Liberty dime, a shine in black dirt between tree roots. He liked Lisa. So did I, too much, if this weren't a date.

"I have to go," I said, emerging from the bathroom.

"But I made pie," she said. "And I wanted you to see my video."

"Video?"

"I jumped out of a plane last month. It came with a video," she said and then rolled her eyes with embarrassment. "It might seem kind of stupid, but it was an important thing I did that I can't explain to you unless you see it."

"Okay. But no pie."

"Why?"

"I'm full as a tick," I said patting my cramping, sweaty stomach. "And I have to help Carole pick up trash at the Shakespeare Fest."

"Wait . . . you work at the Shakespeare Fest?"

"No, I just promised Carole I'd help her."

"Carole?" she said.

"I sit with Carole at church. Second row balcony."

"Oh yeah. I remember. Well, I don't want to make you late, but I wouldn't leave without a piece of this pie. The peaches were so ripe the fruit almost fell off the pit. I picked them myself."

My family had picked fruit at Stephenson's Orchard for as long as I could remember. I knew well the short, tangled trees, the bees that surrounded them. I used to imagine that I hadn't gotten there in our Ford, but on the back of a brown horse, friendly with big nostrils.

"You picked them yourself?" I said. Suddenly, barefoot in my memories, there Lisa stood. She and the horse.

"How about that video?" I said.

We watched her and the man harnessed to her back climb out onto the wing of the airplane, a man who said little other than "dude" and who I didn't like seeing so close to her. I heard the caramelized sugar crust crunch between her teeth. And then dude let go of the strut. They spun in space as if from a spider's spinneret.

"I don't have to do that again, but I'm not afraid anymore," she said. "Of so many things."

I was afraid, especially of knowing what to do after what might come next. So I left, but not before Lisa fixed me a paper plate of noodles covered with foil. All the way to the Shakespeare Fest, I could feel it radiating heat on the seat beside me.

I picked up sodden programs and half-chewed turkey legs while Carole ate my leftovers.

"I just realized all of the sudden how long Lisa and I have been together today. All of the sudden, and then I thought you might wonder where I was."

"This is fabulous," Carole said. "Next time, I wouldn't leave without pie."

✦ ✦ ✦

The next day, Sunday, Lisa and I spent on a blanket, ignoring Carole and the jazz at the festival to which Carole had gotten the three of us free tickets. Like two rare checkerspot butterflies, that out of all the other flying things manage to clap compound eyes on each other in a field, Lisa and I trailed each other from blooming onion booth to the port-a-potties.

Back at the blanket, Lisa said, "Let me spray your feet."

"I have ugly toes," I said.

"Oh, come on. How bad could they be?"

"Terrible," I said. "An evolutionary transition."

"But it will feel so good . . ."

She had the prettiest feet I had ever seen. She had such a high arch. I wanted to touch it to feel what kind of a muscle could possibly hold her that far off the ground. She had perfectly shaped toes with neatly trimmed nails. They were cared-for toes. My second toe is so short it can only bend as a unit with my third toe. In fact the split between my second and third toe looks like an afterthought. I was just shy of having only four toes on each foot. Worse yet, my feet curled up on the end, like an elf's.

I took off my shoes.

"Oh, those are not ugly feet. Almost not there at all. Baby toes." She sprayed water all over them.

Carole leaned forward, disgusted. "I may as well not be here at all. Hellooooo."

I heard her, but as if from behind a crashing waterfall.

Lisa said, "Carole, would you like your feet sprinkled, too?"

"Sure," Carole said, never taking her eyes off of the tiny black woman singing across the hill from us. She sighed and wiggled her feet in mild appreciation.

I no longer worried how I would look or what others might think. I no longer wanted to be careful. When Lisa called Monday night to say she didn't want to wait until the next weekend to see me, I knew there had been no need to worry. "I like you," I finally felt able to say. I told her how brave she'd been calling when she couldn't have been sure what would happen, since neither of us knew the intentions of the other.

"Not brave, really," she said. "I knew you were inclined." Months earlier, Carole had quoted me to a church balcony friend. This friend told the Thundercloud—who I now knew had indeed once been more than Lisa's friend and didn't want anyone to know. The Thundercloud told Lisa. Had I not used such an unusual word, someone along the line would have gotten it wrong. But it had come back to her fresh, just-picked, still warm from my mouth: *Inclined.* As in, bent, leaning toward.

Faced with the sheer impossibility that after a lifetime of dead ends I might be falling in real reciprocal love, I couldn't sit upright. While Lisa unfolded the length and breadth of her affection, how much and for how long, I lay where I had collapsed on my bedroom floor. I listened to her tell me all she liked about me. My sense of humor, my blue sweater with the worn-out elbows.

"I've had that cardigan since 1986," I said. "You're the only person who's ever liked it."

Across three long-distance billing rates from Kansas City to Lawrence, we got a taste of how deeply we would come to understand each other. Not only had we both wet ourselves in the first grade, we had also been sent home after in boy's underwear. We were both childhood neurotics.

"I was an insomniac," I said. "I laid awake worrying about the return of the ice sheets."

"I cried every morning before school," Lisa said. "I thought I should understand income taxes and balancing checkbooks. They took me to a therapist."

"Wow. My family was always afraid of therapy, or at least afraid that somebody would find out."

"So was mine," she said.

"Did it work?"

"I didn't have enough sessions."

"What else happened to you?" she said.

"I ruined slumber parties," I said. "I hated them. I wanted everybody to stop talking and go to sleep."

"You're kidding!" she said. "So did I. People stopped inviting me."

On and on we lined up our lives and held them up to the light. We marveled at how many of the edges met.

✦ ✦ ✦

When she came to my apartment two days later, we discovered our fingers, forearms, and feet were the same length, too. It's a wonder we ever got close enough to find out since I began the evening by showing her way too many home movies. "There we are at Disneyland." Daddy had filmed my particular Dumbo the elephant circling around and around with me screaming inside it.

"You look upset," she said, unfazed, unwilling to stop liking me. "How old were you there?"

"Three. Pirates of the Caribbean ruined the place for me. I remember thinking, 'We're going to die, but they're laughing. No one is in charge here.' Oh, there's me crying at the zoo." When I stood up to thread the film into the take-up reel, something of hers brushed the back of my calf. As far as I could remember, no one had ever touched me there.

We faced off at opposite ends of my couch, our knees pulled up. I prayed for some inkling of what to do next. I'd already moved the folded green blanket off Lisa's end of the couch. It was covered with hair from Mary Todd. The blanket was where Mary Todd always sat, where she was still trying to sit and looking at me as if to say, "Move this." I had not yet had her declawed, something that became clear I would have to do if Lisa were to become a regular visitor.

"So when did you know?" she said, Mary Todd's plume tail swishing across first one side of her face then the other.

"Know what?"

"That you'd be doing something like this, someday, with a woman."

I still wondered what "this" was. "Since I was about four," I said. "I fell in love with my sister's college roommate. What about you?"

"About twenty for sure. But I suspected for longer than that. Something never felt quite right when I dated men. I was always looking at my watch. But with women—with you—" She leaned forward and put her palm on my knee.

We sat in silence, her hand where she'd put it, both of mine still folded in my lap, not ready, quite yet, to let go.

"You've been with men?" I said.

"Yes, and a woman," she said. "And you?"

"I know it's hard to believe, but neither. I should be behind glass in a museum or something. I'm not especially good or anything. It's just never been the right person."

"I think it's unique."

When we were children, Momma had prayed that each of her daughters would meet someone at church.

"I think we need to take this slowly step by step, like a courtship, especially if it is something," Lisa said. "Then if it isn't, we'll have fewer regrets."

I reached forward, finally without thinking, and put my hand on top of hers.

When she gathered her things to leave, I protested.

"But I have to go to work," she said.

"You're quitting in two weeks. Call in sick. Really. It's easy. I do it all the time. Well, not all the time, but on days when I know going to work will make me sick, I call in and tell them I have something."

"What?"

"Anything."

"But I'm not sick," she said.

"In a way you are," I said, smiling. "We both are."

"Where will we sleep?" She'd seen my twin bed.

"This folds out," I said.

I opened the couch and unfolded the bed. Seeing her lying on her back in the middle of it made me tremble, something I hoped she couldn't see. I left the room to wash my face—something I never did at night—and to brush my teeth. Not since I'd lived at home with my parents had anyone asked me where I was going when I left the room. My habits hadn't been noticed for a very long time. Finished washing, I came back and lay down beside Lisa. She had put on the sheets I'd laid out; she had taken everything off but her T-shirt and underwear. She was propped up on one arm waiting for me.

"Goodnight," she said, after I turned out the lamp.

"Goodnight."

The thin mattress did a poor job of protecting us from the metal support bar holding the whole bed together. Nevertheless, we lay on our own sides of it and fell asleep.

In the morning, I pretended not to have woken up while Lisa carefully looked at my grandmother's ring that I wear on my right ring finger. She gently turned the ring around three times and put my finger back down. That was the only time she touched me all night.

"It's time to call in sick," I said. "I'll go first. I always put my head between my knees for a minute. It makes your voice sound sicker."

"Oh what a tangled web we weave . . ." Lisa said.

I picked up my old green rotary and dialed Hyde & Associates. "Linda, I won't be coming in. I feel terrible. Yeah, I will. Bye."

I handed the telephone to Lisa, raised my eyebrows.

"I don't even know what number to call."

"You've never called in sick. Not even legitimately?"

"I've always tried to have perfect attendance. It's my lifelong fear of falling behind."

"Do you have a supervisor?"

"Yes," she said.

"Call your supervisor."

After bowls of cereal, we folded the bed back into a couch and sat next to each other all day, taking turns stroking each other's arms and hands.

At 4:00 in the afternoon, she said, "I can't stay here forever, I guess."

I kissed her top lip and the bottom of her nose, missing my aim in my fear both of kissing her and of never doing it at all. She paused, took her hand off the doorknob, and kissed me fully, on my mouth.

For hours after she left, I sat in a chair, disoriented, wrapped in our bedclothes.

13

Showing My Work

My therapist decided I didn't need any more sessions since I'd reached my goal of being able to give and receive love. As I wrote my last check, she offered to officiate at my wedding. "My what?"

"You never know," she said. "It would be my first same-sex ceremony. You do know I'm ordained, right?" She may as well have been speaking Korean; I didn't understand anything else she said.

Never once in my life had I imagined my wedding, though it wasn't for lack of exposure to them. My sisters had practically cut their teeth on matching bride dolls, one a blonde, one brunette. Each doll had a satin dress, bouquet, veil, and a real, removable wedding ring. My sisters marched them around our musty family room exchanging vows with invisible grooms. All I had wanted to do to the dolls was take their clothes off. In each of my sisters' weddings, I had a role. More times than I could bear recalling, I had been someone's bridesmaid. Depending on the flowers, I wore either a lime or lemon satin gown that made me look like I had liver disease. The silk pumps dyed to match always wound up rain, alcohol, or vomit spattered. At Momma's urging that I might someday need something "nice," I kept each ensemble for a year or so in the dry cleaner bag then left it at the curb for the Federation of the Blind.

I privately clucked my tongue at Momma's, my sisters', and my friends' marriages—at the requisite nagging, the soul-killing inequities, the cases of arrested development in each. I reduced all marriages to a shambles.

Dislodged by the leverage of love, I began to picture myself participating in a very public and sacred absurdity.

That first fall together, Lisa and I spent every weekend from Friday afternoon to the early, sickening gray hours of Monday morning. We didn't turn on the lamp but left each other in the dark as if the night before didn't really have to end until the sun rose on us separately. We touched each other's faces and smelled each other's hair and breath and skin.

In public, we grew increasingly careless. Lisa lay on top of me alongside a trail at the Squaw Creek Migratory Bird Refuge. An older couple with binoculars popped over the rise and nearly stumbled over us. They tried to mask their surprise and embarrassment by saying, "Have you seen the grebes?" In a stand of trees near Old Missouri Town, a reconstructed pioneer village in Oak Grove, Missouri, we neglected even to spread a blanket on the ground before curling up together like chipmunks in a pile of leaves. Lisa wound up with poison ivy so severe that in place of one arm, she had a long blister.

By October, I needed weekends like amphetamines. I barely got through the days in my cubicle listening to mix tapes of singer-songwriters I'd never heard of. I made her classical mixes with big sweeping things like Elgar's "Enigma Variations," Copland's "Appalachian Spring," and bits from the soundtrack to *Out of Africa*. I imagined her driving across Kansas to me listening to them. Writing things for a company working to restore the nation's crumbling sanitary sewers seemed painfully unimportant. In the mornings, I waited for lunch, not to eat, but to check the mailbox for a letter praising my curly hair or the way my skin felt between flannel sheets or remembering something I'd said to her in the dark several days ago that she wanted me to say to her again.

Because I took these letters everywhere with me, I often lost them. After frantic searches, I'd find them in the crisper with the lettuce or under the bathroom counter with the deodorant. In one letter she corrected herself: no, my butt wasn't like bread dough but like bread just out of the oven. She drew things in the margins, such as her face frowning because we had three and a half days until we saw each other. I wrote her back, saying loving things I'd never believed myself capable of feeling.

For a split second now and then, I would worry she was too good to be true—that sometime while caressing my cheek, she would push her thumb through my eye socket, or that she'd try to empty my checking account and buy a plane ticket out of the country to flee the authorities. And that I was having these worries would worry me. How could I be sure my love-addled instincts were right? And like every addict, I needed bigger and more frequent hits.

✦ ✦ ✦

My first winter with Lisa, it snowed and snowed. Normally each of us would have relished snow, but, several times, it threatened to keep us from each other. I tried hard not to see the weather as an old fundamentalist omen that we shouldn't be together. One Friday, both roads into Lawrence were nearly impassable. My selfish spirits lifted when she called me at work to say she was coming anyway. At the stroke of 5:00, I bounded across the drifted parking lot from my cubicle to my apartment to find her lying on the couch, casually reading as if she hadn't almost died. "I drove through a whiteout," she said.

That Saturday night, we stumbled to Dillons grocery store over snow heaps where the sidewalks had been for a quart of milk to make hot chocolate and to rent *Alive*. Lisa had seen it already and warned me before the plane crash. Between spread fingers, I saw two men sail out the back of the plane, the beautiful snow-capped Andes behind them, their seat belts still fastened, their mouths large, dark holes.

"Now who are they eating?" I said later when one of the survivors brushed aside snow from a cadaver and carved a chunk off its buttocks.

"Remember the woman who couldn't move her legs? The main guy's sister? That's why he isn't eating."

Huddled together on my couch, we watched others' disasters, snug in the knowledge that no one could see or judge us. Breaking social rules is exciting until you start to think about the future with its crowds and bouquets and mutual checking accounts. Everyone will be watching to see if you're as happy as you say you are, especially when the cultural codes you've subconsciously obeyed say you and your happiness are abnormal, even appalling.

Like a stroke victim does the alphabet, I had to relearn how to be happy. Not surprisingly, I mistook Lisa's capacity for solitude, which was greater even than mine, for an aversion to commitment. I feared that if she knew how much I loved her, she would feel smothered. Familiar only with crushes, I anticipated exits. I spent the first six months of my first real relationship bracing for its end. The longer it did not end, the more afraid I became about what little would be left of me if it did. If it didn't go on, if it were merely a dalliance with no future, I wanted to be the one to end it.

✦ ✦ ✦

I didn't come up with the idea to get married; I got it from my senior pastor. In typical subversive fashion, he published a pamphlet that not even the most open-minded Broadway Baptist member yet felt comfortable putting in the literature racks at the back of the sanctuary. You couldn't let its baby blue cover and innocuous typesetting fool you; it was a call to revolution. In the first half, he examined the long yet marginalized history of same-sex relationships from biblical time onward. In the second, he demanded that, because the Bible said so little about homosexuality and nothing about the kind expressed in loving relationships, the church should endorse gay marriage. People found out about the pamphlet by word of mouth and bought copies from the senior pastor directly for $1 to cover the cost of copying. I fled the sanctuary with my new copy tucked under my coat as if I were a Muslim with a copy of *The Satanic Verses*. I took the Little Blue Book, as it came to be called, in small doses at night before bed.

At the end, my senior pastor said that refusing to marry your partner out of fear amounted to rejecting God's call to love and commitment. With the Little Blue Book open over my chest in the moments before sleep one night, Imaginary Jesus whispered to me about happiness. I needed to bear public witness to the wonder of it, to how grateful I felt for Lisa and the long-buried wholeness I had recovered in her presence. I realized I must tell her how much happier I wanted to be. I got out of bed and pulled my green rotary phone with the long cord into my small kitchen. I sat nauseous on the floor, bracing my feet against the cabinet in front of me, preparing for the worst.

"It's a little late," she said. "Are you all right?"

"Not really. Not yet," I said. "We need to talk."

"Okay," I could hear the fear in her voice.

"I've been reading a book that says gay people need to be willing to risk committing," I said. I had wrapped the phone cord around my hand so tightly that my fingers turned purple.

"Is it the Little Blue Book?" she said.

"You've heard of that?" I said.

"I have one."

"You do? Well, how do you feel about it?" I said.

"About commitment?" she said. "I guess I always wondered if I was capable of it. Now I know."

"That you aren't?" I said. "Did you say am?"

"Yes, am." She sounded hurt.

I had prepared myself for a different answer.

"You mean it doesn't feel too—oh, I don't know—limiting to you, choosing one person out of a whole world of possible people?"

"I don't want the whole world."

"So what you're saying is you might commit to *me?*"

"I'm saying I *am* committed to you."

"You are?"

We went round and round like this with me having difficulty hearing the good news. I wouldn't have to live from fix to fix forever, but might, one day have a relationship based on daily mutual tenderness.

Shielded from the outside world there on my kitchen floor, covered in the crumbs of a graham cracker I had nervously gobbled, I had an algebraic moment, the kind I'd had in eighth grade. I had always become frantically hopeful, halfway through my homework when things stopped making sense. For each problem, I happily came to an answer of my own, usually an improbable number with a decimal and lots of trailing integers, an answer, that since I wasn't designing skyscrapers or bridges, never hurt anyone. Each time though, I would turn with the eraser of my sharp pencil to the answer page to find a mockingly round number. For a moment, I would worry that I might never get an answer right. And then, foolishly, I would turn the page, happy for the chance to take a crack at another problem.

I resolved anew that night to stop worrying altogether about the answer I'd been finding at the back of the book given to me: man + woman = happiness. I decided to settle for my answer, one that I might get partial credit for because I'd so carefully shown my work.

❖ ❖ ❖

The bone-chilling morning after Valentine's night we spent under the comforter on my twin bed, Lisa and I slept back to stomach, like pomegranate seeds. I tried to roll over to face her without forcing her off the bed's edge. Our faces were so close that I saw, as ever, the optical illusion of a third eye in the middle of her forehead. Until I backed off a few inches, my fiancé looked like the Cyclops.

"My mother has been dreaming of this day," Lisa said. "Now it's here. If she knew, it would just make her sick." A year and a lifetime earlier, the moony look on my face would have made me nauseous, too.

Just moments ago we had both been so happy, but then she'd done it. She'd let our parents into the bedroom. I pictured Momma sitting in her pink chenille housecoat about to pop the last bite of breakfast in her mouth, wondering since it was the weekend after all, why I hadn't called yet.

"Neither one of us did what our Mom wanted us to," Lisa said. Her sister had eloped. We hadn't had enough therapy, either of us, to know you can't stop living just to please your parents. Now it was settled; Lisa's mother would not be the mother of the bride, at least not at a ceremony she would want to attend. Lisa had lots of girl cousins on her mother's side, all of whom had married men and moved into houses a stone's throw from their mothers. At Christmas, everyone packed into the Mount Chestnut Presbyterian Church basement for Christmas dinner. The last time she had been to the gathering, someone took a snapshot of all of the cousins lined up in order of age, holding their babies out in front of them. Three-fourths of the way down the line, Lisa held a borrowed plastic doll.

"I was supposed to marry someone tall. A musician."

"I play the piano," I said. "Well, not very well, but I won a musical aptitude certificate in sixth grade."

"Somebody like Tom Netherton," she said. He was the queeny-looking pious man on *Lawrence Welk*, which we'd both watched on Saturday nights with our families.

Lisa's father still wasn't speaking to her for being gay, and her mother had developed TMJD and arrhythmia, both of which, she reminded Lisa frequently, were exacerbated by stress.

I kissed her shoulder and waited for her to stop crying, so we could celebrate our engagement.

✦ ✦ ✦

Little could I have known how deeply into the soft tissue of my psyche Momma had driven this peg: You must not live with someone before you get married. I felt its sharp point every morning break when I pored over the page and a half of rental ads in the classifieds of the *Lawrence Journal-World*, which someone always left on the break room table. Even though Lisa and I hadn't even chosen the right gender, I felt infinitely guiltier about the thought of shacking up. It didn't help either that my parents, who had met and grown to love Lisa, seemed perfectly content with the half-truth that she and I were hunting for a place together simply because we wanted to be thrifty. It didn't help to remind myself that finding a place to set up house together is what engaged couples do. I shared the classifieds with the man who cleaned the sewer field equipment and ran errands. The field techs called him retarded, but I knew better. He was far more advanced emotionally than the other men in the office. He held open doors for people. He smiled and nodded when we crossed paths in the hallway. He remembered his wedding anniversary. I had seen him walking home from the grocery store arm in arm with his tiny wife. They smiled and laughed together. Seeing him helped me set aside my fear and guilt and do what needed to be done. I couldn't wait until Lisa and I had what he and his wife did: time in the same house together and not just on the weekends. True love doesn't worry about what might go wrong.

Many rentals that looked promising from the outside had quirks that would have detracted from our bliss: a kitchen pulling away from the rest of the house or a floor slanting toward one corner of the room, which would be fine if your furniture had seat belts. For most rentals, we had too many cats or too much huge furniture to heft up a narrow staircase.

One rainy Sunday after narrowly escaping having our faces bitten off by a dog, a tenant told us she found out her son's unexplained headaches were caused by carbon monoxide from their improperly vented furnace. "Thank God for my canary," she said, laying her hand on top of her son's dirty little head. After checking off several more red herrings, we pulled into a nearby parking lot so I, the map-reader, could fight back carsickness.

"Maybe we should pray," Lisa said. I thought of myself as the spiritual alpha; I kicked myself for not remembering God. Both of us still believed in what Bishop John Spong calls "a security-giving heavenly parent who hands out threats and favors, rewards and punishments," Imaginary Jesus's cranky father, a distant flipper of switches rather than the cosmos itself, the Creativity ceaselessly expressed in everything, enfolding everything, permeating everything. We did pray, and we both felt something shift. Something within our own selves gave us permission, a blessing even. Suddenly Lisa said, "Maybe we need to change our thinking." The light in her voice lit up both our faces. "Maybe we need to buy."

Just the week before, a social worker friend had warned me not to make any joint financial decisions during the first year of any new relationship. But I trusted Lisa more than I had anyone. I was ready to make a mistake with her. We turned a corner into Old West Lawrence, a neighborhood we couldn't afford, and saw a sign for an open house.

"What about that little one there?" I said. Either of us could have said the same thing at our first glimpse of each other. Inside, a calm man in Birkenstocks sat in the corner of its warm living room in a rocking chair. I half expected to find Momma in the kitchen trying to cook, so at home did I feel. There were the hardwood floors I had longed to see again since my parents had covered theirs with green carpet. But what made me weak in the knees with homecoming was a wall of pegboard in the basement workshop with painted black silhouettes of a hand plane, a hammer, a hacksaw, and other tools. It was something someone would paint on a place he plans never to leave, a place he has loved and felt loved within.

"That's it," I said, once the door had shut behind us.

"Yes," Lisa said.

In the month-long window before I gave my notice in my desperation to leave Hyde & Associates to make way for a misguided retreat into the English Lit doctoral program at KU, I had the proven income. Lisa had enough for the down payment, though she could not have been approved with only one year of freelance behind her. We filled each other's financial gaps. Within three hours, our offer had been filed in a folder in the realtor's office.

"I've spent more time picking out socks," Lisa said, giving voice to my own panic.

I spent the next week of morning breaks on my office phone holding my voice down with mortgage bankers, pretending to edit a progress report on sewer repairs in Tulsa. At the place with the lowest interest rate, I introduced myself to a woman named Caroline. When I gave her my full name, she said, "Kelly Lee Barth . . . Barfie Baby, well how the heck are you? This is Caroline Smothers. From Trinity. Trinity Church." I heard her clap and rub her hands together, just as she used to during our church youth group meetings at Trinity Presbyterian.

The last time we'd seen each other, I wore tube socks and T-shirts with pictures of kittens.

"So there are two cosigners. And what's the other person's name? How are your parents, by the way?" Trinity was a small gossipy church. Caroline would figure out Lisa and I weren't just roommates, and before long, everyone, including my parents, would know.

At that moment, I needed Caroline's approval for more than just a loan. And I needed so much more therapy.

"They're fine. My father still has heart trouble. The name's Lisa Jo Grossman."

"That's Lisa. L, I, S, A?"

I prepared to give a defense of my relationship. Caroline's Aunt Sandy had been my Brownie leader.

"And that's Gross?" she said.

"As in gross," I said.

"Man, as in man?" she said. "We can lock you in at 7 and 5/8. We need $7,700 down."

She asked no further questions. *Why would she*, I thought. *They're probably told not to.*

"Now, from each of you, we'll need bank statements, pay stubs, employment history, all that good stuff. Oh, and we'll need to run a credit check. I have to tell people that. That's done through Freddie Mac. So your parents are fine? So are mine. I'm engaged, by the way."

"Freddie who?"

Three years earlier, before I had learned to balance my checkbook, I had bounced five checks right in a row, a chain reaction. With the luxury of a steady income, I had used the cushion method of financial management. In paying for some plane ticket or double car payment or another, I had pulled too much stuffing from my cushion, and my paycheck didn't make it in time. I paid a $15 fee for each returned check. Apoplectic with shame, I scurried all over town writing new checks and swearing on my honor to people who couldn't care less that this was the first time this had ever happened to me and that it would be the last. "I always find it strange," said the receptionist at the vet, whose smock had pictures of puppies all over it, "that people who have written you a bad check try to make good on it by writing another check." I promised her I would learn to balance my checkbook, which was none of her business. She had rolled her eyes. I didn't want Lisa ever to find out I had such an accident.

An old high school friend, Whitney, now worked as secretary for the chief of police. I looked up her number as soon as I got home. While I waited for her to answer, I imagined having a loan officer lean across a desk to say Lisa and I had no financial future.

"I've bounced some checks," I said.

"Where? Do you need money?" she said.

"Not now," I said and explained.

"You bounced five checks, that's all, in your entire life?" Whitney said. I had crawled between the kitchen cabinets again, my green rotary phone between my knees.

"Is that a lot?"

"Oh, honey. You don't even know bad credit. How long ago?"

"Several years."

"You want to talk bad credit, there are people bouncing checks, skipping town, unpaid child support trailing behind, five-figure credit card bills. Interest payments bigger than their monthly mortgage. You're a bad-credit virgin."

"How do you know?"

"Do you pay your bills?"

"Yes."

"Car paid for?"

"Yes."

"Angel. Noncriminal."

As Lisa and I signed more than twenty pieces of paper that said we would be mutually responsible for paying for the house, a loan officer paused in his paper shuffling, "You each have the highest credit rating I've ever seen." Neither he nor anyone else in the lending industry cared one iota what we planned to do inside the house they had approved us to buy. On paper, we looked like an excellent risk.

"The exact same number," he said.

I fought the urge to ask for that number. I remembered repeatedly asking Momma to tell me my IQ. "It's best not to know," she would always say. "You just live your life. Do your best. I love you. No number will ever change that."

When I pressed her, she said. "You're above average. Is that enough? There. Are you happy?"

✦ ✦ ✦

As is true for any couple, actually living together took us quickly from bliss to reality. Though we loved sharing not only the same town but also the same home together, we had to get used to each other's habits, social needs. Coming from a family of six, I was used to putting myself in the center of the fray. The first week or so in our little house together felt to me like the first few days in heaven. With my love right there, I followed her from room to room like a baby duck. To help me see her problem, she changed the name of my favorite of Kabat-Zinn's books, *Wherever You Go, There You Are*, to *Wherever I Go, There You Are*. We worked out a plan. If she didn't want me with her, she would close the door behind her. It needed to be that obvious.

She, too, had to get used to my way of being. As an oldest child, Lisa was busy all day long, hammering this, adjusting that. A youngest child, I, on the other hand, could sit for an hour or so looking at a patch of sunlight moving across our wood floor. I liked slowing down in the midst of commotion, pondering things. Initially, Lisa found this puzzling. Eventually, she found it disturbing. "What are you doing?" she said when she found me leaning against the wall looking out our new picture window.

"I don't know."

"You're doing something, aren't you?"

"I think," I said.

"You're thinking?"

"Sort of."

I pictured Gandhi but did not mention him.

It was what had drawn us to each other—Lisa's ambition and my guilt-free periods of inertia.

Eventually, we had what we realized were actual fights. They often seemed lopsided, with one of us screaming or crying and the other one watching from a distance like a rabbit flushed into the open by a lawn mower, trying to be invisible.

Here's what one looked like. First let me say, when on task, I am impulsive, rambunctious, and easily frustrated, again, the classic youngest child foil to Lisa's delicate persistence and unshakable sense of responsibility. As an oldest child, it's all she knows. At the first sign of trouble, tools fall out of my hands and learned helplessness sets in. It's why Momma got an A on my wraparound skirt for Home Ec, because I couldn't see through my tears of frustration to finish it. It didn't help that I had a tornado of a father who got a good deal done, most of which died or fell apart. One look at the ruins of his cold frame, an outdoor passive solar structure where he had hoped to start his own tomato seedlings, is evidence that I came by my slapdash nature honestly.

I have part of his technique down cold, the do-things-as-quickly-as-humanly-possible part. If something doesn't fit, force it just a little bit and maybe you can, by sheer willpower, nudge the laws of physics. But I did not inherit Daddy's bare-chested bravado though. He never had to worry what failure would do to his self-esteem. He would never have had a second thought, as I did, that the solid, shiny steel sauce pot I'd inherited from Aunt

Lucy just might not fit inside the colander and leave enough room for the drawer beneath the oven to close as well. As I shoved, I heard the saucepot's handle click into a ridge inside the drawer, wedging it shut.

The episode that then took place on the floor in front of the stove can only be partially explained by the fact I was about to menstruate and had not yet. Though my hands were, as Lisa unwisely pointed out, small enough to fit through the inch gap, I could not move my fingers once inside the drawer. Determined not to cry out for help as I always did when anyone else was handy, I began to alternately yank and jiggle the drawer, listening for the slightest shift in the long, hard, black handle. I began to curse it for being longer than necessary.

Lisa stepped in to help.

"No. I've gotten myself into this mess," I said.

She continued to stand where I could see her.

"Don't watch me." Before I could get control of myself, I saw one of my own tears drop onto the spattered metal handle of the stove drawer and mingle with a spot of something I had cooked for us and spilled.

She backed into the living room murmuring reassurance, her palms raised as you might at a sow grizzly.

"I can't do anything right," I screamed. "Now, I've entombed our pots."

"No," Lisa said from the other side of the room, still foolishly participating.

"Yes," I said. "We just need to face some hard facts. I'm good for nothing." I gave the drawer a hard yank. That month's egg began its descent of the fallopian tube. The pot handle broke off in my hand. The oven drawer opened, and I fell backward onto the floor.

"Our best pot," I shrieked. "Everything I touch, I ruin. You do *everything* right!"

"I don't," Lisa said, patting my head, a brave thing to do considering I held a sharp broken piece of Bakelite, some of the first plastic ever made. I hated myself for wanting the comfort that she wouldn't have needed.

"You don't what?" I said through clenched teeth, tears collecting in the corners of my mouth.

"Do everything right," she said. "And we have other pots."

"We may as well throw this one away," I said berating myself one last time for the hideous waste of natural resources. I reminded Lisa that the handle had been made from petrochemicals, probably the carbonized body of some beautiful dinosaur.

The next day, she took the broken pot handle to Ernst Hardware. The cranky owner found a new handle and screw that would fit. She fixed it and set it quietly on the stove when I wasn't around, so it appeared to have been repaired overnight by mice or Brownies or that nothing had happened at all.

Over time, we learned how to be together. If I found myself wondering why she would methodically sand a surface a third or fourth time before painting it, I told myself that hers was not my life to live. Lisa too learned to look away when she saw me, for instance, folding laundry or cutting carrots. Nothing would ever have the sheen of perfection she required, unless she did it herself. We reached a place where we could imagine a life of compatible difference.

✦ ✦ ✦

We bought *The Essential Guide to Gay and Lesbian Weddings* at Terra Nova Bookstore. We tried to follow the book's overarching rule: "Be true to yourself, darling." We would not bring up the rear of a train of bridesmaids. There would be no sculpted nightmares of the two of us atop the cake. In fact, our baker looked like a pirate, and he raised boa constrictors in a Victorian near the university, a hobby I couldn't get out of my mind when he brought over our first samples. His almond marzipan and dark chocolate with raspberry filling he planned for the alternate layers dispelled my fears. The cake was just one item on a long list of very real things we paid for. So were the rolls of postage stamps we affixed to our hand-printed invitations that we sent to very real guests.

No matter how often the book reminded us how fun it would be, how sacred, how many had gone before us, I feared otherwise. When the RSVPs trickled in, I learned I wasn't the only one struggling with the palpability of it all. Writers group Janet wrote in her RSVP, "You're not going to wear a big ole rainbow petticoat or something, are you?" I finished her unspoken thought: "What the hell do you think you're doing?" One of Lisa's former Hallmark coworkers penciled on her RSVP, "So, is this like a *real* wedding?" Then there were the lesbian friends who qualified their attendance with "this seems all right for you, maybe," but they would never mimic such a tyrannical, misogynistic charade. "Why ingratiate yourself to the oppressor? You still won't make sense," one said. Quite a few people didn't even RSVP. "Maybe the card got lost in the shuffle," Lisa suggested, in her usual role as optimist. I assumed they didn't want to participate in a public spectacle. We planned to hold the ceremony in our new backyard, just as my parents had in theirs, right in front of God and everybody.

On most days I held firm in my convictions. I wanted to marry Lisa. I could almost picture it. On bad days, I rode a tide of mental illness like a dying jellyfish, stinging any who brushed too near. The glaring omissions on the guest list showed just how ready I wasn't. From my disastrous kindergarten Maypole performance to my interminable graduation, my family had witnessed my every life passage. "I can't believe you're not inviting your parents," Lisa said. "Yeah, we saw how well inviting yours went," I snapped. Her mother had written at the top of her letter announcing our engagement. "What next? I had just about gotten your father to talk to you again." They wouldn't be coming. To leave my family off the guest list meant I hadn't invited my whole self either. I feared my family's "no" too much to set my plans aside until I'd explained myself to them. As with many mistakes I would make in my life, deciding not to invite my family was partly right. I didn't need anyone's official blessing of the best thing that had ever happened to me.

Lisa had her own share of prenuptial fits. She had one at Pottery Barn. The bridal registry clerk couldn't make the computer understand there were two brides.

"One of you will have to go in the husband box," she said. "I'm not saying what you're doing is wrong—that's not it at all—it just won't work with our current system."

She turned the screen around for us to see her struggle to force the box that said bride to accept two names. "Bong, bong," her computer said each time. "See, it's too long—too many characters," she said.

"You can be the bride," I said to Lisa.

"No. Then if people who know you call up and give them your name, Pottery Barn won't be able to find us."

"Does it cross-reference by husband?" she said.

"Well, if a person asks us to, it certainly can," the clerk said, lowering her voice in the hopes that Lisa would as well.

"No one will know to tell them to look in the husband box," Lisa said. "This is ridiculous. We want people to buy things from you. Is that clear? Why does there have to be a bride box?"

"Because there are brides," the clerk said.

"Can't you just write this down somewhere and stick it to the counter?" I said.

The clerk, in a preschool teacher voice, said, "People won't necessarily shop at this particular franchise." Socially, Pottery Barn may have been a lumbering hulk, but technologically, they had us whipped. We should have just typed a list of things we needed for our new home on my 1956 Royal Quiet Deluxe, photocopied it, and tucked it inside each invitation to let the decor chips fall where they may.

The world wasn't ready for us.

"We could try this," the clerk offered. She'd typed "Barth/ Grossman" in the bride box.

"No. That looks like Barth divided by Grossman," Lisa said. "We can't be the first same-sex couple to have registered here. If you don't get this figured out, you're going to lose lots of business. There are lots of us out there." Raised to be nice, Lisa struggles to express anger. "I know this isn't your fault, but your—your damn system isn't right." The whole damn system wasn't right.

Right or not, people found a way to use it. Periodic printouts showed that someone had bought the eight-piece Mexican drinking glasses and matching pitcher, the 300-thread count Egyptian cotton sheets, the heavy, black-handled knife that the wives' tale said we would slice our relationship to bits with if we weren't careful. Not only were people using our bridal registry, they were coming to our wedding.

◆ ◆ ◆

The lesbian at Sunflower Rentals allowed us to borrow the rental tent so we could see how easy it would be to assemble if it rained on our wedding day.

"She's going to figure it out," I said, glancing toward our next-door neighbor's house. Her name was Dorothy, and we left her off the guest list because I worried about upsetting her. She was eighty-seven years old, and I couldn't bear losing the only old person who had ever crossed the line of my lifelong distrust of old people to become my friend. While Lisa and I set the posts for the wedding arbor, Dorothy said. "You two are the workingest girls I've ever seen."

"She can see everything," I said.

"Yes," Lisa said. "Shouldn't we just invite her?"

I'd hoped the huge blue-and-white-striped wad of vinyl and rope at our feet might stretch along the fence between our yard and Dorothy's like the backside of a circus, blotting the inexplicable from her view. Lisa snapped a Polaroid of me holding an armful of tangled rope next to the disassembled heap before we returned it. Our tiny yard couldn't contain such a monstrosity.

You can't hide a wedding. The morning of the ceremony, my only responsibility was to pick up two white balloons and a flat of strawberries. While I tied the balloons to the mailbox, Dorothy came out on her porch, smiling, waving me toward her. I waved back and scurried into the house, pretending I hadn't seen her call me. It was inevitable she knew: the yard was full of white chairs and our trees were wrapped in crepe paper and there were ice buckets and a punch bowl and champagne flutes stacked in pyramids and Jeff the Cakeman had just stumbled over the curb and caught our three-tier wedding cake in midair like the Cat in the Hat. The mix tape of preceremony classical selections Lisa and I had agonized over played loudly into our backyard in a neighborhood of people we didn't know yet, some of whom were college students I'd been known to call the police on because the noise of their lives was bothering me, because I couldn't live and let live.

◆ ◆ ◆

Individual things had gone awry at each of my sisters' weddings. Moments before Daddy was to walk Karen down the aisle, several buttons popped off her dress, which Aunt Lucy had sewn back on with needle and thread pulled from what seemed to me then to be her bottomless white purse. Thanks to one of Daddy's Valiums that Momma had given her, nothing bothered Karen. She only remembered two things from the entire evening: seeing her face reflected in the pastor's shiny shoes and some green pillow mints. At Kathy's wedding, Dovie the organist, in a last-minute ethical crisis, refused to play Mendelssohn's "Wedding March" because it had been associated with something historically gruesome. Kim's ceremony was in August and it was so hot the frosting slid off the cake in the humid church basement. The jubilant wedding party clacked down the stairs to find what looked like three round tiers of foam rubber. Individual, unintentional things had gone wrong at my good sisters' normal weddings. But not only did I not have a groom, I was the groom. I set out to make the kind of mistake no one would laugh about later.

Standing stock still in my air-conditioned living room, surrounded by my "people," as our planner called them, and still wearing my "Conjunction Junction What's Your Function" T-shirt and cutoffs, I suffered a paroxysm of denial. I felt perfectly comfortable avoiding the bedroom where waited the clothes I had selected for the occasion—my linen overalls, vest, and antique men's white shirt and silver cuff links. After our rehearsal the night before, we'd fallen asleep in the middle of *The Absent-Minded Professor*, the one where Fred MacMurray keeps forgetting to go to his own wedding. We stopped the tape just as one of his students used his "flubberized" sneakers to clear the backboard during a game against State. With just minutes to the ceremony, I asked Lisa if she wanted to go downstairs and finish watching it. "Put your clothes on," she said. "We don't have time for your nonsense." She helped me get dressed. I suddenly felt ridiculous. "But I'll look like an Amish man," I said.

"Skin the bunny," she said as she pulled my T-shirt off. I had no hairdo to muss, no tears to run the mascara that wasn't there. I had no one to tell me how beautiful I looked, how proud they were of me. There were no scripted prenuptial scenes, just sweat and absolute, white-knuckle terror.

✦ ✦ ✦

We took a long hot walk across the yard to the arbor Lisa had built while "Jesu, Joy of Man's Desiring" played in the background. I checked in with Imaginary Jesus once or twice for approval as we left the mudroom for the yard, approval that he gave as tangibly as an imaginary friend can, with an imaginary smile, an imaginary hand on my shoulder. But he could only be as encouraging as my own anxiety would let him.

The construction cones at either end of the alley kept all but one car from driving behind our wedding bower. It zoomed by during the monarch butterfly release that, against our better judgment, a friend insisted we must include. We yanked the delicate things from a cooler of dry ice and unfolded them from purple pieces of paper with a quote about the buoyancy of love. Mine sat dazed on the crease for so long I feared we had killed her in our frantic search for meaning. Finally, she came to her senses and fluttered to a lower limb of our pin oak where she would sit through the "light supper" a chef friend had prepared as a gift we would never have been able to afford. As my Baptist pastor/ therapist told us to kiss the bride, we heard the last tray of phyllo beef triangles set off the smoke detector. The sight of us through the kitchen window had distracted my friend's sous-chef. We had made her cry.

"And how does it feel?" I would have a hard time telling everyone who asked me, my cheeks cramped from frantically smiling through blessings and toasts in spite of all I had not done right, in spite of the tempered joy I felt about everyone who I had decided shouldn't be there, people who wouldn't understand or approve. Newspapers wouldn't have printed our engagement announcement if we'd had one. We'd laughed and the world wasn't laughing with us. I wanted what I could not have: for everyone to be happy for me.

A week later, Lisa came in the house white as one of our new Hers and Hers pillowcases.

"I told her," she said.

"Told who," I said. "What?"

"Dorothy. She'd figured it out. She just wanted us to tell her."

Lisa arranged us on the couch, me on one end and herself on the other, so I could see how she and Dorothy had sat. "When she said, 'That was some party,' I said, 'Actually, it was a wedding.' She asked if it was your wedding or my wedding."

When Lisa told her we had married each other, Dorothy quickly found a context to put us in. She told a story about two lesbian friends she used to visit in Russell, Kansas, on a train route that doesn't exist anymore, and remembered how devoted they had been to each other.

Lisa told her how afraid we had been that she wouldn't like us anymore. Dorothy grabbed her arm and said, "I'm so glad you told me. Don't you worry now. You're my girls."

"That's it?" I said.

I'd like to say that my wedding was a spiritual culmination, that I found peace, but I remember the day only as an anxious, bittersweet blur. In going through the motions, I got only a small taste of what Thomas Moore calls in *The Soul of Sex* "the deep fantasy and reality" of the marriage union that couples whose relationships are legally and socially blessed feast upon. I got a small taste also of "the deep repercussions" of the ritual, legal or not, and of all the future would both give and require of me. I had been entrusted to explore the uncharted territory of a soul I barely knew and of my own as well. Though we benefitted from the freedom from rules and from defined roles that prevent true knowing of the other, we would also suffer from the loss of the protection legal marriage provides against those who would try to undermine the very real bonds it created. I knew we would need all the help and encouragement we could get. Whether I was ready for them to check my work or not, a few important people in my life knew I had arrived at the correct answer.

14

Hush Little Baby, Don't Say a Word

I thought I knew for certain my family would never change their minds about homosexuality. I stored proof of this in a mental folder swollen with records of everything I had ever heard them utter on the subject. I had absolute recall of setting, wording, and what I and the other person had been wearing. Whenever I needed a cautionary tale against self-disclosure, I had any number of flashbacks to choose from. The recollection of each stung like a paper cut.

Here's the first one: I am six and Kim is ten, and we are sitting next to each other in our musty family room in matching corduroy slacks with elastic waistbands. An *Encyclopedia Britannica* is open across our laps. Something in a picture seems queer to me. Kim slaps my face to reset my moral compass, which she often took it upon herself to do. She says, "Don't ever say queer again." "Why?" I say. "It means odd, yes, but it also means a daddy who likes a daddy or a momma who likes a momma, which they shouldn't, ever. It's a bad word about bad people." That afternoon marked the first time in my life I made the connection: I was a bad person.

Just eight months before I came out, I vowed never to actually do so to my family because I could not quite yet bear the thought of saying goodbye to them. I had every intention of spending the rest of our lives pretending not to love Lisa in front of them, not to be married to her, even though for the last five, she and I had lived in the same house.

Though no stranger to lying, I was now competing in a division I hadn't properly trained for. Out of sheer necessity, I'd built a falsehood so tall and ridiculous that I held my breath for fear of the crash that never came. No matter how many rickety stories I jerry-rigged, everyone continued to buy the fabrication. When my family toured our new house during the Memorial Day picnic we hosted, Karen's ultraconservative husband, Roger, said, "Where does Lisa sleep?" Thanks to an innate reluctance to think deeply, he swallowed the hook that she slept on a futon in our damp basement, which was full of crickets. Momma, who followed Roger on the tour, didn't seem to remember that I'd already told her Lisa slept on the sleeper couch in the living room. I made a mental note to self-flagellate later for not keeping my lies straight.

I needn't have worried. My family preferred the lie. What's more, they even helped with its construction and maintenance. Despite evidence to the contrary, I remained everyone's little Kelly. I still mentioned Jesus, whom they believed would keep me from straying as far away as it appeared I might already have. We ate hot dogs and hamburgers, which I pretended to still like, on my new patio as if not a thing had changed, as if two grown women purchasing a house together happened all the time. That last Memorial Day as little Kelly, I channeled Shirley Temple. I was sunshiny.

"I thought about calling the police to report you missing," Lisa said after everyone left.

So badly did my family need to believe my tall tale, they told it to others. At the Easter Sunrise Breakfast at Trinity Presbyterian, I listened to Daddy tell it to Mr. Wade, a frowning, liver-spotted church elder. I sat across from them at a newsprint-covered fold-

ing table in the freezing cold basement dining hall, which smelled
of forced daffodils, coffee, and sausage.

"It's just so much cheaper for her to live with Lisa," Daddy said
pointing at Lisa and me one at a time with a forked sausage. "They
save money, such money. You wouldn't believe the cost of houses
in Lawrence. It just makes so much good sense."

An unconvinced Mr. Wade nodded at us in our wedding slacks
and shirts we'd worn for the past three Easters. Daddy looked
across at me and smiled, his face still red with effort. At that moment, I forgave him everything in our troubled past.

When the unexpected visit Lisa and I had feared getting from
Kathy finally occurred, the lie threatened to topple. Before I
could react, she'd "helloed" her way through the front yard into
the back, where I stood wearing my ball cap backward and a wife-
beater and shorts that exposed armpit and leg hair. I was covered
with bicycle grease. I looked up with Edenic shame. In a futile attempt to preen, I turned the mangled greasy bill of my cap around
where it should have been. I could hear Lisa stumbling around in
the house sliding apart dirty sentences of magnetic poetry, taking
down our framed wedding invitation from its place on the shelf
over the toilet, removing the Hers and Hers pillowcases a friend
had embroidered us, and cleaning obscure art books I would never read off the end table on her side of the bed.

I don't know what I thought Kathy would discover that I hadn't
already told her. In the eight years since I'd tried unsuccessfully
to convince her I was a lesbian, I hadn't given Kathy much credit.
She'd seen everything. For a while longer, we played let's pretend.
I changed into pants even though it was too hot to wear them, and
we talked about nothing for an hour while Lisa watched, pretending to be just my best friend.

Lisa had searched for any resemblance between my sisters
and I, but found none. It's as if my parents closed their eyes and
plucked me from a grab bag barrel. They had to have been surprised by what they pulled out. In childhood pictures, I am all
scabs and big new permanent teeth, ridged so deeply they look as
if someone has taken a rasp to them. I am uncombed, confident,

and replete. There is no problem my parents can't talk me out of or fix; between the two of them, there is no need they cannot meet. I wanted to remain like that for them forever. I wanted them always to love me. I wanted them always to let my strangeness in their house. More than anything, I feared being unwelcome.

As I began to entertain the smallest of thoughts of my seventy-something parents finally knowing the tomboy foundling in all the pictures, I sought ways to test the strength of our connection. One visit, I quizzed them about my birthday and my age. Daddy could come up with neither. Momma nailed the birthday, but had to use paper and pencil to work out the age. "What's my middle name," I blurted out. Pressured, both of them drew a blank, and then she said, "You're Kelly Lee, my youngest, my last. I don't even need Vitamin E to remember that."

"What's my full name," Daddy said, "and my birthday?"

"Robert George, but you go by George because there were too many Roberts and Bobs and Juniors in the family already. October 6."

"What is October 6?" he said. "Please phrase your answer in the form of a question."

◆ ◆ ◆

With the holidays bearing down, Lisa bartered a painting for nine hours of therapy. During one of these hours, I announced to both her and our therapist that I thought it was time for me to come out. Our therapist leaned forward, her eyes gleaming. "I just knew you'd come around. You won't regret it."

Lisa, however, sat at the other end of the couch from me, stunned. "This is the first I've heard," she said.

"I know," I said. This would, after all, affect both of us. We'd reached a delicate peace with my family. People had stopped welcoming her effusively as if she weren't ever coming back. My nieces had stopped asking me why I wasn't married. They even, in a deep, teenage way of understanding, threatened to show Lisa my engagement picture with fat Royall Baker, who no one had liked a fraction as well. Not quite a member of the family, Lisa felt no guilt curling up on the carpet behind Momma's La-Z-Boy like an aging retriever after Christmas lunch to nap for a bit while we opened too many packages.

"I just can't go one more holiday pretending," I said on the drive home. "And I have a family now with you if I'm no longer welcome in theirs."

My therapist made me set a date so I wouldn't substitute intention for actuality. I chose July, two weeks after the 4th. I didn't want them to associate the detonation with any national holidays. Should things go badly, we'd have a good long stretch of days to see clearly across with no obstructions until Labor Day and their anniversary, neither of which we celebrated anyway.

In February, I sent out a query letter of sorts to friends. In it, I explained my plans and asked them to write back telling me why they liked me. Throughout March, responses came in. Several people offered to legally adopt me if worst came to worst. I put all of the letters in a manila folder and read one a day like a religious devotional. Throughout the spring and early summer, my panic continued to rise. Finally, there was nothing left to do. I'd read all the books. I'd memorized all my affirmations and used up four therapy visits. "Not that you have any reason to worry," my therapist said, "but I'd save some of these sessions for after."

One sweltering day in July, I sat down at my desk to write the letter I swore I never would. It was my way of exposing my roots, so my parents could examine all that had been hidden. I wrote one draft with no erasures—the vocabulary and handwriting of a twelve-year-old. I wrote variations of the same letter to my three sisters.

Mail sent from Lawrence arrives in Kansas City the following day. By early afternoon, I knew they would all be opening their business-size envelopes—my way of warning them of the contents. I half-expected to feel seismic activity from the east. For lunch, I bicycled to the Merc, our local co-op, to buy something reminiscent of the Jeno's pizza rolls of my childhood. Inside them were organic white bits that weren't cheese and brown bits that weren't pepperoni. Despite the heat, I fired up the oven to bake them so they would taste more nearly like what I remembered. Lisa and I ate them quickly, marveling at the puddles of organic orange grease each one left on our plates. I wiped my mouth with a paper towel, pulled all the blinds, stripped to my underwear, and sat in the dark waiting for the phone to ring. Three months later, the first sign of the ulcer that began to form because of that afternoon would manifest, a burning pain just below my sternum. When the phone rang, I felt as if someone had run me through with a sword. Kathy's first words were, "We all knew. Of course, we all knew." It was 3:00 p.m. Everyone knew. How dumb did I think they all were?

"Momma and Daddy even?" I said.

"I put a few bugs in their ear a while back," she said.

"Bugs?"

"I tried to prepare them a little bit. I said I thought you were a couple."

I checked my pulse. It was in the 150s. "And what did they say to that?"

"They didn't believe me. I told Karen the same thing."

"You told Karen?" I shouted. I imagined Karen watching me slowly backslide, sloughing off Jesus and the robes of righteousness on my way down.

"Well, you'd told me a few years back. Remember? So I just started hinting to make this all go a little more smoothly."

"This? You knew *this* was coming?"

"Everybody's okay. We all knew." I didn't believe her, but it was her way of calming us both. It was like in the movies when men in white coats plunge a needle into the hysteric's arm and she quickly stops thrashing.

I told Kathy I loved her, which only made her cry. The only time anyone in my family besides Momma ever says "I love you" is when someone is in intensive care.

I hung up the phone and sat in the dark again. The phone rang. This time I felt a sharp pain in my medulla oblongata, my lizard brain. I answered it on the half-ring.

As if watching an egg timer, Karen hurriedly said, "I have three things to say, and then I don't ever want to talk about this again: I don't understand, I don't approve, but I love you to death." She said she couldn't wait to see Lisa and me again. We didn't see each other enough. That was all she wanted to say, and then she hung up. What she did not say rang in my ears: What about my eternal salvation? In the kingdom parable, I was the seed that fell among weeds. My love of truth had been choked out by the cares of the world, by my own desires. I would find out later that her whole family knew, even Roger, who wrote checks to people who blamed my kind for the increasing number of tornadoes, hurricanes, and other rumblings of God's displeasure. She'd opened my letter around the lunch table, and her family had demanded to know why she had gone sheet white.

My oldest nephew, Luke, said only this: "Well, duh."

Kim's letter would arrive a week later saying that, though I went against everything she had ever been taught, she wanted to know when Lisa and I were coming back down to the Ozarks for a visit.

Until my parents called, the pizza rolls sat in my body as if in a holding tank, not digesting, simply pausing before expulsion. I imagined that Momma was on the "big numbers" phone in their living room; Daddy was on the extension fastened to the dining room wall. He told me what they'd been doing before and after they opened the letter, just as people recount how, on the day John F. Kennedy was shot, exactly what they were chewing, what street they'd been crossing, what color their math teacher's shirt had been on that day. They had been finishing up a lunch of tomato and peanut butter on toast, a concoction Momma ate as a child that apparently tastes better than it sounds, and one that would probably never taste the same to them.

"I'd just set my plate off to the side over there by the violets," he said. On a walnut table my great-grandfather had built with a hand plane, saw and pegs, my parents grew a circle of potted African violets. Underneath the table were ancient burns from stubbed out cigarettes left by my great-grandfather, my grandfather and my uncles and aunts, all of whom played Hearts there after family dinners. Once, Daddy had taken my finger between his own, like a paintbrush, and run it back and forth across the burn marks so I would know they were there and who had made them.

"We'd just finished *All My Children*," Momma said. "I still had some apple left."

"Do you still?" I said.

"Well, yes. It's brown now, but yes."

"Are you all right?" I said.

"Well, yes, of course," she said. "But tell me this—why would you think we wouldn't want to see you again? I don't ever want to stop seeing you. It worries me that you don't know that."

"Things like this can change things," I said.

"Well, they shouldn't."

"So you're all right?" I said.

"Well, I'm not going to pretend we weren't surprised. Isn't that fair to say, Nadine?" I could picture Daddy looking up toward Momma, checking to make sure he hadn't offended me. He'd offended all of us without knowing it too many times to mention. That was his *bête noir*, and Momma's job was to alert him before he said one word more.

Daddy's irritability and general lack of social skills had been attributed to heart trouble. It had been suggested to us as children that Daddy shouldn't get angry. He had free rein to say anything he wanted to us. We were to absorb any words we felt we needed to say in self-defense. We were not to fight over the soap as we washed up for dinner. Neither were we to sing or laugh at the table. We were not to ask "why" more than once. We were not to have difficulty understanding his explanations of our math homework. We were not to use a footstool for anything other than a footstool. We were not to have insomnia. We were not to stir our ice cream, something we were all obsessively driven to do. When in doubt, we were not to do anything he would not do.

✦ ✦ ✦

"Remember," said my therapist. "Your father would have been a much different man if he hadn't had four children. You all drove him crazy. He wanted your mother; she wanted children. She won. That's it. I'm not saying it's your fault or that you could have done anything about it."

I'd long known there was more to Daddy than heart disease and irritation since the day he carried home the neighbor's dog in a bloody sheet from the busy street by our house. It was a memory I alone had of him—no one else had been there—and the one that tripped me up whenever I wanted to write him off. He'd taken me on his lap, something he never did, to see if I needed to talk to him about what had happened. He'd taken our not-small dog Cindy on his lap, too. The two of us sat wriggling precariously, one on each of his knees. Was there anything I needed to ask, anything at all? "Is Sparky in heaven?" I said. He knew the official church doctrine. "Daddy thinks he is," speaking of himself in the third person, calling on a higher, nicer authority than himself. His face was wet with tears.

Still, I couldn't have relied on occasional lapses into kindness and empathy. My sisters and I said we didn't believe we should be held responsible if something one of us said or did caused the heart attack Momma had always feared. We said that, in life, everyone must manage his own anger, but none of us believed it.

I had only one recollection to gauge what his response might be to my announcement. Watching *60 Minutes*, we'd been blindsided by an interview with Mel White, ghostwriter of the biographies of Jerry Falwell, Oliver North, and Billy Graham. After White finished writing these biographies, he came out of the closet. In my parents' dark, air-conditioned living room, Daddy and I watched White describe how he told his loving wife that he could no longer keep up the façade.

I remember setting my half-finished Salisbury steak TV dinner on the coffee table. I moved carefully, slowly forward as you do when you want to get a close look at a flighted insect without frightening it away. I wanted to check my Daddy's face. I saw no reaction at all, which, at the time, I thought, was good for a man, for any man.

I didn't have as hard a time imagining Momma's reaction: shock, tears, and eventual equilibrium. I'd sifted through my memories of her comments about homosexuals. Gay and Lesbian Day at Worlds of Fun amusement park had always brought the same complaints. "They can be gay, I don't care, but this is a family place. Children shouldn't be made to see that." About the precise meaning of "that" I didn't press her. I remembered her fascination with a high school gym teacher who looked like a man. "Even then, even in those days, we knew," she said. "But we didn't talk about it." She missed the days when women could walk down the street holding hands, linking arms, like she used to do with her girlfriends. "Now people get the wrong idea." She'd said all these things with the confidence that I, a Christian young woman, wholeheartedly agreed with her.

In college, I'd asked her to videotape episodes of *Leave It to Beaver*. I watched them on days of bad writing workshops. I took them like opiates. Nothing could go wrong in the twenty minutes I watched pencil-waisted June icing a cake for the boys to eat when they got home from school, pouring them cold milk from a glass bottle. But then, in the middle of the one about Beaver trapped in the soup bowl on a billboard, was a surprise. Momma had, I'm sure, popped in any tape she could find to record a *Nightline* that featured a panel of men on either side of the late '80s debate in the Presbyterian Church over whether gay people could be ordained, a debate they still haven't quite settled. It snapped me back into the world, her world, her anger at people like me. "The gays are splitting the church," she wrote in a letter to me about the same time. I was destroying her church. She had been destroying me.

I weighed the risk. I wagered we'd pull through, she and I. No one but Imaginary Jesus valued me more highly, loved me more fiercely. I still had the emotional bruises to show for it. She kept the last toothbrush I had used at the house until its bristles turned gray with dust out of fear, I suppose, that if she threw it away, I'd think she no longer expected me home.

Now that they both knew, she wasn't sobbing and his heart was still beating. "We've got lots of questions, Kelly, and I'm sure you've got lots of answers," he said. "When you come over, we'll see if any of them match up." Instead of angry to the point of cardiac arrest, he'd chosen to act goofy. Maybe he understood what it had taken for me to be the first to wave the white flag. "Here I really am," I had said. "Over here."

They wanted to meet with me alone. "And we look forward to it," Momma said, with welcome in her voice. "We love you very much, more than ever."

When I stood to hang up the phone, I noticed I had soiled my underwear. It wasn't anybody's fault. Underwear are easily replaced. As mean-spirited as it may sound, I had given my parents a final exam. Not only had they passed, they had aced it. They loved me without reservation. No coming-out books prepare you for that.

◆ ◆ ◆

All important family papers come attached to a clipboard: taxes, my sisters' wedding guest rosters, vacation packing lists, and initial sketches of Daddy's garden projects. So, it came as little surprise to see both he and Momma holding clipboards when they answered the door together. Until then, as I was the only one in the room without one, I hadn't realized how much power clipboards give you, how much order and security they give to secure life's unclippables.

My parents sat in their respective corners of the room studying me in my rocking chair by the television. They'd asked me to sit where they could both see me clearly. No longer simply their youngest daughter, I had become a fragile curiosity. In thirty-five years, how could they have missed so much? In jeans and a T-shirt, I didn't feel properly dressed. I could smell Momma's powder on my cheek where she had pressed hers as soon as I came in the door. As always, the hinge of her big glasses had pulled out a strand of my hair. She brushed it out of her face as she ran down her list.

"First, let me say that Daddy and I are so glad, so happy that you are here today. Happy and . . . gratified."

"I'm kind of nervous," I said. One of the rails of my rocker scratched the baseboard behind me as I leaned backward. "Sorry," I said. Daddy never liked what his children did in rocking chairs.

"Don't be nervous," she said. "We love you very much, don't we, Daddy?"

He nodded and made a tick mark on his clipboard.

Struggling to sit up straight in the squishy La-Z-Boy she'd inherited when my Aunt Lucy died, Momma referred to her list.

"First of all, did we do something wrong? I mean, was it something we did?"

Coming out books said that first parents pity you for being the recipient of the pain they have inflicted on you, and second they pity you for living a life that terrifies them. What parents don't understand is that if parenting mistakes caused homosexuality, everyone would be gay. I'd practiced this answer.

"No, you did something right. I always felt loved and safe. I'm very happy," I said, and then pushed it. "In fact, I'm glad I'm gay. I can't imagine being any other way."

Momma shivered involuntarily and then recovered. She seemed to remember which gay person she was talking to.

"I don't think of myself as your failure."

"No, no, no, no, no," Momma said. "I've always been proud, so proud of you. I haven't bragged about you because I don't think that's right. But I always wanted to."

"It wouldn't have hurt anything," I said. "You were a good mother, after all."

She wiped a tear off her papers. Daddy took the lead. "How long have you known?" he said.

I'd expected this one, too. Everyone, especially parents, asked it. "Since I was about four, I think."

"Did you feel like a little boy?" she said.

"No, just a human, I think. Just a person."

"Because, you remember, you wanted the cowboy, not the cow-girl outfit, and you loved all those little metal cars. I should have known," she said. "And then that Army man, that cheap little thing you had to have from Cosentino's."

"You remember that?" I said. And there I was, holding my most perfect toy in my hand again, the hard green body with the pink and red face. At the grand opening of Cosentino's Thriftway, each child could choose from a huge spinner rack of free toys to keep her mother as a loyal customer. My Army man had accessories that came off. There was a canteen, a knife in its own sheath, a tiny grenade, a flashlight, and a handgun, which I never really recovered from losing. Also, there was a perfect green helmet with a chin strap that I helped him use for other things like eating a thimbleful of soup, just like the one Daddy said he ate from while in France during the war.

It was Daddy's turn. "Who plays the male role in the relationship?" and then he reconsidered. "That's okay if I ask? I don't want to pry. We're just trying to understand."

"Actually, we don't play roles, and do you know where I learned that?" I said. "Here. You two. There never was a real division of labor."

Despite this clarification, Daddy would continue to slap Lisa on the shoulder with camaraderie and say things like, "Are you going to let her treat you like that?" Once he asked her if I gave her the money he'd sent to cover a meal we fixed for Momma's birthday. "I'll bet she just spent it all shopping, didn't she?"

She leaned forward, peering over her clipboard. "Are you having safe sex? That's what I'm worried about. It doesn't seem safe. You can get sick. Have you thought about AIDS?"

Not since I was twelve and Kim exposed the fact that I still didn't know the sexual difference between boys and girls had Momma said the word *sex* regarding me. As far as she knew, there had been no context for it. I'd showed no authentic romantic interest in anyone.

Here, I thought, I could reassure her.

"Actually, Lisa and I have very uncheckered pasts."

"I don't understand that kind of sex, and I don't want to," she stopped me cold.

"All I meant was that we haven't had . . ."

She held her pencil hand up.

". . . multiple partners."

She put her free hand over her ear.

"We've both led pretty boring lives as far as that goes."

"As long as you're safe, that's all I want to hear."

"Also, are you careful in public? People aren't nice, Kelly," she said, coming out from behind the safety of her clipboard. "You could be in danger."

I don't know if Momma ever had violent thoughts. But I know she imagined violence. So vivid were her imaginings that she played little mental movies of them, the plots and outcomes of which she recounted to me before I left the safety of her presence. "You could be pulled into a passing car, off your bicycle, brutalized, left for dead in a ditch." Not just a ditch, a water-filled ditch. I didn't know if she ever had violent thoughts about homosexuals and what should happen to them. But I do know that now that she knew one, and now that that homosexual was me, her youngest, everything had changed. Whatever disgust she felt she digested finally with the coming of my letter and released from her body forever. She had comprehended the incomprehensible for me.

Ever practical, Daddy covered finances. Did we have a joint checkbook? How did we pay our bills? Did I have enough money in the event that things didn't work out, not that he didn't want them to?

"Do you have a will," he said, "medical power of attorney?"

The questions didn't astound me, but that they knew to ask them did.

"Because if you don't," Momma chimed in, "the hospital staff won't allow you to see each other in intensive care. You know that, don't you? You have to be family on paper."

"Yes, we have all that written down."

"And an executor."

"Yes, Carole."

"Carole Bradley?"

"Yes."

This relieved my Momma. Carole was one of my few friends she still knew.

"She's gay, too, isn't she?" she said.

"Yes," I said. I hoped Carole didn't mind, but I would have confessed anything. The 75-watt bulb in the lamp over my rocking chair had begun to make me sweat.

Daddy smiled. "Still nervous?"

"A little." I felt my face relax, my brows lower.

"I just have a few more," he said. "How about you, Nadine, about finished?"

"Yes, I think I'm almost finished. I'll check for strays."

Daddy ran his flat, silky fingertip down the list I couldn't see, then stopped, "Oh yes, are you planning to have any sort of ceremony?"

I said, "Well, actually, we already had one. A really small one, just a few friends. I wanted to tell you, but I just couldn't then. I wasn't ready. I'm so sorry about that, but . . ."

Momma leaned forward in her La-Z-Boy. One of its springs groaned. "That's all right," she said.

"I would have if I could have. I want you to know that."

"That's one of the things your church has been trying to decide, whether to allow same-gender unions, right?" Daddy said. "We think that's real good, that you have a supportive church." He read about Broadway Baptist frequently in the newspaper since it got so much free publicity from the protests of Fred Phelps and the congregation of Westboro Baptist.

Who was this progressive and where had he taken Daddy?

"Yes, it is," I said. "We're still working toward that, I hope."

Seeing me pick at a cuticle, Momma said, "Not the fingers again, Kelly."

I realized right then why I'd chewed my fingers all those years. I'd needed to inflict my own compelling pain, pain that I could control, to distract me from the pain I could not.

"And, last but not least," he said with a flourish of his pencil, "will you be having children?"

Only then did I realize how barely we knew each other.

"Just wondering," he said with as much of a smile as he can manage with lips that, like mine, naturally turn down at the corners.

"No, no." Then for a laugh, I said, "A thousand times no."

I didn't look at Momma after this question. Only just that Black Friday after Thanksgiving, we'd covered this topic in the car in a Wal-Mart parking lot while she, Karen, and I waited for Kathy and her son Travis to fight thousands of other shoppers for one of only fifty $40 DVD players. "She'll act differently when she has children," Momma said when Karen asked how I could stay so calm all the time. "No, that's why I am calm," I said, "and I'm not planning to change that."

"Oh, you'll meet a man and fall in love and have children."

"Let me say it again. I'm never going to have children. Never." And in case she hadn't heard me, I said again, "Never."

A silence fell and then she said, "Well, that's sad."

"Not for me," I said.

"For the rest of us then," she said.

I still worry today that Momma mistook my reluctance to take on anything as difficult and heartbreaking as child-rearing as a rejection or disapproval of the job she herself had relished. It was one of the many conversations we were never really to finish.

◆ ◆ ◆

"Well, I guess that's about it," Daddy said.

"What's the diagnosis, Doc?" I said.

"No diagnosis," he said. "You're ours, and we love you. Nothing wrong. We just go on from here."

I excused myself to the hall bathroom. Diarrhea again.

"See there, that's why you have stomach problems like me," Momma called down the hallway. "That comes from keeping things inside too long, carrying them around, worrying about them."

Daddy picked up his clipboard, found a clear sheet of paper, and started a letter to Lisa, officially welcoming her to the family.

They both followed me down the stairs just as they always did. We moved slowly, descending one stair, climbing two again to say something else. Finally, at the threshold I had crossed thousands of times, at the door with the tarnished brass plate screwed to it that read "The Robert G. Barths: As for me and my house, we will serve the Lord," Momma laid her head on my shoulder, as the baby I planned never to have might have done in a moment of exhaustion and trust.

Daddy trailed behind still clutching his clipboard, his pencil behind his ear. He gave me the same hug I always get from him. Only one side of our chests touched and part of the side of our faces.

More stunned than usual from the goodbye, I took crab steps down their terrace, where they could never get grass to grow.

"Careful, don't slip," she said. "Daddy fell the other day mowing."

I looked back again and again to wave. We had done that, she and I, since the first time I began leaving her. She waved longer than all the other mothers. I would look up to see if she had gone, tired of watching me. But each time I looked, she waved. She watched as I walked past the Logemans, the Coombses, the Smithsons, and the Pernices. She waved as I reached to the tip of the cul-de-sac where the Munozes' sycamore finally blocked her from view. She stood framed in the glass of the storm door, looking, and when I looked back, smiling and waving. In all the times I left the house, I never saw her leave the door. In my mind's eye, she is still there, black-haired and beautiful, watching for me.

That day, she and Daddy, the R.G. Barths, served the Lord. They served *as* the Lord to the stranger they had never really known, treating me as Imaginary Jesus always had with love, understanding, and respect. They made room for me.

Just as I had with my biological family, I had to risk giving my church the same chance to really know me, to welcome the stranger.

15

Swarming

For Daddy and other Presbyterians, the lure of doldrums is strong. Pastors come and go as their ideas either become stale or outgrow the church. Rather than attempt the rare and painful pastoral extraction themselves, Presbyterian congregations rely on a larger governing body, the Presbytery, to act on their behalf. They themselves don't have to fight the battles over what they believe and over who will lead them. Presbyterians take their religion warm with a little milk and sugar, nothing fancy, no surprises. They know what they do not know and are content.

My sisters and I were raised on liturgical worship, responsive readings, rote confessional prayer, and short, smart sermons of extended metaphor. Such predictability allows people of a phlegmatic and intellectual temperament to better approach the Sacred. God isn't always in a lather, popping out from between the seams of reality with an interpretive dance or a doxology played in cut-time with a screaming electric mandolin interlude.

Unlike Presbyterians, Baptists appreciate and anticipate spiritual disruption. Their services are regularly interrupted with spectaculars starring sock puppets with button eyes and missionaries bringing slide shows of tidings from jungle or desert. And

Baptists are restless, Daddy says. When things get too hot, a little too tight, a bunch of them pack up themselves and their problems and swarm to a new church where, if only for a while, they can live in the illusion of blessed agreement. To my Presbyterian parents' chagrin, both Karen and I consorted with Baptists. Perhaps because the word reminded us that we had rejected our religious heritage, Karen and I had trouble spelling our adopted denomination. "I think you just have to say it to yourself," Karen told me. "It's spelled like it sounds. It's not Babtist, but Bap-tist with a *p*." This didn't help me. People mispronounce it. I'd mispronounced it. That's another thing that bothered Daddy about Baptists; they were too open to misspelling and misinterpretation. Denominational shape-shifters, they could be anything or nothing at all. Big or small. Collectively gentle or strident all at once. As such, they weren't easily governed and couldn't get along in large groups.

Karen's hive was very different from mine. Though we would both eventually swarm, there our Baptist paths wildly diverged. She had a stern, unhappy pastor who inflicted his dwindling, already-saved congregation with lengthy altar calls every Sunday, as if he didn't believe they were really in the fold. Children in her church were encouraged to make pumpkin and corn centerpieces for Mother and eat caramel apples at their Harvest Party instead of "messing around" with Halloween. (Here Karen used her own discretion. Her two sons and daughter went to the Harvest Party, yes, but she also let them trick or treat within a three-block radius of their house. As far as she could see, Smarties and Tootsie Rolls had nothing to do with Satan.) For fun, youth group members at Karen's church stood atop planters at a local shopping mall to preach and hand out tracts. After, they went out for pizza, and they left a tract for their server with their collective wad of dollar bills. My niece told me that she and other girls in her youth group made a commitment never to show their knees.

When she first became a Baptist, Karen had an epic argument with my parents about infant baptism that never really ended. She didn't understand how a baby could intentionally sin. Babies couldn't understand, need, or want the real death and rebirth baptism meant for the Christian. My parents explained that it just represented the Presbyterian parents' desire to raise the baby in the church and to be a person of faith. "Then why not a baby dedication?" Karen said. "I'm sorry, I just think that's wrong. It's misleading and unscriptural." Karen's preacher, Carl, preached Jesus Christ and the crucifixion, and that water baptism killed the old person and gave birth to the new one, nothing more, nothing less. He took his Sanka crystals, which he kept at her house, boiling and black. He took his religion straight up, too. He didn't water it down with metaphor. Supernatural things were always black and white to him and to Karen.

Unlike Karen, I was drawn to my particular swarm of Baptists precisely because of their comfort with uncertainty, mine and everyone else's. I knew little other than that my friendship with Imaginary Jesus had been the longest and truest one of my life. I needed a church that could let me sit with my doubts and questions and, occasionally, my poorly held convictions as he had always allowed me to do. According to our pastor, doubting and theological wrestling was endemic to Baptists. Rather than the doctrinally rigid, repressed Southern Baptists that had by the 1980s come to be viewed as the only true Baptists, the denomination's founders were rebellious, fiercely independent, loosely organized, and "theologically curious." In America, they had even associated themselves with freethinkers. Our pastor quoted people like the Reverend George Truett, a notable early-twentieth-century Baptist pastor who said of his brethren, "They have forever been the unwavering champions of liberty, both religious and civil. Their contention now is, and has been, and, please God must ever be, that it is the natural and fundamental and indefeasible right of every human being to worship God or not, according to the dictates of his conscience, and, as long as he does not infringe upon the right of others, he is to be held accountable alone to God for all religious beliefs and practices."

"That's your heritage, people," said our visionary senior pastor who refused to wear a suit and tie or preach from a pulpit.

"Be true to your ancestors. Doubt. Ask questions. Cause trouble. Seek justice. Love mercy."

The Southern Baptist Convention, the organization run by Karen's kind of Baptist, threw mine out of the denomination. We didn't look like the kind of Baptists they had become, powerful enough to force all churches to resemble them. Not only did we welcome gays and lesbians as members, but our pastor also pushed his congregation to question the Southern Baptist refusal to allow them to marry.

A growing commitment to doing justice and loving mercy meant that my church attracted more gay people. We no longer had the room to avoid the contentious question of marriage equality, even if confronting it would crack us down the middle. Not that many of my fellow members believed that gay people shouldn't marry, but most of us believed that no one should be forced to believe that they should be allowed to marry. This was something our visionary, heartsick, and impatient pastor tried to do—force people to change. In the process, he overstepped his authority and contradicted his own passion for independent thinking, intentional listening, and consensus building. From the pulpit, he taught that we needed each other. Each and every one of us was a member of Christ's body, he said, and, as such, had powers both to teach and to heal: "Shall a toe say to the foot, I no longer need you, no, but rather when one part of the body hurts all hurt with it. The eye cannot say to the hand, I have no need of you. . . . And if one member suffers, all the members suffer with it; if one member is honored, all the members rejoice with it." We no longer needed someone to instruct us how to live our faith, he said. We needed, instead, to acknowledge our own gifts and God-given wisdom and to use them to build each other up. We all believed him. Right or wrong, we believed we needed to hear, understand, and love each other, no matter how frustrated we became in the process.

Lisa and I agreed to participate on a committee organized to build consensus around the issue of marriage equality. We quickly learned that as freethinkers, we must share our house with paradox. We must stand by our own convictions while at the same time allowing others to give voice to theirs. In a stuffy upper room of this church founded by freethinking immigrant Swedes, we had to learn to hear as well as be heard. We had to keep our wits and our tempers in the midst of incongruity. Though small in number, a vocal group of biblical literalists felt uncomfortable dismissing Levitical codes against homosexuality and the Apostle Paul's warnings about abomination. They openly shared these concerns with our committee. Elbow to elbow with these literalists sat a heterosexual woman, an elder—an office that, in the Southern Baptist church, she could not have filled—who protested that she could not see the barest minimum of logic in holding gay couples to the same standards of monogamy and faithfulness as heterosexuals without allowing them the same right to have their relationship blessed and respected. No one changed anyone else's mind right away, but we had created a forum where we could agree to disagree.

As the token lesbian couple on the committee, Lisa and I could speak to the significance of marriage and our unwillingness to wait for the church to tell us it was okay. After a score of meetings, we finally won the trust of a man who had shared during the first meeting that he didn't like lesbians. In time, he revealed that a lesbian couple his wife had tried to recruit as Sunday school teachers had impolitely refused. The incident caused him to jump to all sorts of prejudicial conclusions. After several months of meetings, he took me aside at a church greeting time to say that watching our relationship had blessed him. Other recalcitrant minds might have changed if we had been given enough time.

Progress was slow, but we were making it until the senior pastor ran out of patience. He wanted injustice to end immediately, and he abused his position and violated his principles to make that happen. He visited an associate pastor, the convener of our slow-as-molasses-in-winter committee, and fired him without consulting anyone.

It all came to light, and the church had a series of volatile meetings. In his own defense, the senior pastor composed sad, self-aggrandizing letters about his five-fold vision for the church.

He said that those who did not follow his vision were no longer following Christ. In his urgency for the church to hurry up and become affirming, he went slightly mad, which can easily happen to someone still trying to remain quiet in a closet they have outgrown. I can testify to that.

And so, we swarmed. Roughly ninety percent of us on the church membership rolls signed a roster at the back of the sanctuary at the last congregational meeting. We found a temporary place for the hive in the bar down the street until we could figure out what else to do. When a gay man, who had swarmed with us despite his fear that we might never resolve the issue so he could marry his partner at church, saw how many of us there were, he said, "Shit, this is a church." This phrase appeared on the first overhead projected onto the wall of the clubhouse of someone's housing division the next Sunday, where we would meet until we could decide where else to go and what else to do. For the next year or so, we carted around our ark of grief, confusion, and excitement; our podium and sound system; and our drums, amps, keyboard, and guitars wherever someone would let us pay them to worship there. We met in a lecture hall at the local Jesuit college, and a place called the Dream Center, which was part YMCA, part soup kitchen, and part church, a place with no air conditioning and a sanctuary that slanted back toward the audience instead of the other way around, as we were used to. Trying to make prophetic sense of our homelessness, some members compared us to the Israelites in the wilderness. We would learn to need no dwelling place but God, a term which had begun to mean different things to each one of us, which inevitably happens to my kind of Baptist. Given enough time, we can talk ourselves out of anything, even being Baptist. That's the risk and the gift of freethinking.

Eventually, we signed a long-term agreement to rent a basement worship space from Wornall Road Baptist, a church with a huge building and a pastorless, elderly, conservative, shrinking congregation that was having difficulty meeting its financial obligations. Even their young choir director and his new wife looked wizened and concerned. Opening the door to us gave them even more reasons to fret. In a moment of what they would finally decide was doctrinally unsound desperation and faithlessness, they had let a host of demons into their once clean and holy place.

They had had fair warning. From the beginning, we had made clear to them that our congregation contained real live homosexuals. They also knew that we would be clapping and playing drums and other loud instruments in their basement. Our worship rehearsal took place during their quiet service upstairs in the mint-green sanctuary with ivory brocade draperies over the windows and hard white wooden pews; George Washington would have felt comfortable there. We musicians had to be continually reminded to enter the building quietly on our way down the large hallway to worship rehearsal. We tiptoed past their wooden racks of tracts and the map pierced with white lights that indicated where in the world they were trying to convert others. Next, we snuck past the locked church office, past the hot, rumbling drinking fountain and then the closed green door to the sanctuary. Inside, they sang hymns to organ music played by an Asian graduate student wearing flip-flops over her panty hose. Our raucous service overlapped with their Sunday school hour, the beginning and ending of which were announced by a deafening buzzer outside the ladies restroom. We met each other coming and going. The spiritual alpha ladies from either group shook hands, hoping Jesus would do what he needed to fix the other. Where Wornall Road ladies envisioned repentance and salvation, the woman from our as yet unnamed church prayed for open hearts and minds.

Wisely, Imaginary Jesus chose to leave well enough alone. Even with these little bits of strained contact, patience wore brittle-thin. Eventually, we shared only a seventy-five-cup coffee pot and pained smiles. Wornall Road Baptist hired a great bull of a pastor and paid him with our rental money. We made one last disastrous attempt at cohabitation at an Easter service. We were permitted to play our "nontraditional" music if he were allowed to preach. In his sermon, he relied heavily on the metaphor of an ugly painting. Imaginary Jesus, thinly veiled as an art collector, bought this painting for such a heavy price that he put himself in financial jeopardy. We were the ugly painting; no one but Imaginary Jesus wanted us. We needed to accept Jesus's gift of salvation, stop being loud and homosexual, or stop leasing their basement. A twenty-minute altar call failed to produce any converts from our ranks, people the pastor could rest assured had now heard the unadulterated gospel. He urged his remaining congregation to "come out from among them and be ye separate." This meant they should stop relying on money from a godless, perverted fellowship and terminate the rental agreement within six weeks. Tossed out on its collective ear again, my new congregation began to feel what its gay members had always felt: unwelcome at church. With each rejection, our healing, understanding, and solidarity quietly grew.

We moved into yet another struggling midtown church, St. Mark's Lutheran. Its thirteen members turned a blind eye to our beliefs and offered to meet in their tiny chapel, allotting us the main sanctuary, since there were about 150 of us.

One Sunday's offering money we earmarked to hire a Mennonite to lead us in an identity formation and consensus-building workshop. In all our moving around, we had neither the time nor the energy to face the fact that, though we all agreed we could no longer be "forced" to believe something, that was the only thing we could be certain we did agree upon. After nearly a year of meeting together, we followed the Mennonite's advice and named ourselves. Crossroads Church's new logo could be viewed either as a four-way intersection or a cross. It left plenty of room for both entrance and exit.

We also put our consensus training to work during three months of Saturdays that we met in St. Mark's fellowship hall to decide what, if anything, we believed in common. We set out to conduct what we hoped would be a less hierarchical, less male-dominated variation on the fourth-century Council of Nicaea, which was ordered by the first Christian Roman emperor, Constantine. There, church leaders were charged with resolving the early church's factional squabbles over what Christians believed. They wrote the Nicene Creed, a statement still recited by many Protestants Sunday after Sunday, which proclaims the things they are to believe about Jesus, Jesus's mother and father, resurrection, and where their physical bodies will wind up. The Council of Nicaea decided things like what books—and there were many—would wind up in the Bible and which ones would be cast out into the Gnostic cold. Some were rejected because they were written by a woman or some other suspect person like the Apostle Judas. Some were rejected simply because they revealed too flamboyant a Jesus, clapping his hands to turn stones into doves for no apparent reason. As the church did to these fourth-century Christian leaders, our new church felt doctrinally unmoored to many. For those members uncomfortable with the unknown, the rest of us agreed to try to put our beliefs into words. Our council required a scribe, flip-chart paper, masking tape, and Magic Markers (the permanent, toxic kind that lay down a good supply of ink). We sat in folding chairs around ten folding tables, with an array of Crock-Pots full of hot dogs and chili (vegetarian and non) nearby.

Early on that first Saturday morning, a profoundly loving and organized man, who was deaf in one ear, called us to order and wrote in black marker "What Do We Believe About . . ." With the vigor of the uninitiated, we decided to tackle Jesus first. People held up their hands and shouted who they knew Jesus to be into the moderator's good ear.

After a tense thirty minutes of deliberation, we finally empowered the moderator to articulate four permutations: 1) Jesus is the Christ, the only begotten son of God, sinless and perfect, the way, the truth, and the life, who, in dying on the cross, paid the final sacrifice for our sins; 2) Jesus is one of the best pictures of what God is like and, though he was killed by the Roman state, he somehow lives on in our midst, empowering us to give and receive love, healing, and forgiveness; 3) Jesus was a wise person from history, who, like Gandhi, embodied the Sacred more fully than most people can, and the world would be a better place if all would follow his example; and 4) Jesus was a nice person. He wrote each one in large black letters on a separate sheet from the flip chart, tore each one off, then taped each one up in the one of the four corners of the room. After a ten-minute bathroom break, we all stood under the statement that most closely resembled our own beliefs. We were allowed to take snacks and drinks to our corners, as no one really knew how long whatever came next would take.

The distribution between the four groups wasn't even. Far and above the largest was Group 2, the one I selected. I didn't choose it because I feared separation from the herd, ostracism, or worse, having to defend a heretical viewpoint, but because I then honestly felt most comfortable with this right-of-center point between the two extremes. I chose Group 2 instead of Group 3 because I feared I would lose Imaginary Jesus and the part of me that arose from long following his path, inspecting his choices, and marveling at his freedom. I wasn't quite ready to admit that Jesus wasn't a supernatural being living in my psyche so much as a social radical, a wise subversive whose teachings and example had changed the trajectory of my life, had saved my life. I wasn't ready to admit that Imaginary Jesus wasn't someone separate from me but the very best part of me that had followed his path. Putting myself in Group 3 changed the kind of Christian I assumed I should be, the only kind of Christian you normally hear about. The people I suspected didn't quite like the idea of gay people feeling like there wasn't anything wrong with us made up a large portion of the biblical literalist Group 1. The nice missionary couple in their seventies who did the best they could to attend homophobia workshops but still wanted to hold their collective finger in the dike where Jesus was concerned joined Group 1, as well. I understood their vigilance. To them, without a risen Jesus, traditional Christianity was an egg without a yolk.

Those with the most vague Christology, Group 4, convened in the back corner near St. Mark's ancient machine that sold dusty cans of Vess soda. The two people in it preferred to stand, even though people from Group 1 offered them chairs. One member was a brilliant schizophrenic who for thirty years had sorted mail at Kansas City's main post office. His comrade was a jolly white-haired man who liked to clap and improvise piano solos before the church service that he believed would address the needs of a person he picked out of the crowd without his or her knowledge. When, during church service, we sang the bluesy song "You Are God," instead of facing forward, head uplifted like others, he turned around and pointed his finger at people who would make eye contact. "You, You Are, You Are God," he would sing and point.

After forty-five minutes or so of writing down beliefs, each group appointed a spokesperson who took their group's list about Jesus to the microphone and read it. Then the dialogue toward consensus began. No group but Group 1 felt comfortable saying Jesus was the only way to God. They bolstered their position by quoting the one, admittedly firm, bullheaded sentence attributed to Jesus that could be used to support it: "No one comes to the Father except by me." It's a verse that people from the Jesus Seminar—a group of scholars who meet to vote on which verses sound like something Jesus would in fact have said about himself—have consistently blackballed. This verse is, they say, something Jesus's followers and, thus, the writer of the Gospel of John came to believe about him after his death.

Group 2 overlapped with Group 1 in that we weren't quite yet ready to stop believing all sorts of things about Jesus that contradict the laws of physics. We found ourselves always apologizing. "I'm sorry, I know it doesn't make any sense, but I don't have trouble with the virgin birth. Not right now anyway." That was before any of us had gotten hold of "new paradigm" thinkers who could let us believe not so much *about* what had happened to Jesus but *because of* him. As Frederick Buechner says, "Life is complicated enough without confusing theology and gynecology." Our group of good-natured, recovering fundamentalists also couldn't let loose of the idea that Jesus, our friend, was killed, buried, and somehow brought to life again. I believed in the literal resurrection then, and some days when I can find no other explanation for the love I feel, I still do.

Group 3's moderator, a nervous but friendly person, had recently transferred her membership to Crossroads from Unity because she wanted her church to be "more about Jesus than not." Her group's presentation took the form of a bubble diagram rather than a list. On behalf of Group 4, Michael, the schizophrenic, brought three blank flip-chart pages to the front of the room and smiled. Given all we can really know for certain about Jesus, his was the most honest presentation of the four.

Our maiden value discussion stopped short of disaster. When hard-pressed, even Group 4's members said they might tolerate a statement with some mention of the resurrection if it indicated everyone didn't believe in it. Similarly, Group 3's moderator said, "Okay. Group 3 concedes that strange things happen."

After all four presentations had been made, no one knew what to do next. Finally, someone suggested that we sequester a representative from each group in the kitchen to talk about Jesus until they came up with a statement they thought every group could live with. We sent them away with a prayer in the name of the one we were trying to discern through the fog. It was an excruciatingly diplomatic solution.

Already, we had learned our lesson. While they argued about Jesus in the kitchen, we decided to hammer out some easier statements. For example, did we value the careful teaching and nurture of children? Yes. We also decided that, though we could extend one another help, each individual was ultimately responsible for his or her own spiritual health. The consensus-builders emerged to tell us what we believed about Jesus. Here was the gist: He was the closest picture of God we had (though we still couldn't agree on God either); He loved us and wanted us to know where to find God. His life and ministry were our models. Though most of us did not like the emphasis on the substitutionary death—Jesus as sacrifice for sin—the kitchen group had kept it in because they didn't want to alienate Group 1's members, for whom it was essential. Defining Jesus had taken three hours. By this time, the chili in various Crock-Pots had begun to crust along the edges.

Saturday after Saturday, we went on like this, wrangling one sacred cow after another. Every Friday night, Lisa and I screwed up our courage. We had to speak out about things important to us, things we worried that someone else did not value so vehemently that they might try to stop our voices from being heard in the final recording of values. More than once, someone tried to silence the opposition. One day, the quantity of water and manner of its application caused so much disagreement among the majority—those for whom water, as opposed to flower petals, dirt, etc., must be the medium of baptism—that the moderator had to pull a new Mennonite consensus-building trick out of the bag. A Samoan Circle was a circle of folding chairs like a boxing ring in the center of the room. Only those occupying a chair could speak and only one at a time. Ideally, the technique ensures that everyone who wants to has a chance to voice an opinion without fear, interruption, shame, or reprisal. We quickly learned that Samoan Circle moderators must be vigilant. They must spot things like the man with a firm belief in the inerrancy of scripture, who not only stood behind but also put his foot on the rung of the chair of a reticent woman while she explained why she believed her Presbyterian sprinkled baptism had worked just as well as immersion. When she felt his foot make contact, she quickly gave up her seat and her voice. Rather than have a difficult but potentially fruitful conversation with her, the man, in effect, removed her from the circle. Without her, it was occupied only by people who agreed with him.

After this woman took her seat outside the circle, this man dominated the discussion. But then, by applying another rule of Samoan Circles, another woman made the circle work. She put this man in the listening chair where he was allowed only to echo back what another had said until he got it right. Only then could everyone be sure he had truly heard.

It was with just these kinds of hounds yapping at our heels that Lisa and I ate our Saturday oatmeal. If we didn't go—which we would rather not have, given the wee hour—our voices would not be heard and the kind of church we wanted to attend would not take shape around, but outside of us. We felt a responsibility to help create a church that the children we had decided not to have would be able to attend. We wanted to found a church without malice or judgment and based on the ways modeled by the Jesus that Lisa and I could agree upon: the radical, the lover, and the emancipator. Taking a church apart and putting it back together again isn't Presbyterian, and it isn't impossible, but it does require all the tenacity, tolerance, and vision a group of people can spare.

On Lord only knows which Saturday, the next value on the docket—one we'd saved for next time because everyone had been too exhausted to contemplate—was the sacrament of marriage and who could partake of it. I'll admit that I'd braced myself for, if not outright rejection, then strained tolerance.

Though I felt more at ease in a progressive church, fundamentalism was, for me, a dormant virus that lurked in my psyche and waited for lowered spiritual resistance. Each outbreak was usually less severe, but nonetheless debilitating. I regularly woke disoriented and discouraged from dreams about Celeste, a British missionary friend who I had fallen privately in love with during my Southwest Bible Church Singles group years. She had come to the states for a year to provide hospice care to her cranky, toothless American grandmother. A straight-backed young woman smelling of Ivory soap, Celeste railed against any number of things—Darwin and abortionists and the transgender woman we saw together on a BBC profile. "Rubbish," she said. "How can a person just decide he isn't who God made him to be? All the physical evidence is there." I hadn't been brave enough to say in a voice louder than a whisper, "Not anymore it isn't." The dreams always went badly. Celeste would discover how much I had really been attracted to her because I finally made the play for her that my wakeful, vigilant self had tried not even to fantasize about. She would rise up in all her clanging religious fury to say how inexplicably sick and wrong I was.

My inner fundamentalist used whatever means necessary to air her grievances. If she had to wait until I was asleep, just as my once-closeted lesbian had used to have to do, so be it. Instead of dreaming I was ripping an Asian woman's clothes off behind the woodpile in my childhood backyard or causing my Sunday school teacher's wife to climax, I heard British sermons. I would wake from them feeling surprised at how guilty I could still feel for enjoying how Lisa's skin felt in the nest of our pale green flannel sheets. Like a

newly erupted cold sore, such dreams came often enough to remind me that my inner fundamentalist needed reassurance.

This inner fundamentalist took advantage of my weakened
spiritual immune system two days before Thanksgiving when,
still reeling from Momma's sudden death from colon cancer, I
took a phone call from Brad, the friend who had introduced me
to Living Waters. I hadn't seen or heard from him in more than
a decade. Though the complete lack of context did concern me,
Momma had raised me to take telephone calls even when I didn't
want to, even when the caller neglected to ask if I had the time.
There would never be a good time to talk to Brad, but I naïvely
hoped he had called to tell me he was questioning his beliefs. For a
brief while, I even entertained the idea that this troubled, beautiful man had finally allowed himself to be authentic.

For several minutes, I relaxed into a Lord-free conversation.
Then he asked me what I'd been doing. As I used to with Momma
before I came out, I carefully edited out any mention of Lisa. I'd
forgotten how tedious and demoralizing lying could be. I remembered, after all those years, to ask about his schizophrenic brother.
And then the conversation took a turn. The brother had died, but
only after Brad had the opportunity to "really share the plan of
salvation with him." Deep inside me, a gland secreted adrenalin. I
did not heed my body's short, simple warning. I stayed on the line
pretending all was well and that I could handle whatever came up.

My inner fundamentalist liked to know what was going to
happen; she liked to brace herself. She didn't "read the daily horo-
scope for entertainment purposes only." She was certain Something out there was trying to tell her something and that that
Something would use anything—traffic lights, astrology, or sidewalk cracks—to let me know what could happen to me if I didn't
heed the warning. My fundamentalist kept me on the line with
Brad, who said the Lord had told him to share something with me.
He wondered if I wanted to hear it.

"I've been hearing from the Lord a lot lately," Brad said. "I've
gotten messages for several people. I think it's because I've been
so close to the Lord. It's been a really sweet time." He said this to

establish himself as one with a reliable connection, cable or DSL, rather than dial-up. The message had come across complete and ungarbled. "Do you want this word?" he asked. Would I want to hear what, in my heart of hearts, I knew Brad had to say? Any ex-fundamentalist worth her salt knows that when someone says they have a word for you, it's never good news.

"I know you've made lifestyle changes," he said. I could hear his throat tightening with fear as he began his speech. Thanks to my inner fundamentalist, rather than wonder *why* Brad would so grossly violate my boundaries, I wondered *how* he had. Probably, like a few billion other people, he knew how to use the Internet. I hadn't made any secret of my relationship. I had even gone so far as to speak on behalf of Lawrence, Kansas's proposed domestic partnership registry and to allow the newspaper to take a picture of me posing next to Lisa on the eve of its initiation. The caption below us expressed my plans to register as one half of an all-but-married partnership as soon as the doors of City Hall opened the next morning. Figuring out where Brad had breached my boundaries was the first of many things I would obsess to a powder in the coming days.

We both knew the rules here. Brad mustn't let me get a word in edgewise. "The Lord told me to tell you that you shouldn't deepen your commitment—I'm getting March pretty clearly here," he said, pausing for a second to adjust his antennae. "So what I get strongly is that you shouldn't, absolutely should not go through with whatever you'd planned—what do you call them—commitment ceremonies?" To have said the words like he knew what they meant would have leant them credence. "Were you planning something in March?"

I didn't tell him he'd gotten bad information, that Lisa and I had already been deeply committed for the last twelve years and extralegally married for ten. With a last fleeting grain of sanity, I felt sorry for him. "We were planning on maybe getting a couple of kittens," I said. "Does that sound like what you might have heard?" Had I known both of these March arrivals would manifest the first signs of ringworm after we'd already worn them like boas for a week, I might have thought Brad had simply gotten the ceremony part wrong.

"No. This is coming through loud and clear. It isn't about kittens. I distinctly heard ceremony.

"Anyway, I also heard the Lord say that you need to change your life and leave your partner. I know it will be hard, but you need to do this. God says to let Him fill the empty place inside you. Let Him offer you the love you're seeking because His love is enough after all. I seem to remember you saying a while back that you weren't sure whether God really loved you. And I remember thinking at the time, 'Well, I'm not that sure God loves me either.'" Here, he swallowed involuntarily. "But now I know He loves me beyond what I can even ask or think. And Kelly, He wants to love you that way, too." From what I remembered, Brad had always talked like that. God was always speaking to him and telling him he was loved. Maybe Brad hadn't been lying exactly, but hoping just by repeating that he felt close to God would make it so.

"You need to know we're on very different paths now, Brad," I said. Like a fly bitten by a spider, I tried to fend him off, but my struggles were pointless. His venom knew its mark. It went there and commenced its work. He spun me around, his gossamer words tightening around my brain.

"I know, but this is our Father God we're talking about here. You know He meant men to be with women. It's the way He designed us," he said. Imaginary Jesus called out a contradictory warning to me that already sounded like it was coming from the bottom of a well. "You know that," Brad said, appealing to my common sense.

I had never known that.

"Anyway," I said, a bowel movement urging me onward. "I'll talk to you later" even though I had no such intention. I could be caught, but I didn't have to like it.

"I love you, Kelly. I really do," I heard him hollering, frantic and fervent, as I set the phone in its cradle.

✦ ✦ ✦

"I hate to sound blunt here," my therapist said when I called her the next day in a panic, "but he's nuts. This is his shit, not yours. He found out you were happy being something he couldn't let himself be, and he had to make you stop. If what you're doing is all right then his whole life ceases to make sense. He's close to fifty, right? Tick. Tock. Do you see what I'm saying?" She sounded like she was calling from the bottom of a well, too.

"Uh huh," I said.

"This is garden variety religious abuse," she said. "Sometimes you just have to tell yourself I have to do what's right for me. Also, you have to tell yourself the truth. You're in a loving partnership." Lisa and I had fought that morning. "You have a good life. You're happy."

While my therapist talked, my inner fundamentalist strutted about, wagging her finger. She didn't want me to suspect for one moment that the recent collapse of my libido might not be a direct result of God's disapproval. I'd been depressed before but never when I had the opportunity to have sex. I didn't yet understand that depression and libido don't like each other. It's one of life's natural safeguards lest someone should conceive a child feeling like I did.

"As soon as this guy said God told him something, he took away your voice," my therapist said. "It's the oldest trick in the book. Are you feeling better now?"

"Much," I lied. I didn't want to disappoint her. I wanted her to like me. I wanted Brad to like me. I wanted everyone to like me.

I tried to make immediate use of the sense she had made, but viruses don't respond well to treatment. You can try to manage symptoms, but ultimately, they have to run their course.

The first week or so after the phone call, the only thing I could do for myself was take to my bed, not to sleep but to hide. Each morning, I put my feet on the floor determined to get something done, but exhaustion and terror would get the better of me and back under the covers I would go. There I lay contemplating the life of misery I would live again once I had the energy to make the required destruction of my current one. God Himself—the mean Big Daddy with the booming voice I had been well on my way to not believing in—had sought me out to tell me he wasn't pleased. For my sake, he wanted to take my life, as I knew it, away from me. If I obeyed this God, the love I felt for Lisa I should try my level best to no longer to feel. The home we had made together, every soft and beautiful thing around me must go. No more writing, because without Lisa's emotional and financial support, I would need a full-time job. No more reading or environmentalism or bird feeding or hanging clothes on the line. I wouldn't have a clothesline. They don't let you have them at the ugly apartment I would be able to afford where God would fill me up with television, which is all I would have energy for. I didn't feel loved but imprisoned and punished. Click went the latch, away fled my appetite and my mind.

During a second phone call to my therapist, I said, "I think I might be depressed. It's only 10:00 in the morning and I want to go back to bed."

"I don't think you're depressed exactly," she said. "It's exhausting to tell yourself the truth when you been handed such a sack of religious lies. You may need to write true things down. Keep a pen and paper handy. Write them down and carry them around in your pocket with you."

I didn't know the first thing to write.

"Just go to bed if you need to—watch movies, relax."

I went back to bed, but I didn't relax. I hardly slept at all either, day or night.

When our Mac technician first connected us to the Internet because one of my freelance jobs demanded it, I had scoffed at his warning. "Be careful," he said. "This can be addictive." Addicts can be the most puritanical of people. My parents voted against gambling in Kansas City. They railed against the Catholics for relying on bingo proceeds to fill their coffers. They predicted organized crime, explosions, and blood in the streets. That was before Station Casino started giving away free T-shirts and vouchers for all-you-can-eat breakfasts and before my parents started stashing their winnings in Topsy's popcorn tins all over the house.

By the time Brad phoned, I already had great practice cyber-obsessing, usually about my health. Every year, it was something else—breast cancer, colon cancer, a rare neuroendocrine disease. Every year, it was a fresh look into the abyss, and after, great rejoicing.

In seeking electronic reassurance from the Christians who did not believe I was a hapless deviant, I found all of those who did believe this. I found NARTH (North American Association of Reparative Therapy) with a picture of its towering ex-gay complex and impressive list of psychiatrists and doctors who said they could, through the use of any number of clandestine procedures, retrieve someone's "normal sexual orientation." I found Exodus International with its gee-whiz web site full of shiny faces of hip people who almost don't look gay anymore saying how happy they are now that they've found the "help" they needed. I was vulnerable all over again to the ex-gay gospel. In the few seconds I allowed myself to look at this site—it was like looking at the sun; I knew it wasn't good for me but I couldn't help it—I saw big pulsating letters that said something like, "ARE YOU READY FOR THE JOURNEY?" It's what someone says to you as you stare up at the shiny rails of a five-story roller coaster. It's a dare, really. Once you're strapped in, it feels like the most exciting thing you've ever done. Dropping over that first hill, it feels like your skin might be pulled off and that your bones might come unhinged. Eventually you realize though that it doesn't feel good and that you'd like to get off and do something else. The ex-gay journey is one that threatens to drag you over the same track of self-loathing so many times that you'll never feel well again. The web site doesn't tell you that. I found numerous other sites with pictures of less hip people with captions about their hideously abusive childhoods and history of sexual abuse that drove them to the unfulfilling wasteland of homosexuality. All of these sites had links to each other.

By the time I'd visited enough of them, I couldn't take in help from the Christian organizations and individuals who had reconciled homosexuality and Christianity. Nor did it matter that the American Psychiatric Association, the American Psychological

Association, the American Counseling Association, the National Association of Social Workers, and the World Health Organization all agreed that any mental disorder I might have had nothing to do with my homosexuality. I couldn't take any of it in. My brain was hardpan.

At the suggestion of my beleaguered therapist, who finally said enough times that people with my tendency to obsess could more easily get through a bad patch with a short-term dose of anti-anxiety medication, I got a prescription. The last domino fell. I was caught between a rock and a hard place. I could either take the moral high ground, insist on getting through this on my own as my family always had and risk complete mental collapse, or I could contribute to the already measureable level of anti-depressants pissed into the waterways. Because I chose the latter, I am still here to write this. With the help of a little pink pill, I gradually returned to my senses.

Among other things, my therapist forbade me to browse since, she reminded me, my sexuality wasn't a disease I needed a treatment plan for. Otherwise, she offered me weekly paper cups of hot tea and let me look out the window at a neighboring chip-and-tar roof and try to figure out why I'd been blindsided again. In between sessions, I came home and finished a book I'd been paid to write. I made and ate meals. I slept beside Lisa and I quit thinking of a future without her. My daily anti-anxiety pill allowed me to tolerate the pain I'd never allowed myself to feel. Unlike most people who find themselves languishing in an ex-gay ministry year after year, I had snuck away after one academic year. I'd sequestered the trauma others continue to feel someplace inside me and pretended to have gotten away unscathed. Ironically, Brad's awful phone call left me capable of suffering not only *because* of other people but also *with* them. I had finally processed the shame of being an ex-gay graduate, of having anyone know I'd ever hated myself enough to go through it. I felt everything through protective fathoms. I could hear the drilling, the cutting; I could feel the pull of thread through psychic skin. Healing voices took deeper root—Marcus Borg, Elizabeth Stroud, Peter Gomes, Frederick

Buechner, Sister Helen Prejean, and Shelby Spong. Their encouragement gave me compassion for Brad, who in his fervor to believe his self-induced deprivation and suffering had meaning, hadn't heard God at all, only his own fear and despair. On bad days, I called him names.

As I healed, I had extremely lucid dreams. In one, I wandered the upstairs of Trinity Presbyterian, the church I'd grown up in. I walked past the choir rehearsal room, bell tower, and Sunday school classrooms toward the sound of construction. I passed the pastor's study, beautiful woodwork exposed. The sanctuary had been completely gutted. I could see frame and joist. I could see the pulpit, open end out. Everything was exposed. I could see and be seen. People from my past—loving, strong people—strained to pull out rotten floorboards and replaced them with new ones. The whole place was being restored.

If I came to believe the lesbian raw material of me was thoroughly loved, supported, and equipped, I'd have to find something else to worry about. Could it be that, at least in part, I'd clung to a lie that everyone disapproved? Believing it kept me ineffective, yes, but it also kept me off the hook. No longer a hapless victim, I would be without excuse.

✦ ✦ ✦

I knew that though some in the Crossroads congregation believed God blessed same-sex marriages, others did not. What did I want with a church marriage anyway, when most had such moth-eaten views about it? Every one of the fundamentalist churches I'd attended had offered a Young Marrieds class. I'd read about their social activities—Bible studies, bowling tournaments, and potlucks—in countless bulletins. I'd watched the clique of them sit apart, compassionately eyeing the bedraggled remains of the singles group to which they had once belonged. I had spent the better part of my Christian life fighting back nausea over what the Young Marrieds learned in their Sunday school class. I needed to confront the scriptures the church has boxed people's ears with for nearly two millennia.

I reread the Apostle Paul's dictates for a Christian woman. She was to remain single if possible to spare not only herself but also, and more importantly, some poor man, the encumbrance of earthly love and responsibilities. If she found herself married to an abusive apostate, she was to remain so to "please the Lord." If, while sitting in a church meeting, a question or an insight began weighing on her small mind, she was to button her lip and wait until she got home to share it with her more discerning husband in the silence of their own house. From the looks of it, Paul was a very happily unmarried man—possibly a gay one—who wanted nothing to do with what amounted to half of his fellow Christians, not even women willing to have their bodies beaten and torn apart beside his for the sake of the gospel. In his defense, he probably had no idea these letters he wrote to a smattering of churches would be bound into a book used to judge right behavior for the rest of Christian life on earth. It helps a little, too, that he sometimes qualified his harshest comments by saying that, unlike the rest of what he said came from "God," the epistles came out of his own pointy head. It helped a teensy bit more to hear that some of the harshest letters attributed to Paul may not have been his at all. Some scholars have suggested that these sexist passages from letters they do believe he wrote were likely added later by a follower of Paul. Paul or not, some knucklehead now hallowed in the canon *had* written these words, and I was tired of cutting him slack. I'd watched too many people wield them like a cleaver against another.

This is why I wanted church marriage. I wanted to know that if my marriage failed, it wouldn't be for lack of my church's support, accountability, and blessing. I wanted to attend a church with people who really knew us and could show us that they weren't better than we were or more spiritual or more married just by virtue of their heterosexuality. I wanted the church to acknowledge that I already was married.

I asked Imaginary Jesus to turn his head while I scanned the crowd for the people I suspected still thought of me as machinery in need of parts and service. I knew for sure how one couple felt. They spoke openly in meetings and committees and at every opportunity to tell anyone who would listen that homosexual behavior was a sin, an unhealed malfunction. They said this with sad, soft looks on their faces like parents who have caught their child misbehaving. I made a mental tally. One. Two. And then my eyes rested on the virulently fundamentalist man who had dominated the Samoan Circle. His teenage daughter had written a letter before she went to Yugoslavia with Campus Crusade for Christ that she didn't want Crossroads to condone homosexual marriage out of a desire to keep the peace. What was wrong was wrong, she said, and God knew it and God never shied away from telling people what they should hear, even when it hurt. Three. A gay man on the worship committee assured us there were more. He just didn't feel at liberty to reveal who they were. I couldn't be sure if they had brought a Crock-Pot of chili, if they'd smiled at me that morning, or if they'd touched my forehead with oil and prayed for me when I'd asked, and, if they had, what they had really prayed for.

That Saturday, the most important Saturday of all, my lizard brain took control. We sat at the same table with another couple who we resembled in few ways other than that we were all lesbians. They loved shopping and perfume, their cars and jobs. We had little in common but lots at stake. Also, at our table sat Carole, who still had no partner but wanted one. Next to Carole sat a middle-aged woman who looked like a teenage boy and wore a T-shirt with a monarch butterfly caterpillar in the shape of a question mark. Filling out the table was a gay male couple who had been waiting around for several years while the church decided whether or not they could be married in it. One black, one white, they had already endured plenty of opposition from their own families. One had raised two daughters with his wife for the first decade they attended Broadway Baptist. When he couldn't pretend anymore, they divorced. One daughter made the cheerleading squad, and the other began wearing men's wingtips and neckties. On a church ski trip to Colorado, she found Lisa and me at the front of the bus. She developed different crushes on both of us while playing a word game that would have anesthetized the rest of the youth group, who all lay at the back of the bus in piles, their ears plugged with headphones. She and her junior high girlfriend formed a gay/straight alliance at her school. She was thirteen. Unlike me, she had grown up in a church that made her feel perfectly comfortable being gay.

All of the gay people sat at or near this table in a little ghetto. We had books with pages dog-eared for the quotes we planned to read to substantiate our beliefs that we should be married in the church. We came jittery and dry-mouthed, prepared with a lifetime of explanations why people shouldn't feel burdened by what they thought God thought about us. We wanted them to know we weren't worried. We all wanted especially to get on with our lives, to have them be about so much more.

◆ ◆ ◆

Thirty minutes after discussion began—without the need for a Samoan Circle, our note cards, or impassioned speeches—by a vote of most to a few who even agreed to coexist in disagreement, the church adopted the following value statement: "We believe all members of the church, regardless of sexual orientation, have the right to full participation in the life, events, and ceremonies of the church, including baptism, communion, ordination, and marriage." Ordination we hadn't even dared to hope for.

"Well, shut my mouth," I said.

Within the year, Crossroads would call its first interim pastor, a stocky gay man, who did not feel as comfortable as the rest of us with casual Sunday dress. Out of respect for our customs, he suffered through his first sermon in a pair of Bermuda shorts that he fastened beneath his large stomach. They left his dimply knees exposed, the one part of his body he said he hated. The congregation unanimously encouraged him to wear whatever he liked.

He performed the marriage ceremony for the mixed-race gay male couple. Standing in line for cake and punch at their reception, I saw my high school American government teacher. He didn't work for Raytown High School anymore but as a textbook consultant for Houghton Mifflin. Also, he was no longer married to my former English teacher, but to a tenor who sang in the Heartland Men's Chorus with one of the grooms. He and I had to cut our conversation short to hear a toast from the best man, the groom's teenage daughter, who, in true rebellious Baptist fashion, was wearing one of her father's ties and a rented purple tux.

In this new church I had only dreamed could exist, I learned to appreciate hearing about the early church's experiences of the Jesus who seemed not to have died, whose influence was still somehow being felt. I joined an ecclesiastical huddle grateful finally to find our feet on solid ground. We no longer had to balance on the high wire of literalism, contorting ourselves into whatever posture it took to continue to believe that the scripture—regardless how unloving or violent—came from the mind of a capricious and very human God we should entrust with our lives. I came to see the Bible as a description of one group of people's experience of the Sacred.

Epilogue

One afternoon, I felt the awkward hush before a final departure I'd been anticipating really for years. The picture of the tiny, imaginary, and supernatural friend hiding in my heart had to go. I needed to let go of the tiny Jesus I'd shaped just for me to embrace the uncontainable person he was and the life he had lived as an example for me and others. Imaginary Jesus suggested it, in fact. If I ever needed this more tangible sense of him, he said, "I'll be right here, quick as a whistle." In return, he left me with his words, his compassion, his thoughts, his narrow and often unpopular Way. He also left me with his open heart, the ability to know others and to be known for who I am. Where many of his followers offered me not love but judgment they mistook for it, Jesus left me with a sense of the wideness of mercy. He left me my life as a follower, a Christian, one who has left the binding confines of the traditional church. That I am here, loved, and sane is thanks to who I imagined him to be. That is its own kind of testimony, its own kind of miracle.

Biographical Note

Kelly Barth lives on very little money in a very small house with her partner, Lisa Grossman, in Lawrence, Kansas. She was a fiction fellow in the University of Montana's creative writing program and has received fellowships from the Missouri Arts Council and the Kansas Arts Commission. Her work has been published in anthologies and literary journals, most recently *Coal City Review*, *Literary Bird Journal*, and *Muse & Stone*. *My Almost Certainly Real Imaginary Jesus* is her first book.